PRAISE FOR SUSAN SHAPIRO

For *Secrets of a Fix-Up Fanatic*

"This is a fantastic book." –Candace Bushnell,
author of *Sex and the City* and *Lipstick Jungle*

"Compelling . . . reliable, honest . . . encouraging."
–*Women's Wear Daily*

"Fast, funny, sexy." –Glamour.com

"Funny and direct, candid but warm. . . . Shapiro is passionate
on the subject of matchmakers—not least because she owes her own

"Enthusiast   *Weekly*

"Shapiro . . . can dissect excuses for your sorry state of singleness. . . .
She orders you to shift your focus away from the superficial, which
can blind you. . . . Ignore her advice at your own peril." –*Newsday*

"Shapiro . . . is a way better matchmaker than one of those creepy
dating sites. . . . Keep this book under tight watch." –F

"Smart,

"Feisty and funny . . . with war
author of *50% Off* ar

"Susan Shapiro is a serious and gifted fix-up fanatic."
–Lisa Loeb, musician

For *Lighting Up*

"Frank and darkly funny." *—New York Times Book Review*

"A mind-bendingly good read." *—O, the Oprah magazine*

"Four stars." *—Jane* magazine

"A great voice. . . . You can't help liking her, and waiting eagerly for the next installment of her memoirs." *—Newsday*

"The truth, the whole truth, and nothing but the truth about substance abuse. . . . A wickedly funny memoir of how we love our addictions and how difficult it is to bid them adieu." *—Illinois Times*

"Warning: this book invites serious overidentification. . . . Not only do I feel like I've known this woman since birth, I'm starting to think maybe I am her. . . ." *—Nerve.com*

"Hilarious." *—Gothamist*

"Shapiro's funny and nakedly honest voice is irresistible. . . . . Another great reason to lose sleep besides sex."
—Susan Jane Gilman, author of Hypocrite in a Pouffy White Dress

For *Five Men Who Broke My Heart*

"Susan Shapiro's promiscously readable guilty pleasure of a memoir has a caustic, urbane feel.... It's a Seinfeldian quest to settle accounts with five exes ... a comedy of manners." *−Elle* magazine

"Sly, candid ... disarmingly frank ... what is best about this memoir is Shapiro's desire to tell the whole truth about her delusions and obsessions, as well as her breakthroughs and triumphs." −Pam Houston, *O, The Oprah Magazine*

"Playful ... entertaining." *−New York Times Book Review*

"Shapiro is bitingly funny and revealing." *− USA Today*

"A *Bridget Jones Diary* for the Married Set." *−Washington Post*

"Shapiro's often funny and always heartfelt recollections of past relationships are so entertaining, it's a shame she doesn't have an endless supply of material.... A delightfully kaleidoscopic autobiography of an impulsive and passionate woman who comes of age with style. " *−Publisher's Weekly*

Only as Good as Your Word

WRITING LESSONS FROM MY FAVORITE LITERARY GURUS

SUSAN SHAPIRO

SEAL PRESS

Only as Good as Your Word
Writing Lessons from My Favorite Literary Gurus

Copyright © 2007 Susan Shapiro

Published by
Seal Press
A Member of the Perseus Books Group
1400 65th Street, Suite 250
Emeryville, CA 94608

9 8 7 6 5 4 3 2 1

Library of Congress Cataloging-in-Publication Data

Only as good as your word : writing lessons from my favorite literary gurus / Susan Shapiro.
p. cm.
ISBN-13: 978-1-58005-220-7
ISBN-10: 1-58005-220-7
1. Authorship—Anecdotes. 2. Authorship. I. Title.

PN165.S53 2007
808'.02—dc22
2007016662

Cover and interior design by Domini Dragoone
Printed in the United States of America
Distributed by Publishers Group West

In memory of my favorite teacher, Jack Zucker

my favorite cousin, Howard Fast

my favorite boss, Helen Stark

Author's Note

Some names and identifying characteristics of
people portrayed in this book have been obscured so
they won't divorce, disown, hate, kill, or sue me.

Contents

13 ..... Introduction

31 ..... My First Muse x JACK ZUCKER

73 ..... All in the Family x HOWARD FAST

119 ..... Institution Within an Institution
x HELEN STARK

169 ..... A Quiet Brother x IAN FRAZIER

227 ..... The Rescuer x RUTH GRUBER

271 ..... Asinine x MICHAEL ANDERSON

317 ..... Not Related x HARVEY SHAPIRO

351 ..... How to Have a Protégé

387 ..... How to Get Great Gurus
of Your Own

Introduction

"You made me sound like a bimbo, and I'm writing a rebuttal about a daughter who lies about her mother all the time."

That was the message my mother left on my answering machine right after I published my first personal essay, about our close albeit complex relationship, in *Cosmopolitan*. Getting paid $500 from a national glossy women's magazine was a very huge deal for a twenty-three-year-old Midwestern girl who'd dreamt of being a writer from the age of three. I had assumed Mom would be proud and get a kick out of being immortalized. Listening to her less-than-thrilled reaction, I was shattered. Yet what could I do – but steal her line?

"You're funny, I'm gonna quote you on that," I called her back to say.

"Off the record," she soon learned to add after sharing anything juicy with me, an annoying habit she uses to this day.

I'm only half kidding when I now warn all of my journalism students that the first time they come up with a piece their family hates means they've found their voice.

"Why don't you write about science, or business, or a biography of an important politician who's dead, like a real writer?" my father grumbled.

But I didn't really feel passion about science, or business, or any important dead politicians. I was completely self-involved, preoccupied with poetry, my sex partners, close friends, and emotional conflicts I constantly psychoanalyzed, as well as books, articles, and poems about friendship, sex, and psychoanalysis. ("Being in therapy is like getting a Ph.D. in yourself," one fellow therapy junkie opined.) When anyone accused me of myopia, I merely quoted the lyrics of an Edie Brickell song: "I'm not aware of too many things, but I know what I know, if you know what I mean."

Luckily, when searching for subjects to explore, I was given the extremely helpful career advice to "exploit your obsessions" and "write about people you love." I've been eternally obsessed with the people I loved, and combining the two has so far provided me with material for countless clips and seven books, five still in print.

Everyone in my conservative clan worked in "normal" fields and kept their deepest emotions quiet. So through the years they've been absolutely mortified to watch me spill the turbulent ups and downs of my inner world in poems, provocative first-person essays, and revealing memoirs they've stashed away in hidden closets, like they were smut. My family did fly to Manhattan for a book party celebrating *Five Men Who Broke My Heart,* my sex-drugs-and-marriage memoir chronicling my journey to remeet my "top five heartbreaks of all time." For the theme, I'd envisioned a dimly lit Valentine's Day soiree, with invitations that said: BRING AN EX — FOR JUST DESSERTS.

My folks' version was more like *Fiddler on the Roof.* They insisted I invite all our aunts, uncles, and cousins and serve real food, not just chocolate and champagne. Greeting the Michigan branch, all the New Yorkers hugged my parents and asked, "Are you okay? How are you holding up?" as if they were paying a shivah call for someone who'd died in a tragic accident. My father's mantra was, "We're moving to Alaska." Even my beloved husband, a TV writer/producer not thrilled to be used as a recurring character, got into the act, threatening to pen a rebuttal called *The Bitch Beside Me.*

Still, after watching me on *The Today Show,* my kin called to say I looked cute and thin on TV. My brother Eric even stuck the interview on my website and showed me how to view my mini-me, smiling at Ann Curry, with QuickTime software. When the book was optioned by Paramount Pictures, my siblings took to cybercasting the movie version. (Brian thought Mary-Louise Parker was kooky enough to play me. Eric cast fellow former redhead Ron Howard as himself and chose Carroll O'Connor for my father, but he was disappointed to learn that O'Connor was dead.) When students express fear that their family will disown them if they divulge too much, I tell them to just make sure they become successful, since most people are starfuckers and vanity often overrides privacy.

In my experience, nothing good comes from keeping feelings veiled, hidden, or repressed. Thus, the first and favorite assignment I give to my classes is to write a three-page double-spaced "humiliation essay" about the most humiliating thing that's ever happened to them. These are always by far the best crafted and the quickest to get published. Jeff, a thirty-year-old married student in my adult education course, confessed in his gut-wrenching piece that a family friend had sexually abused him as a teenager. After I helped him whittle his seven-thousand-word rough draft to a more polished nine hundred words, he sent it to *Newsweek*'s "My Turn" column, one of the premier first-person columns in the country. After the editor said yes, Jeff then made the mistake of showing it to his dad prepublication.

"My father was furious, insisting this not be printed. So I called the editor to take it back," was the message greeting me early one Saturday morning. Oh no! I attempted an intervention, insisting it was Jeff's life, his story to tell and sell as he pleased. I told him to get an emergency double session with his shrink and quoted my shrink, who said that to be happy and healthy, one must "lead the least secretive life you can." I repeated what my lawyer told me – that to stop someone legally from publishing nonfiction, you'd have to prove he or she lied, with malice intended, and show damages. Although Jeff's memory seemed totally true, I suggested he delete the three lines that mentioned his parents, not let them in on his decision, and call the editor back with the new version. He did, and the essay ran with Jeff's picture.

It was his best clip, the most he'd ever been paid for his work, and he was quite proud of it. Interestingly, the next time I saw Jeff, he'd shaved his beard and had shorter hair. He looked more hand-some and clean cut, as if airing the pain from his past had literally cleansed him. He told me that his father later apologized, admitted he felt guilty that he'd done nothing to stop the abuse, and feared what the neighbors would think. Ultimately he told his son that "printing that story was courageous."

Unfortunately, not all such conflicts have happy resolutions. In other situations I've advised students to tone down, turn into fiction, or ultimately not submit pages that could lead to unemployment, divorces, custody battles, ugly press, or expensive lawsuits. Even in less dramatic cases, it's confusing and hurtful when your loved ones don't approve of what you do. My relatives' befuddlement about my chosen profession was probably why I so desperately needed to find encouragement elsewhere. To paraphrase a certain politician, it takes a village to raise a writer. Through a series of well-aligned stars and small miracles over two and a half decades, I've been able to develop a candid, semi-distinctive voice, despite my family's disappointment. But I found success only with the constant aid of several important mentors close by, influencing my ear.

A mentor is a wise and trusted teacher or guide, honoring the Greek mythological character in Homer's *The Odyssey*. Unlike the old East Coast trend of finding a long-term therapist, or the current West Coast craze of paying a short-term "life coach," with mentors no money changes hands. The seasoned sponsor gets appreciated and glorified, while the youthful protégé gains support and wisdom.

The counselors I looked up to warned me straight off not to become a scribe to make a fortune or find fame. Better motivations: because there's no choice and there's nothing else you'll ever want to do nearly as much. They said it'll take a long time to make a decent living, told the story of how Ernest Hemingway accidentally left a suitcase filled with his first thousand-page manuscript on a train, never to be found again, and suggested all young writers do the same. (Good advice. I'm sure the first thousand pages I wrote were humiliatingly bad and probably illiterate.) They asked if I never made any money, would I still do it anyway, letting another trade pay for my writing habit? When my answer was yes, yes, and yes, they said, "Mazel tov. Now look for a day job." As the poet James Wright told his son Franz after reading one of his poems at age fifteen: "I'll be damned. You're a poet. Welcome to hell."

While scrawling my every thought and feeling into narrow-ruled spiral notebooks until dawn, I resigned myself to spending my nine-to-five hours proofreading, copyediting, working as a receptionist, secretary, personal assistant, or teacher. That way there was less pressure to earn money from my poems, humorous essays, and reviews. Surprisingly, even after my freelance checks could cover all my bills, I found that I enjoyed the combination of toiling alone all day at my typewriter (and later, laptop) and then teaching big, fun evening classes at the New School, NYU, and most recently Mediabistro, an exciting national journalist organization based in SoHo, just a dozen blocks from my apartment. Unlike freelancing, teaching came with an easy equation – I showed up and they paid me. Methodically, on the first of every month. It also turned out that my classes perfectly fit my nocturnal and stubborn type-A personality – they were at night, downtown near my home, and I was in total control.

It was good that I found another way to finance my writing, because it's never been just a job for me. It's been an intense, all-consuming calling that's defined, reflected, revealed, and saved me, engrossing me ten hours a day, every day of the year. As a Reform Jew who follows very few traditions, I've let work govern my existence. Although none of my mentors were actual religious leaders, I listened to them as if they were beloved spiritual advisers whose words and ethics I lived by. In elevating my literary luminaries to almost godlike status, they became my personal rabbis, the only authority figures I've trusted and still listen to, in three cases even after their deaths.

These interconnections were cerebral, not sexual, but the dependency was as extreme as a romantic fixation. Often it felt like having a secret escort who'd usher me into a higher universe that I couldn't enter alone, a savior who understood me and could thus rescue me from the dark, confusing sea of rejection and depression. My mentors made me a better writer, a better teacher, and a better person. Since no good deed goes unpunished, I've structured *Only as Good as Your Word* around seven generous champions who hired, inspired, read, reread, edited, encouraged, and made me who I am. My take is ridiculously one sided and not intended to be unbiased or definitive, though how wonderful if it incited full-fledged, well-deserved biographies. ("Real books," my father would say.)

I'm sure it's no coincidence that Jack Zucker, my esteemed Michigan high school English teacher, whom I met when I was fifteen, had the same first name as my father. Jack was also born in my dad's old city, had gone to City College like my mother, and knew Anne Sexton before she killed herself. So when he told me I was a talented poet, I believed him. At twenty, I had the original idea of moving to the big city to make my mark. Who knew it would take me twenty-two more years of working eighty-hour weeks to see my work published in hardcover? (And that I'd spend the rest of my days fighting to keep it there?)

Soon after I moved to Manhattan, I latched onto new role models: my best-selling cousin, Howard Fast, and Bette, his artist wife. In the summer of 1981, I showed up at their Connecticut doorstep with flowers, wine, and raw need, along with a bunch of his books to sign. While Bette fed me, offered fashion advice ("Stop with the all black! It's morbid!"), and gave me red blouses, lipstick, and scarves, Howard read and critiqued my work on a regular basis. He'd challenge me by asking, "Why are you only writing poems and short essays? Write a whole book already! Come on, Susie, let's see some more pages. A page a day is a book a year. What are you waiting for?"

I used to moon over Howard's vast bookshelves, overstuffed with copies of the more than seventy books he authored. Not surprisingly, my parents loved his historical novels *Spartacus, Freedom Road,* and *Citizen Tom Paine* but detested his two risqué, confession-filled memoirs, *The Naked God* and *Being Red* (which I preferred). Howard was so prolific, he penned mysteries under a pseudonym to avoid flooding the market. His *New York Times* obituary ended with his quote: "The only thing that infuriates me is that I have more unwritten stories in me than I can conceivably write in a lifetime."

I was grief-stricken when Bette and Howard passed away in the 1990s. But they left me someone special who tied me to them genetically – their auburn haired granddaughter, Molly Jong-Fast. While I'd been the youngest guest at Howard and Bette's art openings and book events, Molly soon filled that role at my attempts at a literary salon. When she was fourteen, she became the youngest member of my Tuesday night writing workshop. The first pages she brought in for critique chronicled the difficulties she had finding her voice when *Fear of Flying* author Erica Jong was her mother, the novelist/screenwriter Jonathan Fast was her father, and the notorious communist-turned-capitalist Howard Fast was Grandpa. When Molly published her first novel at age twenty-one, Howard told her, "I sold my first book when I was eighteen." So maybe I'd actually had it easy growing up in a clan of conservative Midwest doctors. At least my elders never competed with me! Molly became the compassionate little writer sister I'd longed for.

Meanwhile, my real, not-so-sensitive brother Brian, a trauma surgeon in Grand Blanc, Michigan, used to taunt me by telling everyone that I'd made more money from typing than from my master's degree in English. Yet it was precisely because I could type one hundred words a minute that I landed my first great full-time job in the library of *The New Yorker*. Okay, so I was a peon who spent my days summarizing articles on three-by-five index cards and gluing copies of cartoons into big black scrapbooks for $13,000 a year. I would have paid them to let me work there. My boss, Helen Stark, was the magazine's wonderful and eccentric head librarian, who became a great friend, encourager, and guardian angel to me. She'd been at *The New Yorker* since World War II, knew where all the ghosts were, and wasn't afraid to tell. I wasn't afraid to listen – and take notes. Now that she's gone, along with half the cast of characters, I feel entitled to share our enlightening dialogue – as well as the dirt. As Joan Didion – and my mother – know, "A writer's always selling someone out."

Helen used to jump to attention whenever there were requests from her favorite staffer, Ian Frazier, author of the hysterically droll first-person collections *Dating Your Mom* and *Coyote v. Acme*. A decade later, I invented my own "instant gratification takes too long" school of journalism. The goal I set for my students was to sell a piece by the end of class to cover their tuition. The rule was, if they got $1,000 for it, I got dinner (I've since had hundreds). I'd invite them to "Rejection Slip Parties" where the cost of admission was a rejection slip they'd received to tape on my wall, joining many of my "Sorry, this just isn't right for us" letters. I made sure to point out the ones from the publications I wound up writing for, adding that in this biz, "no never means no." (It means rewrite, retitle, respin, add a more timely lead, and resend it to the hopefully nicer editor at the next cubicle.)

The heads of my teaching programs allowed me to offer $75 stipends for guest lecturers, so I begged Ian Frazier to speak to my

Monday night humor class. After charming my students, he asked me to co-teach a special Wednesday afternoon writing group with him at Holy Apostles church in Chelsea. It was a funny place for a nice Jewish girl. I didn't know what it would entail, but here's a good rule: When in doubt, emulate those you admire. That workshop, whose members were one-time addicts, the infirm, and formerly homeless people who chronicled their gritty lives on the street, has lasted more than a dozen years. It led to *Food for the Soul,* a special first-person charity anthology Frazier and I published together that wound up on *The Today Show,* NPR, and at Yale Divinity School.

As if to counter my Episcopalian adventure, I simultaneously befriended Ruth Gruber, a Jewish activist, one-time confidant of Golda Meir, and the oldest member of my writing workshop, who joined when she was turning eighty. A former foreign correspondent in Israel, Russia, Germany, and Alaska, Ruth was working on a memoir called *Ahead of Time.* She wanted to schlep from her vast Central Park West apartment to my tiny West Village one-bedroom to get chapter by chapter critiqued each week.

"But Ruth, you already have twelve books out! You're too advanced," I warned, afraid the motley crew of popcorn-crunching poets and critics I'd assembled in my living room would offend my fantasy grandma. Ruth held her ground, joined, showed up with fresh pages each week, listened carefully to the feedback offered, and diligently revised her opus. The first project she workshopped garnered the best reviews of her amazingly accomplished career. To think I used to walk around reciting, "Dying / is an art, like everything else. / I do it exceptionally well," from Sylvia Plath's "Lady Lazarus." Gorgeous lines, yes. But Plath finished only three books before she died at age thirty. Ruth, who at ninety-five has her nineteenth book out, became a better role model, teaching me about grace, fortitude, longevity, and many other essential truths.

While so many authors got famous and then lost their touch in their later books, she showed me that the way to keep improving was to keep asking the right people for criticism – regardless of how old or acclaimed you get. She said some authors, like Simone de Beauvoir, published multiple volumes of memoirs, insisting, "You can do anything as long as it works," and keep going as long as you have something important and useful to say. Ruth was so successful and fulfilled herself, she never begrudged her younger peers their own books and success. At her fancy uptown party for *Ahead of Time*, she invited the entire Tuesday workshop, who greeted her with a huge, warm group hug. It occurred to me that I'd created my own idealized, intergenerational writing family.

My teacher Jack was clearly a parental replacement, a poet dad I could pick. With Ian Frazier, a male mentor just five years older than I, it seemed like I'd bestowed on myself a helpful, artistic older male sibling, a nice concept for a firstborn female who was followed by three brilliant, sarcastic, science-brained brothers. Ruth was fifty years my senior, the age of a grandmother. Since they were giving me permission to be just like them, I chose substitute grandparents, mothers, fathers, and siblings who shared my passions much more than the biological ones, who to this day still hope I'll come to my senses and go to law school. In some ways, my instructors shaped my direction more than my relatives, friends, and lovers.

That was especially true of Harvey Shapiro, a shrewd, tough-talking editor I pursued as my poetry guide, pal, and protector. Though we shared the same last name and he came to seem like family, he was no actual relation. If at first his brusque manner intimidated me, I didn't mind, since he wound up printing my words in the country's best newspaper, with a circulation over one million. When a student in my course asked him if the writers he'd seen make it during his fifty-year career at *The New York Times Magazine* and *Book Review* were the ones with the most talent, Shapiro said, "No. It was the ones who were most obsessed." That word again. Talk about rapture! I could see my class thinking what I was thinking: *I can be obsessive. There's hope for me yet!*

Harvey was the one who commissioned Joyce Maynard's first splashy *New York Times Magazine* article in 1972, "An Eighteen-Year-Old Looks Back on Life." Her pixie-like pose on the cover led to a letter from J. D. Salinger, a meeting, and her subsequent exposé of their odd relationship. Upon prodding, Harvey will repeat the colorful story of discovering Maynard to remind my students that most editors are dying to find fresh talent. And since full-time staffers are often white, gray-haired, and bespectacled, they prefer young, diverse new voices.

These days about half of those in my classes every term manage to get ink, an internship, or a job during my fifteen-week course. So many of my former students have published books that I made a new rule: Though I am thrilled to write endorsements for the projects of my protégés (one of my editors refers to me as a "blurb whore"), if any of the books sell better than mine, they have to give me a blurb. It's already happened — twice!

With the right instruction and encouragement, it is not hard to improve your work and have it see print. Okay, I admit that after selling five books and a movie in the last four years, I am one of the luckiest writers on the planet. You are meeting me in my most upbeat, optimistic phase, twenty-five years after I landed in New York City, clutching a batch of bad poems to my chest. One student handed in a parody of my class in which a bouncy brunette teacher reads a humor piece and says, "This is fantastic, really great! Now just rewrite the whole thing and make it a whole lot funnier." But so what? You have to be a little insane and self-deceiving to make it as a freelancer in an art field. I'm just emulating my mentors by offering a map.

Stumbling home after being bullied in elementary school, my mother told me I was the smartest kid in my class and my tormentors were just jealous. (Clearly they were just being jerks.) At a gala filled with beautiful women, my husband whispered, "You're the best-looking woman in the room." (Clearly we've been in couples' therapy.) I have a theory that the unspoken mentor-protégé pact involves the use of similar benevolent falsehoods to soothe feelings and insecurity. I bet that to build my confidence at times my mentors fibbed a bit or offered exaggerated hope or applause. Did believing their praise create a self-fulfilling prophecy? Fascinated by this cycle of benign deception, I wondered which falsifications defined each of my relationships with my gurus. It reflected the link my teacher Jack Zucker described in a poem to his grandfather Flexo, when he wrote, "Lies hold us together, like bandages."

Now I'm a writing teacher, the same age Mr. Zucker was when we first met, with many pupils and trusting disciples seeking my counsel. I've included an account of my fumbling attempt to impart hard-won knowledge to one of my acolytes. I don't know if my true-life sagas are idiosyncratic and distinct, or if they dissect the anatomy of any creative career. They certainly argue for the incredible sway the right mentors can have. At the end I added strategies for how to obtain, cultivate – or at least not alienate – a band of trusted advisers of your own.

I hope to be as sage and helpful to young students as my exalted elders have been to me. When I try to pinpoint their exact influence, I recall my second-grade music class, where I kept singing enthusiastically, loudly, and horribly off key. My poor frustrated instructor, who didn't want to hurt my feelings, had an idea. She placed me in the middle of the most melodious singers in the room for the entire term. This proximity to true talent so improved my pitch that I was given a solo in the school play, and I have sung relatively in tune ever since.

My First Muse

JACK

ZUCKER

"I need you to help me type some poems,"
Jack said, surprising me after the first day of my high school modern literature class. He stopped me at the door, handing me a book open to T. S. Eliot's poem *The Love Song of J. Alfred Prufrock*.

Who was this weird little guy, pointing to the goofiest title I'd ever heard? Why was he singling me out, punishing me with more work when I hadn't done anything wrong?

In September 1976, I was a tall, dark-haired, chain-smoking, lonely fifteen-year-old who could easily pass for the nineteen years my fake Michigan driver's license claimed. I was five foot seven, 125 pounds, and fully developed, so I felt like a giant towering over the boys my age. In my purse I actually had several phony IDs I used to get into local bars, where I'd puff on mentholated cigarettes, drink white wine, and dance with older men. I noticed I was about the same size as Jack Zucker, my new English teacher, a rumpled nerdball in khaki pants and a white button-down shirt. He had green eyes and dark wavy hair framing his baby face, which made him seem way younger than his forty-one years. It was like we were both stuck in the wrong age.

He'd spent the initial hour of class lecturing on Hemingway and Hardy and the second hour defending himself against the raucous argument that black and Asian female students raised about why his syllabus was filled with dead and boring white guys. I'd agreed with their screed but had stayed silent, busy finishing a poem. It was about a girl who carried around a deck of false identification cards; in case of an accident, nobody would know who she really was. So I wondered how this Jack person could have possibly known that I was a fast typist, or that the only thing that fired me up more than sex, drugs, and rock 'n' roll was poetry. I was an insomniac who stayed up all night in my pink bedroom, scrawling notebooks full of confessional poems and prose, envisioning myself as a cross between the Jewish Sylvia Plath and the feminine Bob Dylan.

Early that evening, inside my parents' white brick house in West

Bloomfield, I went upstairs with Jack's book, which included Eliot's long epic, and the ditto master Jack had given me. While tapping the keys of the IBM Selectric my father had brought home from his office for me, I reluctantly became interested in J. Alfred Prufrock, the geeky, self-conscious antihero. He was afraid of aging, knew he looked silly eating a peach, and longed for the mermaids who would not sing to him. Like me, he always felt he was wearing uncool clothes. Although he was old, male, and seemingly British, the overly cerebral, sad, paranoid Prufrock cracked me up; I could relate.

Hating shallowness and xenophobia, I zeroed in on Eliot's lines: "Should I, after tea and cakes and ices, / have the strength to force the moment to its crisis?" Amid inane social rituals I couldn't bear, I'd forced a crisis myself, five years before. I'd begged my parents to get me the hell out of the rigid, hall-monitored-bells-ringing-at-seven-thirty-in-the-morning public system, where I was lost, friendless, and flunking. Ironically, I hated attending the same well-endowed local school as all the rich white mean kids in the area, imploring my mother to send me to Roeper, the most diverse, radical educational institution in the state of Michigan. Its open classrooms "for artistic and gifted children" were full of minority kids on scholarship, bussed in from Flint and Detroit. The headmaster, George Roeper, was a left-wing advocate of Amnesty International. My Republican father wanted no part of it.

But my mom knew something was off. I was too sensitive, didn't fit in with my peers, and needed special attention. She'd feared I was learning disabled and had me tested, which proved just the opposite. Then she convinced Dad there was something amiss when a ten-year-old girl, who had a sophisticated vocabulary and loved to read, kept getting detentions, cried every day during recess, and was being demoted to the lowest reading group. "You can't fit a round peg into a square hole," the Roeper admissions officer told my folks. "Susan will be much happier here."

Upon landing there in sixth grade, I immediately made pals of all races and backgrounds, aced college-level English courses, and felt better. I later realized this was because Roeper didn't begin until ten-thirty in the morning, so every day I was functioning on three or four hours more sleep. Also, Woodward Avenue, where Roeper was located, was on my doctor father's route to the hospital. So he drove me to school every day, which gave us rare, much-needed time alone together. My favorite part was when his silver Cadillac would race down the twenty-mile-an-hour zone on Lahser Road and the same redneck cop would give him a speeding ticket. "Don't tell your mother," he would say every time, paying the secret tickets at his office. I never told (until now).

George Roeper, the German-born headmaster, had escaped the Nazis to become an outspoken voice against anti-Semitism, racism, and the Vietnam War. He rallied for his pet cause, Amnesty International, at daily assemblies he convened by beating on an African tin drum. He had a thick accent and looked like a cross between Sigmund Freud and

Grandpa on *The Munsters*. He insisted we call him, and all our teachers, by their first names. His experimental "learning laboratory" was in the tony town of Birmingham, housed in a woodsy, semi-dilapidated country mansion. George and his wife, Annemarie, had bought it in the 1940s for a progressive nursery school and then expanded.

There were no mindless bells, dress codes, gymnasium, or glee clubs, and few desks and chairs. Instead an art camp atmosphere reigned. There were impromptu bongo drum concerts in the halls, constant rehearsals for musical theater shows, a modern dance instructor whose silk parachutes filled the cafeteria, talent shows with mimes and clowns, and an annual weekend Trampolinathon to benefit the scholarship fund. Kids walked around in gorilla, army, or monk costumes, no questions asked. We met downtown police officers in a class called Emphasis Detroit and beat pillows with tennis rackets in Transactional Analysis.

Switching to this idealistic, politically correct environment did not come without culture shock. My first new friend was Tammy, a warm and gregarious black sixth-grade classmate who turned out to be the daughter of a doctor colleague of my father's. I visited her at her home in Palmer Woods, a fancy Detroit area. When Tammy slept over at my house, some kids I grew up with called her a *"shvartzeh."* I asked my mother what it meant. "It means our Jewish neighbors are stupid assholes," she said. Even though I figured it out and told Tammy it was a derogatory term for people of color, she thought the word was funny. Back at school the next day, every time she saw a group of black students, she'd call out, "There's some *shvartzehs!*" really loud. Then Shirley, another Detroit girl in our class whom I barely knew, called me "whitey" and "kike" and threatened to beat me up. Luckily, Shirley soon left Roeper, Tammy stopped using Yiddish, and things went back to being fairly harmonious.

Best of all, for the eldest of four siblings born in the space of seven years, Roeper respected privacy. It was easy to sneak away to read in the tree house, doghouse, garage, garden, or a room in one of the Martin Luther King domes, the igloo-shaped buildings of the lower school. I embraced the wannabe hippie stereotypes that annoyed my parents, wearing torn jeans, painter pants, and peasant blouses, smoking cigarettes and dope, swearing, and calling myself a raging feminist poet. But I earned good grades and remained clean cut and well mannered enough to confuse authority figures.

"Do you know T. S. Eliot's work?" I asked my father at dinner that night. I expected him to make the same gagging gesture he had made when I mentioned Sylvia Plath, while my brothers ran to the stove and took turns sticking their heads inside. I waited for another tedious lecture on how I should give up poetry to study law, medicine, or business, like everybody else with a brain.

"*Shantih shantih shantih,*" my father said, smiling.

Having just been introduced to *Prufrock*, I had no idea what that meant. After we finished eating, my dad led me downstairs to his den, an unusual act since he always wanted to be left alone in there. From amid the thick medical tomes and historical biographies stuffing his bookshelves, he pulled out an oversize hardcover I'd never seen before. It was a facsimile edition of corrections that Ezra Pound had made on the first draft of Eliot's poem *The Waste Land*. I thought *Prufrock* was long, but this poem was way longer, book length. I'd never seen a book-length poem before. Everything about my father's volume fascinated me, especially that one writer would take such liberties with another writer's work – crossing out entire stanzas, rearranging lines, scrawling notes in the margins. Wasn't that blasphemy?

Mostly it amazed me that my father, a Lower East Side New York street kid who'd morphed into a conservative Midwestern doctor who trashed my admittedly unusual school by calling it "a kooky communist country club," would have such an obscure poetry book in his vast nonfiction collection, let alone light up at the mention of T. S. Eliot. I'd almost forgotten that it was my father who'd first taught me poems, singing me stanzas in lieu of lullabies when I was a baby.

The rare times Dad was home, he was preoccupied with discussing diseases with my three younger brothers. But finally we were bonding here – over something really important! My father read me pages of *The Waste Land* out loud. I looked at his face and realized he wasn't reading; he had whole sections memorized. I didn't understand a word of it, but I guessed that its gloomy tone appealed to his pessimistic side.

"My teacher said it's the most important poem of the century," I told him.

"Is your teacher from New York?" he asked.

How did he know? "His bio said he was born in Brooklyn but grew up in Inwood Hills. Where's that?"

"Way uptown. What's his name?"

"Zucker." My father had never paid attention to who my teachers were before. "His first name is Jack, like yours," I added.

"Don't know him," he said. "Now get your old man a cup of coffee." He ruined the emotional connection, as if we'd reached his threshold of intimacy for the day.

"You already have one subservient female waiting on you in this household," I tossed out. "Don't be a chauvinist pig." (This sounded quite sassy and provocative in the '70s, at least to me.)

"This chauvinist pig is paying the tuition that allows you to learn that feminism crap," he countered, totally unfazed. "So get me that cup of coffee."

In the kitchen I poured him a cup, adding the sprinkle cookies he liked to the saucer. Rushing back downstairs, I handed it over – on the condition that I could borrow his yellow Eliot/Pound book to show to the other Jack at school the next day.

My teacher was impressed with my father's book, which he'd never seen a copy of before. He showed it to our class, which consisted of a ragged bunch of teens who sat on chairs, the floor, and the windowsills, swearing, arguing, eating potato chips, and puffing on cigarettes. Soon Jack was directing questions at me and asking me to help him type on a regular basis. When I asked why he couldn't just get the poems copied, he said it was better the way I typed it, with several poems fitting on one page, which saved a lot of paper. I never knew why he'd picked me for this chore, but I began to enjoy typing poems, which helped me study and memorize them. I also kind of liked being singled out for the extra attention — until he started reading paragraphs from my papers out loud and criticizing them in front of everyone. Like Pound did to Eliot, he slashed my words, jotting down messy, combative notes and challenges in the margins, as if my writing were not a solitary art but a collaborative sport, like boxing with a lesser opponent who could cream you.

"I suppose you think this is humorous, but it's so overstated it falls flat," he wrote. "Pretty forceful stuff, but you have yet to prove your case," he added. Along with: "Tell me why it's ironic or don't throw the word around"; "Your first sentence seems awfully general. What's your point? You must have one hiding somewhere"; and "Your theme here is ridiculously obvious. Can't you even aim for something semi-original?"

At first his blunt and sometimes public criticism embarrassed me and hurt my feelings. He was being mean, picky, and horribly intrusive, trying to get between my head, my hand, and my paper. But soon I saw that his tactics worked — he was making me think about every sentence I wrote in a new way. I was arguing with Jack constantly in class, after class, in my pages, and in my mind, editing and overediting. It wasn't like fighting with my dad and brothers, who were always preoccupied with math and science, speaking in medical jargon I didn't understand, interrupting and talking over me. Jack was challenging me in a language I loved and then listening carefully to my responses. Debating over words felt fun, intense, and stimulating in a way I wasn't used to. I became desperate to prove him wrong, improve each line, and be rewarded with any crumb of his praise.

Reading and writing were the only areas where I felt smarter than my siblings. I'd been memorizing poems since I was two and my Aunt Ettie had given me Robert Louis Stevenson's *A Child's Garden of Verses*. Now I'd skip biology, chemistry, and algebra to hide in the tree house, get stoned, and scrawl songs, poems, and diary entries. My sometimes rhyming, sometimes free verse encompassed the typical tangle of adolescent traumas: debating whether it would work out with this handsome, eighteen-year-old potential boyfriend, Mark (a senior who had a mustache, glasses, and a slick Trans Am), envying the fuss over my brothers' bar mitzvahs, trashing the suburban roles of wife and mother I already felt were being shoved down my throat.

As with many misguided young poets, my favorite topic soon became writing about writing. Poems about making poems infiltrated my notebooks for all my other subjects. It was hard to concentrate on anything but the next lines I was working on, as if reality merely existed to provide me with material. Even during Jack's lectures, I pretended I was taking notes, when I was really just continuing to record my internal saga. One day, at the end of such a class, Jack slipped me a poem called "The Black Art," which began: "A woman who writes feels too much, / those trances and portents! / As if cycles and children and islands / weren't enough; as if mourners and gossips / and vegetables were never enough. / She thinks she can warn the stars. / A writer is essentially a spy . . . "

Oh my god. It was totally about me! I was transfixed. I xeroxed the poem and reread it hourly. Who was this all-knowing witch, Anne Sexton, the biting, smart, and bitter twin sister I'd never had? The forty-three dark and complex poems in Sylvia Plath's slender collection *Ariel* had enthralled but also confused me; they were like an elitist, elusive code I couldn't quite crack. Sexton's work was more out there, rougher, less academic, easier to take in, filled with blatant psychology references (the only other subject I could stand and understand). Plus, there was tons more of it. Reading her nine volumes, I felt as if I'd stumbled upon a stack of my best girlfriend's endless diaries. I devoured everything by Sexton I could find. Still hungry for more, I asked Jack about her. He said that he'd actually been friendly with her in the '60s, when they'd hung out during a teaching stint in Boston. He'd been shattered when she killed herself. She'd read some of his poems and proclaimed them to have "great value." Wow, a famous dead poet's praise. At the time it seemed to me the ultimate badge of honor.

After that I'd hog Jack's office hours to discuss and deconstruct Sexton and Plath, along with Ted Hughes, Robert Lowell, Allen Ginsberg, and Gregory Corso. I was excited by these angry, open voices, pouring their guts out about real things that nobody in my milieu ever mentioned in public. I was lost in the poems, found in the poems, shaken, yet I felt like I'd just come home. I emulated them — horribly, of course. Jack said my poetic voice was improving, though my grammar and punctuation "still really sucked."

That winter I impetuously decided I needed to get to college right away. I was sixteen, but I had enough credits to graduate and good enough grades and test scores to get into Vassar or NYU, my dream schools. On my side were Jack and my adviser, Schavi, a young, pretty black teacher with a big afro and bright-colored kimono-style dresses who'd turned me on to Langston Hughes, Nikki Giovanni, Rita Dove, and Maya Angelou. The opposition was the old, bald, white, Buddha-looking headmaster, George, and the stern WASP college adviser, Barbara, who was pale and wore oversized glasses and a fake-looking beehive hairdo. She'd nixed my marvelous escape plan with one stab: "Susan, we think you're not emotionally mature enough to handle college." I was insulted, heartbroken, and mortified to learn that my square parents would have the deciding vote.

"Jack, Barbara says I'm not emotionally mature enough to handle college! Can you believe that?" I lit a cigarette, holding back tears. "Do you think she's right?" I put him on the spot. "You never lie to me. Tell me the truth."

"All the students here are emotional basket cases," Jack offered. "They may have high IQs, but there is way too much freedom at this *meshugganeh* place. You all need more discipline and structure so you stop running around like wild maniacs. You show no respect for your teachers or the learning process. Frankly, I find it upsetting to be teaching in such a circus."

He didn't answer my question, and it was the first time I noticed how nonlinear and off the wall he could be. Since he was a left-winger who'd complained about the rigidity at his last job, Phillips Academy in Andover, Massachusetts, it surprised me that Jack suddenly sounded as conservative as my dad. I feared that if he didn't help me, I was doomed to hang around Roeper for another year – even though I'd already taken every English class the school offered, along with a few at the nearby Oakland University. I couldn't compete with my brainiac classmates' 1500 and 1600 SAT scores. I would have to give up my only possible distinction – being the youngest graduate that year. Worse, since there were only thirty kids in each grade, I'd already gone through – and alienated – mustache Mark and all the other decent, cute guys. I would have to spend a whole year English-class less and dateless.

I'd heard that Jack lived in Birmingham with a journalist wife and two artistic daughters he was close to. Was that why he understood me? He and my father had both come from poor immigrant clans in New York. Was that why I understood him? I pondered the connections. Both Jacks had put T. S. Eliot on some kind of weird postwar pedestal. They were both loners wavering between being the establishment and abhorring the establishment. I determined that the second Jack — anti-Roeper rampage notwithstanding — was my best bet for an ally who'd be able to sway the original Jack to see it my way.

"Would you try to convince my father that I can handle graduating this spring?" I begged Jack. "Please. You have to help me. My family has no idea who I am. I feel like an alien stuck on the wrong planet. I need to leave home and go to college in September. I might be immature and *meshugganeh*, but I'm always right about myself."

Meetings were hastily arranged between my eccentric headmaster, disapproving WASP college counselor, hip adviser Schavi, and the dual Jacks. I was not invited. I waited in the tree house, smoking and reciting Sexton's "The Black Art" twenty times for good luck, French-inhaling between stanzas. When my dad emerged from the main office on that cold Friday in February, he looked solemn. We walked down the hill toward his silver Cadillac. I awaited the bad news: that even in the practically lawless realm of

Roeper, I couldn't break some dumb rules. That the principal and college adviser had deemed me a juvenile idiot unready for higher learning. I even feared that Jack had been a turncoat and shared his rant about how students here were undisciplined maniacs.

But my father informed me that I could graduate early — on two conditions. I could not apply to Vassar, NYU, or any out-of-state schools, and I first had to get officially accepted to a respectable local college. I hugged him, jumped up and down in the parking lot, and agreed to apply to the University of Michigan, only an hour away in the mellow land of Ann Arbor, home of the annual Hash Bash. It didn't occur to me that those stipulations — not moving to my father's old city and staying in the state — had been invented by my protective dad and not by anybody at Roeper. But I never pushed for more details. Handed an escape route out of Jewburbia, I wasn't pressing my luck. Nor did I tell my father I'd already sent in my application to join the Woolverines (which my mother had clandestinely signed).

I assumed Jack had gone to bat for me and felt intense gratitude. Instead of a hug or emotional exchange, the next day he merely nodded when he heard my news. How cold! It occurred to me that by leaving Roeper I'd be abandoning him and his domain. I might never see him again. Was he rejecting me before I could reject him? Then, on my way out of his next class, he slipped me a poem with his byline.

The Last Dead Animal Poem,
  or *Searching Through the Sink*

A fly got in behind the Ajax can.

Not the kind of big fly

That buzzes around and drives

you half mad, just an ordinary fly.

How he got there I don't know,

But there he was,

dead and all

When I made my biannual cleaning

Behind the sink.

Should I have written a poem

On this poor *shlemiel* of a fly

Called "All the Lonely Trapped Ones?" telling how

I pushed him over the sink's brink

To the terrible darkness below?

Well the truth is,

I sprinkled him with Ajax

And said one original Hebrew blessing:

Goodbye,

Old fly!

Jack had introduced me to my favorite gut-wrenching, powerful poetry of pain, sadness, suicidal feelings. Now, through his words, he showed me that writing could also be funny, satiric, Jewish, colloquial, and address less-than-grand subjects. You were even allowed to throw Yiddish in there! From my parents' conversations I sort of recalled that a *shlemiel* was a "foolish person," while *shlemozzl* referred to someone who was a "born loser." When I checked with Jack, he clarified: "A *shlemiel* is a man who keeps spilling hot soup on a *shlemozzl*."

With me on my way out of Roeper's door, the floodgates opened. Jack showed me his poetry series about the loud, intrusive clan of Jewish loony tunes he'd left back East: his grandmother who baked challah bread she fed to her fifteen cats, his angry commie uncle who shook his fist at God and all the rabbis, his Grandfather Flexo, the grocer who hid the bad tomatoes under the good ones. It was as if Jack had turned Isaac B. Singer stories into poetry.

Jack said that good writing "started in delight and ended in wisdom." I thought his work was good because it made me laugh, cringe, cry, and think. Not only because the people he vividly captured were endearing, human, and maddening, but because I recognized the characters from the lunatic, Yiddish-speaking extended family my parents couldn't wait to get away from. I had relatives just like that! I had an angry communist cousin who'd gone to jail and two obese, loudmouth aunts. My Grandfather Harry, who owned Shapiro's Window Shades on Delancey Street, had been tricked into marrying Grandma Yetta, who was sicker and a dozen years older than he had been told. Harry hated most people, preferring to talk to his pet parrots, which scared me as a kid.

I hadn't yet nailed down why Jack's intensity, brains, and sly dark humor fighting off depression felt so comfortable and familiar. Now I knew. We could have been from the same village (which he'd call "shtetl"). If a male mentor were a father figure, I'd stuck pretty close to the gene pool. In picking Jack I'd chosen an uncle, or older brother. Or perhaps I'd stumbled upon a warmer, more verbally expressive version of my father – the guy my dad might have been pre-doctor, years before I was born.

I graduated from Roeper in May, two years early, at sixteen, the youngest in the class. (There were two other sixteen-year-olds, but I was younger by a few months. Ha!) In September 1977, I enrolled at the University of Michigan and adored everything about the school – except lecture classes with two hundred students where you barely met your teachers. I took an independent study with an eccentric poetry professor who liked my work. But he had time to read and edit only one poem a week. I was pouring out twenty or thirty. Out of those, only one would be halfway decent, but I couldn't yet tell which one on my own. I needed someone with better critical eyes to show me.

By my second semester I sorely missed Jack, irrationally feared he'd moved on to other pet students and had forgotten me. So I sent him a sheepish letter asking if he remembered me, along with a stack of new poems. I threw in humorous essays I'd published in a campus humor magazine, *Michigas,* and *The Gerbil,* a literary magazine. (Ads for it showed a rodent with leather high heels and a whip and commanded "Submit to the Gerbil.") Of course I remember you, Jack wrote back, launching into great Roeper gossip about George, who was retiring, and Barbara, who was still victimizing seniors. After me they'd stopped letting anyone graduate two years early, he reported. More important, he marked up *all* of my new poems, said several were worth rewriting, and offered his assessment: I was improving and "zeroing in" on myself. He was pleased I was an English major, following in his footsteps.

He was even more pleased in 1981, when I moved to Greenwich Village to earn my master's degree in NYU's English program. He sent me back every batch of my poems and humor pieces completely edited, checking the good lines, putting question marks by phrases he found incoherent, deleting extra phrases, repetitions, and clichés. He told me I was allowed to use every word only once in a poem or an essay, because using the same words twice or more was lazy and dull, and insisted that I consult a thesaurus to find synonyms. Best of all were his goofy, sarcastic commentaries in the margins. "This line echoes Plath. At least steal from somebody less famous"; "Stop using big vague general words like 'life,' 'love,' and 'passion,' you're putting me to sleep" and "The first three lines here should be killed, it's just adolescent throat-clearing." A few starred lines later he added, "But this stanza is fine, fresh, and off-color – now you're cooking."

Jack taught me that the secret to good writing was rewriting. My first drafts were always a mess. I needed a sharp critic to cut out the fat, point out my best lines, and tell me which direction to follow. Jack often said my generalities were trite and boring, and that dialogue and specific details were the way to go. After getting his feedback, I'd rework my lines over and over until I was saying the same thing more specifically and succinctly. Each revision made my pieces better and clearer. "Read what you want to be writing," he'd advise. So whenever I was confused or stuck, I'd go to my shelves and pull out a book I admired in the same genre. I'd scrutinize exactly how the author had pulled off what I was attempting, which I came to see as a free consultation.

In 1983, feeling unappreciated by the new headmaster, Jack left Roeper to become chairman of the English department at a private school in Ohio. We still kept in touch, but his displacement wigged me out. Even though I'd taken off first, I wanted Jack to stay at my old school, lodged safely in my past, where I'd left him. Not that I'd hesitated to move on and seek new mentors.

While finishing my master's degree, I fell for Dan, a very smart, intense, forty-year-old poetry professor who, like Jack, was an astute critic. Dan "fixed all my broken half-rhymes and drew stars for honesty," as I later wrote in a poem. Not knowing I was a walking grad school cliché, I embarked on a whirlwind romance with him. He showed me the older West Village literary scene, initiating me into such essential rituals as eating Chinese food in bed on Saturday nights while reading the first edition Sunday *New York Times*. It felt cool, like we were in a downtown Woody Allen movie.

I was enthralled to be hanging out with Hugh Seidman, Jim Reiss, David Ignatow, Yehuda Amichai, and the rest of Dan's crew of seriously majestic poets, honored to be in the same room as these geniuses. Because at the time I was sharing a big one-bedroom sublet in a chic lower Fifth Avenue building, I offered to throw them book parties and receptions after their lectures and group poetry readings. When I mentioned the first upcoming social gathering to my mother, who'd become a West Bloomfield party planner, she was aghast that I'd been instructed to serve just wine and cheese. She called Second Avenue Deli and (in Yiddish) explained she was from the Lower East Side and entreated the owner to rush over trays of turkey, roast beef, salami, pastrami, lox, bagels, et cetera, to feed her daughter's poor, suffering artist friends. My soirees became quite popular, and I was soon known for throwing the best-catered free poetry events in town. Only problem was the books on my shelves were signed with such salutations as: "Great chopped liver. Hugh 1983."

Answering questions about my generous Jewish mother in Michigan, I found out that my new poetry pals had known my high school teacher Jack from his old days back East. How funny that I'd stumbled into Jack's one-time gang! Jack was also tickled by the literary links, though I didn't tell him I was dating Dan right away. I worried that jumping the bones of a fellow poet his age seemed too tawdry or incestuous — that is, until the connection became more than kosher.

Since my parents expected me to move back to the Midwest after I earned my NYU diploma, I was desperate to land a real job real quick to stay in my beloved big city. I told Dan about an assistant position open at *Soap Opera Digest* I was applying for. "You just spent thirty thousand dollars to study with Nobel- and Pulitzer Prize-winning poets, and you're going to go work for a soap opera rag? Are you a complete idiot?" he yelled. Instead he insisted I send my resume to *The New Yorker*.

"Right, like somebody is really going to hire me there," I told him, rolling my eyes. Nevertheless, I was flattered that he thought so highly of my career potential, and — not being a complete idiot — I immediately mailed my resume and cover letter. Dan then placed a call to highly recommend me to an editor he knew there. By the time I started the job as an official peon in *The New Yorker*'s editorial library a month later, Dan and I had split up and the magazine became my new love.

My impressive gig excited Jack, who acted as if his hunch about me, and the attention he'd lavished on me, had paid off. His long typed yet messy letters were filled with exuberant questions. He sent *Beginnings*, a book of his poems published by a small house, along with new poems, asking what I thought. I marked them up, line editing the way I'd done in my NYU graduate writing workshops. After I mailed them, I worried he'd be hurt by my tough criticism. But Jack was amazed.

"Holy cow, when did you become such a wise slasher!? Kind of bugs me that you can see problems it would take me seven months to figure out.... You're already as good as Jimmy and he doesn't return my calls or letters. So you're stuck with the job," Jack wrote. I was jazzed that he appreciated my newfound editing skills. By studying with luminaries, obsessively reading and rewriting, and listening to smart scribes critique each other's work, I'd picked up more than I'd realized. Since my work appeared to improve by osmosis, I decided to always hang out with writers I wanted to be.

Jack sent me more poems, five or ten at a time, wanting my opinion the way I'd once hungered for his. I ardently obliged. Then he asked me to submit the ones I liked to Howard Moss, *The New Yorker*'s poetry editor. I totally dug the transition from being Jack's needy student to being his esteemed colleague and urban connection. Although I got a few nice "almost" notes, neither of us had any luck selling a poem to Moss. I hated getting rejection letters from my full-time employer, but I was far from alone. Every receptionist, secretary, and *New Yorker* messenger was also quietly submitting their work through interoffice mail.

In the meantime, Jack didn't like Ohio and moved back to Michigan to teach at Oakland University. He and Helen settled in Oak

Park, the neighborhood where my family had lived when I was little. Although I was a thousand miles away in the Big Apple, Jack was residing in my old backyard, which in poetic logic was closer.

When I visited Michigan, Jack and I would go out to eat at a nearby Chinese dive. Our feelings for each other were nonsexual – like father and daughter – but these meetings were more significant to me than dates. We were dying to hear what the other thought of the latest work we had sent. Plus, I'd never gone out to dinner alone with my father, who was always too busy working, or going to sports games with my brothers, to give me the one-on-one attention I craved. So in terms of self-esteem, seeing Jack was better and cheaper than therapy. He viewed me as his former star student and local girl made good, who reflected well on him. Not to mention the second chance I offered him to catch up with his cronies or the cachet of any affiliation with *The New Yorker*.

Jack and I basically adopted each other. When I invited him and Helen to my parents' for dinner, Helen won my mother over by telling stories of how they'd married at New York's City Hall in 1958. My parents, who'd been equally "poor as church mice," had tied the knot there in 1954. Jack played chess with my brother Michael. Before he left we exchanged poems, quietly trading manila envelopes, as if sharing x-rays that would show what was going on beneath the skin.

My salary at the magazine was humiliatingly low, but my first years on the East Coast were crammed with hope. When I could only publish in tiny journals nobody ever heard of, Jack sent long letters of reassurance. "I've been in all sorts of crummy small magazines, it's good to keep getting printed. . . . Took Jimmy ten years of academic journals before he broke into the inner circle, with the help of his big-shot friend John, may his soul rot in hell for saying my poems were corny. . . . Keep cracking the small rags. They'll lead to better. Just crazy or lucky people write poetry for money."

When I left *The New Yorker's* editorial track to freelance in 1987, Jack wrote, "You are a real poet and a real poetry critic, which is rare. Your work keeps getting better. I'm proud of you." My father wasn't so proud and let me know he didn't plan to keep paying my rent indefinitely.

With help from journalist friends, I made the transition from poetry to selling articles, profiles, humor essays, and book reviews to *The New York Times*. Clips from *The Washington Post, The Boston Globe,* the *Los Angeles Times, The Nation,* and *The Village Voice* followed, then glossy magazines whose payments escalated from $500 to $1,000 to $2,500 per piece. Jack responded most strongly to the poems I had printed – even if they were just in the NYU magazine or *Cover* or *The Aquarian,* free underground papers that paid in copies.

My father ignored my poems, except to say that he hated the few about him – "Dr. Daddy," (the one Jack thought echoed Plath) and "Shapiro's Window Shades," about how my bitter grandfather never forgave my father for leaving the family window shade business to become a doctor. Dad was impressed by my lighter nonfiction in *Cosmopolitan, Glamour, New Woman, New York Woman, People,* and *US Magazine.* Earning a dollar per word for ten-page pieces that took a week seemed incredible, especially when ten-line poems that had taken five years earned $20. When my mother informed my father that I had earned $5,000 ($1.50 per word) for an oddly innocent profile of an actor in *Penthouse,* I received a rare paternal call of congratulations.

"Doesn't it bother you that I'm in a X-rated magazine?" I asked my father, waiting for him to make fun of me.

"If they pay you that well, why don't you pose for them too?" Dad kidded.

"Still a sexist Republican, I see."

"Really, it's good," he told me. "You need to make a living with your writing. Not because I can't help you out — which I will — but for you."

"But I would rather be writing poetry."

"Oh, come on, Susie." I pictured my father shaking his head. "You gonna sell poems on the sidewalk to pay your rent? You're almost thirty. Get a life already."

It was clear that my father was still an insensitive, closed-off, middle American clod. Though I did steal his "Why don't you pose for them too?" line for my humor piece "A Feminazi in Smutland." It chronicled how a raging feminist could justify writing for *Penthouse*, ironically stating that the essential part of feminism was being independent, while my father was sending me $1,000 a month for my rent so I could stay in New York.

I saw my longer magazine work as inconsequential, a sideline to make a living. In my heart I was a real poet; Jack had said so. Yet after a decade in Manhattan, it wasn't happening for me. Between part-time jobs, bad breakups, and freelance ups and downs, I went through a downer period where I was totally drained. I smoked, toked, drank, and screwed around, feeling defeated and frustrated.

"Hey, have some patience. I'm way older than you and I haven't made it yet. It takes a while. Don't give up," advised Jack, who'd published his second collection, *From Manhattan,* and had work featured in well-known, classy magazines. But the fact that he hadn't really "made it" yet made me doubt his judgment – when it came to my work and his own. I wanted to give up. I stashed away many versions of each of my poems in my files and stopped sending them out. I'd heard no enough times for one lifetime.

I found a Jack Zucker miniscrawl in the mail in September 1990. It said, "I have incredible news. I'm founding a new magazine in Michigan called *The Bridge.* I've already accepted stellar work from Bukowski, Patty Hooper, Judith McCombs, Phyllis Janowitz, and Jimmy! I'm flying pretty high with this! Will you submit some poems?" Along with the note, he enclosed an article from *The Eccentric,* a local newspaper. It said that the bridge pictured on Jack's magazine's cover, one on I-75 in Detroit, had been designed by Jack's daughter. "For years I've had this foolish longing in my brain to start a literary journal," Jack was quoted as saying. "Like a bridge that spans distant shores, we'll span traditional and experimental genres and dare to take chances."

If he could take chances, so could I. What the hell! I went to my tin file cabinet and spent the next forty-eight hours straight rewriting poems from the rejected series on my crazy Jewish relatives. I sent Jack the ones about my Aunt Celia talking to her dead husband Natie, my grandfather's window shade store on Delancey Street, the ghost of my Aunt Rose, Dr. Daddy, Uncle Sid at the Sukkoth party, and Grandpa Harry walking around the house, listing everyone he'd ever loved who'd died.

In *The Eccentric* article, the fiction editor had warned that for every twenty poetry, short story, or essay submissions *The Bridge* was getting, it accepted only one. I was not intimidated because I didn't really count this as an official submission. I was just sending some work to an old Michigan pal. Jack was safe. Or so I thought. But then I heard nothing in October and November. By December I was despondent. He obviously didn't even have the balls to tell me that I didn't measure up compared to the stars he was publishing. This had to be an all-time low – my first muse declaring that I was a failure. In January a tiny Jack envelope finally came. I hoped it wasn't a standard form rejection, which would be worse than no response at all.

"My coeditor Mitzi ran into my office the other day, holding up a batch of poems." She was yelling, 'Jack! I've discovered a new talent, a genius, a real first-class poet we have to publish! Read these!' Guess who that was? They were yours!" he wrote. "I love them! *The Bridge* would like to accept four!" which he listed. Then he wrote, "Upon publication you'll receive two complimentary copies of *The Bridge*!"

I'd never seen Jack use so many exclamation points before. It was the kind of overpunctuation he would have slammed me for. Fat tears fell from my eyes to Jack's letter, smudging the ink. I was a real poet after all! By the time I read his last line – "P.S. Mitzi disagrees with me, but the last line of 'Dr. Daddy' could be improved" – I was weeping and laughing at the same time. I called my parents, who were relieved to hear me sound human again.

Completely reinspired, I pulled out the forgotten drafts I'd given up on and reworked and resubmitted them everywhere. This round they were accepted by better literary journals, Jewish magazines, and anthologies. When they came out, I sent my *Cosmopolitan* editor a xerox of my *Bridge* poems. Sounding jealous, she said, "You know, we publish poetry too. Do you have any about relationships?" Of course I had tons of love-gone-wrong ditties, and *Cosmo* bought a few – for $100 a pop, the most I'd ever been paid for a poem. The first one *Cosmo* took, about my ex-boyfriends, began: "If all my old lovers lived in a row of dark houses on the same street . . . " I figured it would be my most read poem, since I'd heard the magazine readership was seven million.

I sent Jack a thank-you note, mentioning how he'd made my six years at Roeper so memorable. He wrote back that he'd begun teaching there in 1976; thus, I had been his pupil for only my two senior semesters, not the six years I'd magnified it to. How interesting what we misremember. I then sent him so many rewrites of poems that his next missive said: "We'll take 'The Ghost of Aunt Rose,' 'If Celia Wrote Natie A Letter,' and 'Grandmother Sophie.' But now we have so many Susan Shapiro masterpieces in our custody, please don't send any more for a while or we'll OD on your *mishpocheh,* and your family is even more *meshugganeh* than mine."

Jack published fifteen of my poems in a row. Members of my Tuesday workshop submitted their poems and fiction to Jack, too, and five had work accepted. So *The Bridge* became our official mascot. Since it was a nonprofit that survived through grants and donations, whoever could afford to sent in $50 or $100. I later noticed my parents on the list of *Bridge* donors.

A few months later, my Michigan colleague Lynne recommended I try a small press that had published her first book of poems. I submitted my manuscript (culled from my NYU thesis), and the editor there miraculously accepted my collection, *Internal Medicine*. The title came from the first poem, about my brother Brian's acceptance to medical school, when my father had handed Brian the bones from his old study skeleton, one at a time. The spooky black book cover showed a naked girl dancing with a man in a skeleton costume. This slim paperback represented almost fifteen years of work and made almost no money. Jack had promised *The Bridge* would review *Internal Medicine*. Yet as each issue came and went, my first, hard-won collection was not even mentioned in the book section. Jack said they were overloaded with reviews and told me to be patient, they'd get to it. I was disappointed they never did.

By my midthirties I feared that my father was right about striving for external success. I focused more on commercial writing seen by the masses, which paid my bills. Jack was still on my VIP list, and he and Helen came to my wedding and my Michigan Barnes & Noble poetry reading in 1996. After that I composed fewer poems, and my visits to Michigan grew further apart. I started teaching at NYU and the New School several nights a week. When I uncovered a yellowed stack of my high school English assignments that Jack had marked up, I saw that I'd been editing my students' assignments in the exact way he had corrected mine. There were checks, stars, question marks, deletions, and sarcastic queries scrawled all over the margins, as if Jack had initiated a literary argument that I was continuing in the papers of my own protégés.

After *The Bridge*'s ten-year anniversary in 2000, I heard the journal was not doing so well, and neither was Jack. He had diabetes and other medical problems that left him disoriented and depressed. He sent an incoherent rant in the mail, and we had a few phone spats that didn't make much sense. Helen hinted it was his illness speaking, not Jack. I blamed his dark moods on his medication, wondering if I had underestimated his affinity for Anne Sexton and her work years earlier. I never quite got over *The Bridge's* not reviewing my poetry paperback, which it had inspired.

The fact that even Jack didn't review my book fed my overall discouragement with the professional poetry scene. My friends and I joked that the same group of guys named John and James kept winning all the prestigious prizes. I don't know if it was sour grapes, self-protection, or all my psychoanalysis finally paying off, but images of suffering poets lost their luster. Instead of exalting Plath, Sexton, and other prodigies who petered out young, I began noticing prolific journalists and authors of novels and memoirs who merrily published popular work into their old age. I was probably just disappointed that my own poems never lived up to their early promise.

"Your poetry just doesn't have enough music," said a poet friend. "You leave the scene of the crime too quickly," said another critic I asked. "You find the fire, but then you don't stay long enough, dig deep, and develop. You escape the pain, so your poems are too short and funny." The rare times I could assess my work objectively,

I saw that I was too linear in my thinking, too wordy for poetry, not careful or methodical enough, too messy and rapid-fire. If, as Jack once said, poetry was about the words you left out, I could never hold enough back.

When I was young I thought I had enough fierce honesty, intensity, and obsessive devotion to develop into a real poet. Oddly, as I aged, published more prose, and felt happier, everything that was once agonizing now looked humorous, ironic, ridiculous. I still believed in my writing. Yet I was better at longer work than poetry. All my editors, colleagues, and the world at large encouraged my first-person nonfiction. I wished Jack had also pushed me toward prose and thus spared me much time and heartache. But of course he couldn't. Giving up on my poetry may have meant he'd have to surrender his fantasy vision of himself as the real thing. How unfair of me to expect more than he could give.

Still, I loved Jack, and I called him in the spring of 2002, thrilled when a mainstream publisher made an offer on my first memoir. Helen said he was in the hospital and gave me the number. I called him there, afraid he wouldn't remember me. But he was completely lucid and happy to hear from me.

"It only took me two decades to get a hardcover," I told him.

"Congratulations! I always knew you were a real poet," he said.

Had he misheard what I had told him, or confused a funny first-person memoir with poems? On second thought, I decided what he was saying was astute – that my poetry had gone into my prose, and that one can always be a poet inside.

"My book is pretty commercial," I admitted. I didn't want to mislead him into thinking it was some kind of highbrow masterpiece. "It's about re-meeting my old lovers."

"'If all my old lovers lived in a row of dark houses on the same street,'" he said, quoting my *Cosmo* poem back to me. I hadn't thought of the connection. It was as if I'd unpacked that twenty-line poem, expanding my early theme into two hundred pages. But I feared he didn't really understand what kind of book it was.

"They're calling it 'chick lit,'" I explained. "I used my women's-magazine voice. Only raunchier."

"That's okay. I'm almost finished with my science fiction novel," he shot back. Did I even know he liked science fiction? "And I'm still reworking *Protest for My Uncle*."

"You've been reworking that one for twenty years. It's already been published. Isn't there a statute of limitations for poetry rewrites?" I joked. I must have gone over – and signed off on – that epic rant ten times.

"But it keeps getting better," he insisted. "I'll send you the new version when I finish."

He never finished. A month later, on July 30, 2002, Jack died of pneumonia. He was sixty-seven years old. I heard there was a very small burial, just for family. I was at my parents' house in Michigan on August 18th when a Roeper colleague called to tell me, very last minute, that a special memorial service for Jack was planned in Birmingham that day.

"I have to borrow your car," I told my mother that Sunday morning.

"I need it," she said. "I'll be done by two."

"But Jack Zucker's memorial service is at eleven!" I was teary and manic at the thought of missing it. "I have to go. I need a car. Why can't you get a cab in this town? Where can I find the number for a car service?"

I noticed my father hadn't gone to work at the hospital as he usually did, even on Sunday. "Can I borrow Dad's car?" I asked, though I'd never driven it before. I only came home once a year and barely drove anymore. Truth be told, I'd always been a horrible driver and was lucky to have settled in a city where I could get around by subway, bus, cabs, and on foot.

"I'll take you to Jack's service," my father surprised me by calling from the bottom of the steps.

"But it'll be an hour or two. How will I get home? I don't know who else is going. If I can't get a ride home, by the time you drop me off, you would have to come back to get me."

"I'm coming to the service with you," he said.

I was proud to show up at Jack's memorial service with my father. It implied — rightly — that Jack was so important to me that even my father had come to pay respects. Or was it that, having lost my first substitute dad, having my real father beside me made me feel protected and less alone?

Jack's family, friends, fellow Roeper and Oakland teachers, and former students were among the hundred mourners who showed up for the nonreligious service, which was appropriately *meshugganeh*. The memorial for Jack, a Reform Jew, was held at the Birmingham Unitarian Church and led by a reverend. The opera-singing mother of my old high school boyfriend Mark (the mustache) was crooning in Hebrew. Jack's wife and daughters read his poems. Mitzi spoke of Jack's ten glory years at *The Bridge*.

For me, the most vivid part of the service was learning what I'd never known about Jack. Irwin, one of his twin brothers, talked about Jack's early life. I didn't remember that Jack had twin brothers. I was amazed to note that Jack and I had the same birthday – January 23! He'd been a gifted student at Bronx Science High School, excelling in chemistry. I didn't know he'd been good at science, which he studied for two years at City College, where my mother had gone to school. He'd graduated as an English major in 1957. I'd never realized he had to make a choice between English and science. Irwin also spoke of how their father had been abusive and wondered out loud whether that was the root of Jack's bipolar disorder. His parents had divorced when Jack was eleven, and their mother had remarried, further complicating the boys' chaotic childhood. It was unusual to hear such openness at a Michigan funeral service. Yet it felt oddly right to honor a confessional poet. The program announced that a memorial poetry prize would be established in Jack's name at City College in New York.

On the car ride home I hummed along to the Motown song "I Heard It Through the Grapevine" on the radio, avoiding conversation. I was afraid that my father would poke fun at the psychobabble of the service or the poetry. Instead, he shared details I'd never heard about his own crazy, passive-aggressive father's antics in Manhattan. Rather than ridicule the admission that Jack had been abused as a child, my father was stirred by the confession, identifying with Jack's story.

My father revealed that he'd also written poetry in the early '50s. Three years older than Jack, he too had been a gifted science student (at Stuyvesant, another specialized New York high school) and had to choose between the same two majors. Should he be practical or idealistic? Follow his head or his heart? By picking English, Jack got to do what he loved but sentenced himself to a life with little money. Deciding on medicine, my father worked a million hours and was hardly ever home when I was a kid. Yet ultimately he'd prospered, earning an excellent salary, living in a bigger house filled with more children. For a moment it seemed as if the difference between my father and Jack came down to that one difficult yet crucial decision – instead of *Sophie's Choice*, it was both Jacks' choice.

Analyzing the roads they'd taken led me to question my own direction. Was I following in my doctor father's footsteps by deciding to pursue high-paying prose over poetry? Was that being a sellout or being smart and self-protective? I admired Jack for spending fifty years immersed in poems. Still, I had never felt more of a creative surge than when I was in the middle of one memoir and was already finishing another one. Couldn't I work for passion and money at the same time? Or was I just rationalizing greed?

"Jack was a good man," my father said.

"Yes he was. I'll never forget how he took my side at Roeper when it came to graduating early. Remember when George and Barbara said I wasn't emotionally ready to handle college? I was so hurt by that," I said, thinking that I was now about the age that Jack had been then.

"Immaturity wasn't your problem," my father told me. "Nobody really thought you weren't ready."

"What do you mean?" I turned the radio lower.

"Roeper was a poor school because of all the minority scholarships handed out. They were never as well endowed as Cranbrook or Country Day," he said.

I had no idea where this was leading. "What are you saying?"

"If you graduated two years early, they would have lost two years' tuition," he told me. "That's why they didn't want you to leave. It had nothing to do with maturity levels. It was finances. So I paid it and they let you graduate."

"What?" I turned the radio off, shocked. I pictured the day almost three decades before. George had been dead for years. Jack was gone, too, but it suddenly felt fresh in my mind. "That's what happened in that meeting? They didn't really think I was immature?" It was immature to still care so much what they thought of me so long ago, but I did.

"Nobody thought you were immature," my father repeated. "At fifteen, you were like thirty-five. You're more immature now than you were then."

"Thanks." I stuck out my tongue out.

"Listen, they just couldn't afford to lose two years' tuition. That's all."

What an astounding paradox! My left-wing comrades had lied to me and hurt my feelings while my right-wing father saved me by slipping them money under the table. I was glad to be just learning about it now, when I was an older, happily married grown woman feeling very psyched about finally making it to hardcover.

"Why didn't you tell me before?" I asked.

"You didn't ask."

"Come on, Dad."

"Because you loved Roeper so much," he said. "I didn't want to wreck your idealism."

"Now you can shatter it?" I asked.

"Now you can handle it," he said.

It was true. I could.

"Did Jack know about this?"

"I don't think so," he said. "It was just me and the headmaster in the meeting at the end. I don't think he wanted anyone else to know the exact terms of our deal."

I liked to think there was another reason that my father chose this moment to come clean. When I was fifteen, Jack had sort of taken over the role of father, guiding me in ways my dad couldn't. Juggling his busy job at the hospital, my mom, and my three brothers, he didn't have time for me. Now that he was older, slower, less busy, and Jack was gone, my father could reclaim his place in my heart.

Some people deceive you because they love you or want to avoid hurting your feelings, like Jack with his Grandfather Flexo. I used to think that Jack's insistence that I was a real poet constituted a deception between us. But it probably didn't, because Jack truly believed what he was saying. I know he did, because he published fifteen of my poems beside the words of his more esteemed colleagues in his baby, *The Bridge*. (One or two might have been a mercy print, but nobody you weren't sleeping with would publish *fifteen* poems he didn't like.) I often told my students, "I'll lie to you about anything but writing."

It turned out that the best lie from Jack was one I only recently caught. On the first day of his modern English lit AP class in 1976, he'd told me, "I need you to help me type some poems." I looked up all of his long typed letters to me, which I'd saved in a thick file with his name on it. Thirty years later, in the winter of 2006, I called Jack's widow, who was living in Oak Park, where I used to live.

"I have a question for you, Helen," I said. "Could Jack type well?"

"He was a great typist," she said. "Really fast — on the typewriter and computer. He typed all the time."

"What about in the early days at Roeper?" I needed to know. "Did he type well then?"

"Yes, he could always type well. Ever since I've known him. But at Roeper he had a secretary who typed even better than he did," Helen recalled. "She typed all his work weekly and left it in his box. Why do you ask?"

All in the Family

HOWARD

FAST

Growing up, I heard colorful stories about Howard Fast, my well-known communist cousin who was the best-selling author of *Spartacus* and *Citizen Tom Paine*. Yet, as a typically myopic teenager, I was more interested in my own romantic histrionics than historical fiction. Plus, Howard and his artist wife, Bette, lived eight hundred miles away, and I had so many elderly relatives coming out of my ears, I wasn't in a rush to find any more. When I moved to New York in 1981, my mother handed me their Connecticut phone number and said, "Don't be an idiot. Call them."

Busy juggling a secretarial job, NYU night classes, and self-destructive bed partners while scrawling the bad poetry I thought was my true calling, I waited a few months to make contact. All of a sudden I realized how cool it could be to have a famous novelist in the family and desperately wanted to meet Howard and Bette. As if fearing they wouldn't believe we had common blood, I composed a long letter overexplaining the Goodman-Shapiro-Cohen-Fast lineage: Bette's mother, Lillian Cohen, the best challah bread baker in Teaneck, New Jersey, was my lovely Great-Aunt Lilly. She was the sister of my grandfather Hyman Goodman, my mother's father. Hyman died when my mother was thirteen, leaving her (as the story went) a smart, fiery, poor, redheaded orphan. My mom, Miriam Goodman (nicknamed Mickey), idolized Lilly and her husband, Isaac Cohen, a New Jersey newspaper distribution magnate who founded the Hudson County News Company in North Bergen. Ike, as he was called, was king of the castle, since he employed the poor side of the family as office workers and truck drivers.

Though Lilly had three children who were already grown and married (Bette, Rozie, and Bobby Cohen), she'd offered to adopt my mother. But my mom couldn't bear leaving the City for the Cohens' New Jersey estate. She chose to live with her siblings until she was sixteen and then rented her own Grand Street tenement. Twenty years older than my mom, Bette and Howard were like her fantasy parents. They adored Mickey, partly because she was independent and didn't want Ike's patronage. A further bond was forged when my father rejected Ike's help and went to medical school in the Midwest, since Howard, refusing his father-in-law's handouts, was also determined to make it on his own.

My epic letter ended by revealing that I was an aspiring scribe. I told my cousins it would be an honor to meet them anywhere – even for a quick cup of coffee. I dropped my missive in the mailbox on my way to my midtown job Wednesday morning.

On Thursday they called and said, "Of course we want to meet you, Susie. Come to Connecticut on Saturday. We have to check out Mickey's daughter." I was stunned that the mail had arrived and they'd responded so quickly. Since receiving my letter, which (as I'd hoped) they found funny, they'd already called my mother. I could tell because I'd signed my name "Susan," but on the phone they called me "Susie," the moniker only my parents and best childhood friend used and which I'd started to find infantalizing. Yet hearing my old nickname coming from Howard and Bette now seemed cute and comforting.

Saturday morning I was excited to take the train to Greenwich and wore my best black jeans and black sweater, my latest poems and essay in my purse. I schlepped a huge basket filled with gourmet candy that my mother had insisted on overnighting from West Bloomfield (because you couldn't get candy in Manhattan). They hugged me hello and then looked me up and down. "She's a beauty, just like Mickey," was Howard's verdict. "Dark like Jack, with Mickey's lips and Sophie's high cheekbones," Bette added. I liked that she thought I resembled Sophie, my maternal grandmother who'd died when my mother was four.

They gave me a tour of their stately house, filled with hardcover books, Bette's elegant, Henry Moore–like bronze sculptures of torsos, and ink drawings of naked women. I scanned their original Picasso, antique furniture, sleek black piano, and swimming pool in the tree- and flower-filled backyard. They asked tons of questions about the Michigan sect; I was hungry to learn all about them. For eight hours we ate, talked, laughed, quizzed each other, and looked at photographs of the old Lower East Side, where, like my parents, Howard had once lived.

Bette was in her sixties then, a beautiful, classy, sardonic, straight-shooting, blond former dress designer turned artist. She was understated, in a loose beige skirt and blouse, with two pieces of jewelry – her wedding band and a necklace with an unusually shaped gold pendant. She'd met Howard when they were both art students at the National Academy of Design in the 1930s. Despite her parents' disapproval of her penniless suitor, she'd married him in 1937, had two babies amid many miscarriages, and supported him through the lean years, she said. Bette was a fascinating hybrid –

a feminist Meryl Streep lookalike who overfed like my mother and her mother. "Get your own career and money, so the men can't control you," she immediately advised. "But cooking and wearing a dress won't make you a Barbie doll, Susie. Don't buy into that crap. A woman alone with cats is even more pathetic."

Howard, also in his late sixties, was a funny, bald, slim chronic storyteller who dressed sporty, in khaki pants, a button-down striped flannel shirt with a beige vest over it, and sneakers. Though not conventionally handsome, his confidence, outspoken defiance of all authority, and political acumen gave him a masculine, robust aura. His childhood sounded like a Semetic Dickens novel. He said he was the grandson of Ukrainian immigrants from Fastov, Russia, the origin of his surname. He was born dirt poor in 1914 in the Bronx, where his mother, Ida, died when he was eight. His father, Barney, was an ironworker who left him and his two brothers alone to fend for themselves. In order to eat, Howard took odd jobs, including reclaiming overdue library books from whorehouses. Returning them to the New York Public Library turned him on to reading, and he sold his first fiction to *Amazing Stories* before he graduated George Washington High School at sixteen.

His imposing office was a wannabe writer's paradise that awed me. His floor-to-ceiling shelves were filled with dozens of his books, many translated into different languages. He pointed to the manual typewriter he used in 1932 to type *Two Villages,* his first paperback, a historical romance, published when he was eighteen. "Dial Press gave me a $100 advance for it," he said. He pulled out a mystery from the series he wrote under the pseudonym E. V. Cunningham, in which the nisei detective, Masao Masuto, of the Beverly Hills police force, was a Zen Buddhist, as Howard was. I read the framed rave his 1943 hardcover American Revolution novel, *Citizen Tom Paine,* had received on the front page of *The New York Times Book Review.* He showed me the first copy of *Freedom Road,* which, he bragged, had sold twenty million copies. He made it sound so easy and possible, I immediately wanted to publish a book that got raves and sold twenty million copies, too.

Howard was most impassioned about being blacklisted and jailed for communism in the '50s, which made him so unpopular that he established Blue Heron Publishing Company to self-publish *Spartacus,* he told me. He sold it by taking out an ad in *The New York Times Book Review,* asking people to send him $3 and promising he'd send out the order when he had enough money, a scheme that didn't quite take off. He worked on the screenplay with Stanley Kubrick and Peter Ustinov. But since Howard refused to name names for the House Un-American Activities Committee, the "spineless idiot producers" at first took his real name off the credits. They worked in tandem with the "morally weak" actor Kirk Douglas, whom Howard called "the scum of the earth" because he believed Douglas didn't stand up against McCarthyism soon enough.

Though the movie wound up breaking the blacklist in 1960 and made Howard's novel a bestseller, Howard was still pissed off decades later that fellow communist Dalton Trumbo got credit for rewriting the screenplay Howard had started. I loved his moral outrage, his fierce candor, and his juicy, celebrity-studded story with its triumphant end; I wanted to be just like him.

When I asked about the Emmy he'd won for the TV miniseries based on his Benjamin Franklin novel, he said more than a dozen of his books had made it to the screen. Pointing to a Norman Rockwell painting, he explained that Rockwell had illustrated one of Howard's *Saturday Evening Post* stories. After Howard sent the artist a fan letter, Rockwell had sent him the original artwork. It was now worth a million dollars, he told me, the amount he'd made on his 1977 bestselling book *The Immigrants*. This chronicle of tumultuous generations of a Jewish family led to six books and another TV miniseries, which made him really rich, he reported. For a one-time Red whose Zen master made house calls, Howard sure liked to talk money. "It's the worst profession in the history of the world, Susie," he warned me. "So you better watch out for the vultures."

I was the only vulture in evidence – leaving with six signed books, three of Bette's fat-naked-woman drawings under my arm, a picture of the dead grandmother I'd never met, and fancy leftover food in a doggie bag. Two days later I received a typed letter from Howard. "I read your smart essay and excellent poems. Without question, you are a real writer, Susie," he declared. "But these few pages simply are not enough. You must get down to the job and do longer stories or a book. Society imposes the difference between the dilettante and the professional. The professional enters the mainstream and gets paid. Don't allow yourself to be self-indulgent, just go to work. Remember, a plumber never gets plumber's block." (This struck me as so profound, it became one of my main mantras.)

All of his advice thrilled me, mostly because the size of my output had never been my problem. (Coherence and structure were.) I placed his letter in the special album where I kept my diplomas and first clips from school magazines.

Invited back for a party the next weekend, I met the eclectic cast of characters in the Fasts' inner circle. Their daughter, Rachel, was a slim, pretty, sarcastic blond shrink in her forties, married to a smart, older, sarcastic shrink named Avram, who cracked me up. "A new family member? Watch your back," he joked. (I analyzed what that meant – that one of the Fasts would wind up stabbing me in the back? Or writing about me?) Howard and Bette's son, Jonathan, was a tall, cool, droll novelist married to Erica Jong, whose sexy poetry and landmark novel, *Fear of Flying,* had rocked my world in college. I scanned a framed 1980 *People* magazine article on the Fasts where Erica said, "Howard taught me that writing is a trade, like being a shoemaker. You get up in the morning and go to work every day." It was the same kind of practical advice he'd given me!

I'd never met more publishing people in one room before. Howard's brother, Julius, was a science fiction writer with his own bestseller. "But his latest is just a self-help book," Howard sniffed. Gerry Frank spoke of his Judy Garland and Zsa Zsa Gabor biographies. I asked Patricia Bosworth about her acclaimed Diane Arbus book. *New York Times* critic Christopher Lehmann-Haupt talked baseball. Howard's gentlemanly agent, Sterling Lord, discussed current issues with his TV producer girlfriend. Sterling's assistant, Elizabeth Kaplan, from my West Bloomfield hometown, said to send her whatever I was working on. The president of Houghton Mifflin, Howard's publisher, also told me to send him my work. Was he kidding?

I could not believe my good fortune in landing amid these entertaining, outspoken, liberal geniuses. Hanging out with the Fasts confirmed my belief that I'd been switched at birth and should have always been here, in the East. I chatted, smiled, listened carefully, and laughed at all the inside jokes, even the ones I didn't quite get. Though I sometimes felt like an impostor impersonating a writer who belonged with these sophisticated, arty people, everybody appeared to like and accept me, no questions asked. I was subsequently invited to birthday, anniversary, and New Year's Day fests, book and theater events, award ceremonies, and holiday dinners Bette and Howard hosted at the luxurious city apartment they owned on Fifth Avenue and 74th Street (where I ran into Woody, Mia, and their baby in the elevator) and a series of exquisite

Connecticut homes with swimming pools they kept upgrading. If I didn't hear from them before Christmas or Thanksgiving or Yom Kippur, I'd phone and not so subtly let slip that I had no plans whatsoever, was in fact sitting alone in my apartment, working and ordering food in. I thus perpetually wormed my way into the Fast family picture and refused to ever leave.

An eager caller, I'd show up to all events early, when Bette was in the kitchen, arranging food. "Why, hello, beautiful. What a lovely sweater you're wearing," Howard would greet me. He loved women; flirting was as natural to him as breathing. "He has the gift of gab. He can charm the pants off of anybody," Bette said, rolling her eyes. "You're looking pretty natty yourself," I'd flatter, noting his plaid jacket or bow tie for fancy occasions. I'd hand him an oversize candy basket, flowers, champagne, and other gifts sent via my Michigan mom, with whom he also used to flirt shamelessly.

"Rich people like presents even more than poor people. That's because most of the upper class are cheap and don't bring each other anything," said my mother. A professional party planner, she knew about these things. "Ever notice celebrities and tycoons after charity events getting their goody bags? These multizillionaires step on each other's heads to steal two more of those silly free takeaways."

Howard and Bette went nuts over the goodies I brought. They'd call my mother on the spot to thank her and report on what I was wearing, my latest date, or my haircut. It surprised me that other guests showed up empty handed, and that amid the literati, finances were such a big topic. When asked how he always managed to keep his heated swimming pool so warm, Howard replied, "With money." At their fiftieth anniversary dinner, he whispered that the richest person there gave them a $50 silver-plated Tiffany tchotchke. He gossiped about gossip maven Claudia Cohen, daughter of Bobby Cohen, Bette's brother. Howard and Bette had attended Claudia's wedding to Revlon chairman Ron Perelman at the Palladium. They felt snubbed by the snobby Upper East Side *machers* and seemed impressed only with Claudia's subsequent $80 million divorce settlement. I couldn't imagine how dumb socialites and boring businesspeople could ignore the compellingly fascinating Fasts.

I'd taken to sending Howard a package of my latest poems, essays, and articles every week or two. Whenever I'd come over, he'd call me into his office to give me edited versions of the pages I'd sent, with such criticism as, "This is clever and juicy, but get rid of all those adjectives. It's overkill," or "The really interesting story doesn't get rolling until the third page." He usually told me to add more drama, politics, and sex, and, most of all, to write longer. In Howard's honor I'd tried short stories and scenes from novels chronicling a nice Jewish girl's move from the Midwest to the big city and/or a twenty-two-year-old's messy romantic entanglements – the exact trivial subjects as my nonfiction, only more self-conscious and stilted. Though Howard said, "Good for you for trying a new genre," even my biggest fan had to admit, "It needs a little work," or, "It's a little rough around the edges."

Once, in exasperation after yet another nondramatic story of mine about a poet's bad breakup, he said, "Can we add a murder or war or set it during the Holocaust to make it a little less auto-biographical?" I laughed. Though this was decades before a harsher critic told me, "You have no imagination whatsoever; stick to mem-oirs," I still saw myself as a poet and had little invested in fiction. The mere fact that Howard was reading my work and commenting on it seemed like an astounding miracle.

After our private mini-counseling session was over, he'd reward me with one of his books, or the copy of a screenplay, or a clip of his own op-ed piece from the Connecticut paper. Sometimes he'd ask me to read a page or two and tell him what I thought. (Since the work had already been published, I was rarely critical.) Then we'd join the crowd and he'd introduce me around as "a brilliant new writer in town," adding, "Be nice to her. She's *mishpocheh*." I was jazzed by his compliments on my work and dug having the label of "family" stamped on my forehead. Although I was confident socially, I watched how Howard and his author friends spoke and acted and tried to emulate them to come off as older, richer, more accomplished. Just being at Howard and Bette's events felt invalu-able, boosting my confidence, feeding the delusion that I was amid peers and could be part of this scene.

Yet his two kids were still a bit reserved around me, and I wondered if they were perplexed by the attention Howard was paying me. Did the forced addition to their insular foursome make them uneasy? Were my mom's extravagant presents a bit much? Why didn't Howard praise their work in public, especially when Jonathan was publishing acclaimed novels and selling multiple screenplays? Once, at a dinner party, when I mentioned an excellent review I'd read of Jonathan's latest book, Howard changed the subject to compliment a four-hundred-word op-ed piece I'd done for *The Nation*. Okay, something was up. I wasn't imagining this chasm.

In the apt illustration for "Son of a Writer," Jonathan's *New York Times Magazine* essay, a young man sat at his typewriter while the huge ghost of his father loomed overhead. He discussed the difficulties of being in a clan of writers, including his great-uncle Sholem Aleichem, whom I didn't know was also kin. When he was seven, Fast Jr. had written a novel that Howard had his secretary type. In retrospect, Jonathan wrote, it was either a wonderful gesture or horribly cruel, since Howard knew that seeing his hand-scribbled manuscript in print would hook his son on the family biz. He ended by saying that he didn't show his father his work until his fourth novel had already been published.

It was becoming obvious that Howard was a workaholic with a mammoth ego. His insatiable appetite for female admiration seemed rooted in his mother's tragic death. After she died, his father was too busy working to take care of him and his brothers, whom he sometimes spoke of antagonistically. Since I had an emotionally distant father and three brothers I saw as rivals for my dad's attention, I desperately craved male empathy and encouragement. So Howard and I had perfect chemistry – our early pathologies were so in sync, we automatically fed each other.

He often shared anecdotes from his horrible, lonely youth, linking his childhood poverty to his connection to communism. Yet he was more likely to milk his rags-to-riches saga for pithy punch lines and political melodrama than to muster up deep insight into his own psychology. Howard was competitive toward most men and resented authority figures, but he wasn't conscious of it. He never really admitted how much damage he'd caused his loved ones by spending three months in jail, going off to pick up the International Stalin Prize, or having extramarital affairs, which he recounted too flippantly for my taste in his autobiography *Being Red*.

It couldn't have been easy for Jonathan as Howard's only son, not to mention being sandwiched between a bold, best-selling father and bold, best-selling wife. Interestingly, it was Howard who'd set Jonathan up with Erica Jong, a woman like Bette, Howard's type: ballsy, blond, classy, emotionally generous, Jewish, saucy. It was unclear whether the fix-up was intentional. When Erica, then a hot young writer, flew out to L.A. in the 70s, a friend asked Howard to show her around. Howard and Bette were living out there at the time, throwing as many West Coast parties and literary events as they'd hosted in the East. They invited Erica to one of their infamous soirees, sending Jonathan to pick her up at the airport. The romance was immediate, followed by marriage and a beautiful redheaded baby girl named Molly. But by the time they'd separated three years later, Howard appeared more enthralled with Erica's largesse than Jonathan was.

After the divorce, Jonathan married Barbara, a pretty, blond, preppy, gentile lawyer. In one of her spicy novels, Erica called the new-wife character the less dazzling version of herself. Erica married Ken, also a strong, stable attorney. By the '90s, Jonathan had become a professor of social work and Barbara had left a corporate law practice to be the reverend of a local parish. I was a bit uncomfortable when she said Christian prayers before meals we shared with my Jewish parents, but she was always more than kind to me.

My main recollection of Jonathan and Erica's divorce was that little Molly, at ages four, five, six, ten, twelve, and thirteen, needed a ride from Fast events back to the City, where she lived with her mother. I'd ask whichever date I'd coerced into driving me to Greenwich to make a stop on the Upper East Side. Molly, in the back seat, would trash all the guests she didn't like on the hour-long ride. She was a charming kid with dark wit, obviously hurt by her parents' ongoing conflicts. It didn't get easier when her dad and stepmom had two sons. "Will you keep an eye out for my beautiful little granddaughter?" Howard asked me, with pleading eyes, every time I saw him. I swore I would.

At another Fast "open house," I met Helen Singer Kaplan, a sex therapist, who decided that my destroying my Barbie dolls as a kid was the reason I could have robust sex as an adult. (Rumor had it that Howard and Helen were once an item, but I was never able to verify it.) Helen's husband, Charles, a toy tycoon, shared his business strategy: He was going to sell cribs, but he realized parents only bought their kid one crib but would buy a whole bunch of toys. Helen offered to fix me up with her son. Jonathan whispered that Helen's son had once dated Erica, who'd immortalized him in a novel. I looked it up, excited to meet this stud worthy of literary citation. Alas, Helen's son turned out to be a not-so-studly, anti-Zionist fascist who raged about vague political matters for hours on end. "Are you really mad at your mom?" I psychoanalyzed him over dinner at the Odeon on our first and last date.

Compared to the Fasts' acclaimed colleagues, I was young, broke, hickish, and hungry. But, hey, we all need mascots. As a fawning fan, at least I returned their generosity with sweets, roses, liquor, and love. Plus, they were people collectors and I was a terrific procurer – adding many youthful, energetic pals to their party mix.

That summer, my blond, Protestant USC Law School boyfriend, Tom, moved in with me. Still fostering the inane notion that I might marry a Midwest Jewish doctor, my parents were at first ambivalent about Tom. But Howard was warm and genial. When he learned that Tom liked to sail, he insisted we meet at the *Intrepid,* a World War II aircraft carrier docked by the Hudson River. The men spent the day discussing yachts and ships they'd sailed. (My only reference point was the boat I once took to Bob-Lo, the tacky Michigan amusement park.) Howard was working on a legal thriller and picked Tom's brain for legalese. He went on about his and Bette's glamorous years on the West Coast. For proud Jews, they really dug good-looking WASPs, nicknaming Tom "The Gorgeous One," inviting us over all the time, and bugging me to get him back for a decade after we'd split.

Since Howard and Bette were pretty groovy faux grandparents, I relinquished my rebel-in-the-family role. Not that anything I did shocked them anyway. After my Chinese dinner with friends on Rosh Hoshanah, Howard said he and his commie buddies had eaten in Chinatown on Jewish holidays in the '40s. When I brought over Hal, my new black boyfriend who'd been a Broadway singer, they said Hal was "quite a handsome man" whom I should marry, holding him rapt with stories of Paul Robeson singing lullabies to Rachel in the '50s.

In fact, everything I did in my original home was wrong and caused havoc, but everything I did at the Fasts' was right on and elicited delight. While Dad sneered that I should sell my poems on the sidewalk, Howard said they were good enough to be in *The New*

Yorker. My mother hated the racy story I'd published in the NYU magazine, in which a sexist man used the words "cunt" and "tits," which she found "disgusting." Howard deemed it "brave and powerful," adding, "It's in dialogue, so it shows us who this guy really is deep down." Yes! Exactly! Of course!

While my brothers trashed my social scene, calling me "deb," "party girl," and "socialite," Howard was impressed by my cronies' looks, brains, dough, and/or connections and wanted to meet more. Before Fast events, he'd call with special requests. "Is The Gorgeous One here or in California, Susie? Bring the smart filmmaker and her husband, the history buff. They have a car, right? Can she pick up Molly on the way?" On the bottom of one invitation, in an elegant script, were the lines, "Bring the filmmaker, that lovely architect Donna, the rich Wall Street trader we like, and your musician, if you haven't dumped him yet."

Two guys who escorted me to Fast festivities bought Bette's sculptures, which sold for $3,000 to $6,000. I preferred *Woman on a Cross*, *Man Holding the Baby*, and her other work that made a social statement, but they picked naked women's bodies in burnished bronze patina. This endeared me to Howard and Bette even more. One of the art aficionados, Josh, a cute millionaire I dated, wanted to produce a film of one of Howard's historical plays. Howard asked, "Susie, why don't you marry this one?" I said, "'Cause he's a Republican." Howard shook his head and said, "Forget it, then."

Every time I saw Howard, I'd pull new clips from my briefcase to show him. Howard proclaimed, "You're getting better at structure, but these are still too short. You need to go further, make it book length. You should write about sex, it sells." I tried to take his advice and always wanted to talk about work; he wanted to talk about my sex life, inquiring after The Gorgeous One, or Paul Robeson Jr., or Josh. Was Howard getting voyeuristic kicks from my racy relationships? Or was he adding to his storyteller's inventory? He did like to nail current slang and social trends, and he was quite curious when a gay friend of mine referred to himself as "queer," rather than "homosexual" or "gay."

While I worked at The New Yorker from 1983 to 1987, Howard constantly lauded me for getting a job at the best magazine in the country without asking for his help. His letters praised my poems and essays, but my author profiles seemed to make him jealous. "Susie, why don't you write about me and my new novel?" he'd ask. I hooked him up with Matthew, a publishing reporter pal, who publicized the reissue of his banned book Sylvia. But Howard insisted that I, too, get him ink. I wrote a few paragraphs for small papers and mentioned him in a syndicated book column I wrote for Newsday.

I was afraid he'd disapprove when, after almost four years of grunt work, I quit The New Yorker to freelance. My parents, colleagues, and former NYU professors thought I was crazy. Howard wrote, "You don't need them, Susie. You're a serious writer, good enough to do it on your own." Then he added, "Why don't you pitch your nice *Newsday* editor my latest book? It's a hot one." It first felt weird that someone so well known needed my tiny publishing links. In the '80s he was still getting reviewed in *The New York Times* and major newspapers. But by the '90s, he was past his prime. His literary cachet was diminishing, as my journalistic credentials and clip files were growing. His calls became more frequent: "My book's been out three weeks and not a word has been written about it. Susie, can't you get me any press?" I guessed that actual lines in the newspaper denoted reassurance from the world that he was still important. He didn't smoke or drink much, but press could be addictive and became Howard's drug of choice.

The only time he reacted negatively to my work was when I sent him book reviews, which he called "a stupid genre." He ranted, "Don't waste your time with book criticism! A critic is a eunuch working in a harem. He watches it, but he knows he can't do it." Obviously, it was a sore spot. But when I broke into *The New York Times Book Review*, he changed his mind and decided I should review his work. We were cousins; I explained it wasn't ethical. I introduced him to Michael Anderson, my *Book Review* editor, an African American fan of Howard's 1944 antiracism novel *Freedom Road*. They hit it off, and a brief, positive review of Howard's latest book ran. Maybe it was coincidence, but Howard and Bette treated me like a savior.

I was more like a minor public relations mole, working behind the scenes for free. I didn't mind, as I felt all protégés should be loyal and pay a debt to their mentors with whatever power they eventually obtained. (Hadn't I diligently submitted Jack Zucker's poems to *The New Yorker's* poetry editor, no questions asked?) In some ways I'd felt inadequate around the Fasts and overcompensated with gifts, art sales, newspaper hits. Still, it never felt like our love-fest had to do with money, presents, or favors on either side. If externals enhanced my place in their house and hearts, surely I got the better deal.

Someone close to the scene once offered a different take. As an aging star who'd led a high-profile life, constantly being lionized or demonized, Howard got off on being a famous writer, political activist, and flavor du jour, as well as a sexual magnet for the ladies. Since he never recovered from the dimming of the spotlight, he saw me as a much younger, hot, with-it fellow writer who offered him press, confirmation that he was still relevant, while also being a "kissing cousin" whom he could flirt with before an audience.

Throwing Jonathan a book party at a friend's downtown loft, I had an uncomfortable spat with Howard about the guest list. He wanted to invite my young colleagues and his publishing honchos, but not many of the extended family members I hoped would come. Jonathan intervened, insisting that all Fasts, Cohens and Goodmans were welcome, especially his uncle Julius. My favorite picture that night was a rare shot showing Howard, Jonathan, and Julius, three bald Fast men with glasses, smiling warmly, their arms around each other.

I was initially miffed at Howard's reluctance to include our whole clan, yet I ended up admiring the way he didn't feel obligated to hang out with relatives just because they were related. Why waste precious hours on people you didn't really love or enjoy? Being selfish and discerning with his time was how he'd become a best-selling multimillionaire. I'd rather be a wildly successful writer than a nice person any day.

And how joyous it was to be in the right company. Once a year, when my parents flew East, Howard invited us over for elaborate boisterous meals of Bette's. "Oh my god, you bake challah bread just like my dear late *tanta* Lilly," my mother cried. Bette and her "Howie" showed pictures and swapped Lower East Side sagas of nutty cousins and great-aunts in half Yiddish, half English. They raved about the parade of cute chums I'd dragged to Connecticut. Everyone drank wine. The men smoked cigars and talked business. "You've become a capitalistic pig, Howard, I see," my right-wing father said with glee. Being around the Fasts made even my staid folks seem hip and lively.

During one trip, Howard canceled our get-together, claiming Bette was sick. My father grabbed the phone to see what was wrong. "What? She can't even go out? Why? Where's the rash? Her face is paralyzed?" My dad's voice was raised. "Was she gardening in Connecticut? The test said it wasn't Lyme disease? That doesn't mean anything. They're clowns! They don't know what they're doing!" Mom took the phone and said, "We'll be right there."

We cabbed it to their Fifth Avenue place. My Dad rushed to Bette's bedroom and then paged her doctor at the hospital, screaming at him to have a new prescription of antibiotics delivered right away. Bette did have Lyme disease (which apparently didn't show up on tests). With the right diagnosis and medicine, she was better in a week. "Jack saved her life," Howard often said. "Your father is a brilliant medicine man."

Aside from that terrible health scare – which intensified the Shapiro-Fast bond – my dozen years hanging out with Bette and Howard were blissful. I didn't probe beneath the Jewish Gatsby aura to see the rage or alienation lurking. I attributed any hint of Howard's narcissism to his early poverty and his mother's untimely death. He'd picked himself up "by his bootstraps" and expected others to do the same. He resented his relatives' reliance on him, unaware of how his fame, wealth, and neglect had exacerbated their dependence.

Luckily, I had few needs or expectations. With my own solid dad, who helped support me financially, and an overprotective, nurturing mom, I never asked my cousins for money, jobs, editors, or a place to stay. I merely showed up at their extravaganzas with presents, adoration, copies of books to sign, and dates with deep-enough pockets to buy Bette's artwork. My presence must have provided a relief. Howard could easily please me, with signatures on his books (an author's favorite request) and a little attention, while I reflected his godlike status. I was a fading writer's dream. Plus, I was safe. As a cousin of Bette's who was forty years his junior, Howard couldn't sleep with me. As a failed poet and lowly journalist who often got him press, I wasn't threatening in any way.

On a psychic level, Jonathan and Erica were dangerous – they'd invaded the field of fiction, Howard's territory. Julius had also stepped on Howard's bestseller crown. Even Molly's publishing a novel at age twenty-one threatened Howard's status as the young genius who'd published his first book at eighteen, and he became competitive with his own granddaughter. With brains, outsize personalities, and big hardcover book deals, these relatives could usurp Howard's position as the most famous writer of the family. I wasn't really courting wealth or fame; I was self-effacing, publishing puny three-hundred-word reviews and poems for pennies. I let him remain Herculean, so I escaped his hostility.

Not that my love was totally blind. I preferred the angry, colloquial voice in his 1957 memoir *The Naked God* and 1990's *Being Red*, especially his disenchantment with the communist ideals he renounced in 1956. "When a priest can be a selfish bastard and a rabbi a lecher and a judge a cold blooded murderer in your Communist Party . . . something washes out of you," he wrote. His historical novels and plays seemed grand and passionate, but the tone of his contemporary fiction struck me as purple. Not that I ever told him that. Not that he ever asked. I'd learned never to critique people's work unless they made it clear they wanted criticism.

His daughter asked my opinion once. Retiring from her psychology practice, Rachel took a stab at a personal essay. I was freelancing for *The New York Times Magazine*, so she sent me a potential submission to the *Times Magazine*'s "Hers" section, the female counterpoint to the "About Men" column her brother had sold. On the bottom she wrote, "Please do not discuss this with Father." I thought it was a strange request, since her piece wasn't about him at all. It was actually about an inconsequential fight she'd had with a woman friend. I guessed that she'd subconsciously shunned Howard's juicier subjects of modern marriage and sex, as I thought Jonathan had, thus sabotaging their chances of success. (I hadn't yet examined my own methods of self-sabotage.) But Rachel didn't want Howard to know the details of her attempts at writing and publishing. I never told him.

She had a piece in a Red Diaper Baby anthology and signed with a known agent. We were cordial when we saw each other, but we never bonded. I wasn't quite sure why, until one Rosh Hashanah at home, when I watched my father make a big fuss over a doctor's daughter who was in medical school. I guessed how Howard's kids felt watching their notoriously neglectful father lavish praise on me, a distant interloper who'd instantly won his affection. A continual loser in wars with my three brothers, had I perpetuated a sibling rivalry I could actually win?

Howard and Bette kept moving to different homes, each a few

miles from the last, bouncing from Redding Ridge to Cos Cob to Greenwich to Old Greenwich. He said they'd given one-million-dollar houses to each of his kids, as if this fulfilled his obligation or justified their compulsive house lust. I didn't talk much about finances, but I admitted that my dad still helped pay my rent. "Write a book already, Susie," Howard admonished. "Your short essays and reviews are good, but books are bigger. Take the plunge. How many years are you going to waste with these little pieces?" (I realized how much his advice sunk in when, a decade later, teaching "How to Sell Your First Book" seminars, I pushed many of my young students into expanding short pieces into book-length projects.)

When Howard and Bette were in Manhattan, I visited constantly, showing up with fresh batches of flowers and writing. I'd leave well fed, with a drawing of Bette's, a gold necklace, or a signed paperback. I was bereft when they gave up their Fifth Avenue pied-à-terre, but it was getting too hard for them to travel back and forth.

In the fall of 1994, I took my new boyfriend, Aaron, to their latest classy Connecticut abode for lunch and inspection. Bette wasn't feeling well but told us to come anyway. After food, swimming, and the requisite tour, she called me upstairs to give me a red blouse of hers. "Those boring black clothes wash you out," she said. "You should marry this Aaron. It's time, you're getting old and bitter already." She phoned my mother to report that Aaron was a mensch. For Bette, calling him "a genuine person" was her ultimate praise.

But Howard didn't take to him. When he quizzed Aaron on his TV/film credentials, I assumed they'd find much in common. Alas, Howard belonged to the Writers Guild West; Aaron was in the Writers Guild East. Since Howard had lived in the East for thirty-five years, Aaron said he should join the East Coast division. Howard wasn't interested. I boasted that Aaron had written for *In Living Color*, *Saturday Night Live*, *Seinfeld*, and *The Jon Stewart Show*. Howard, who prided himself on keeping up on pop culture, now feigned ignorance of these shows, bragging about his hit TV movies and miniseries. Aaron said he'd met Howard before, through his friend's father, the biographer Ladislas Farago. Howard said he'd never heard of Farago.

When we took a drive, Aaron sat in the back seat. Howard made a snide comment that Aaron's heft was weighing down his car. I was shocked by my cousin's bad behavior. It was a childish side to him I'd never seen. The Howard I knew was cultured, having traveled the world and met many dignitaries and heads of states. He'd charmed every other (less important) male I'd brought over. I analyzed his insult. He was five foot ten and 160 pounds, Aaron was six foot four and weighed 240. Was this Howard's crude response to feeling threatened by a bigger man? Someone who'd been more successful in the TV/film realm? The one male writer I might love more than I loved him?

"Howard hates Aaron," I told Bette, lighting a cigarette later on the back porch.

"Stop smoking already," she said. Howard usually bummed a few cigarettes and smoked them with me. Bette, who'd quit the habit decades before, hated them. "Howie's just jealous 'cause it's the first guy you're fawning all over," Bette confirmed. "It's about time you learned to be nurturing. All men want mothers, you know. All that therapy but you can't quit nicotine, you dumb jerk. It's time for you to bite the bullet and stop, Susie." It was the last advice she ever gave me.

Bette died of cancer at the end of November. The first time my mother met Aaron was at Bette's funeral. She started the conversation with "My favorite *tanta* said you're kosher" and then cried as Aaron hugged her. My ex-boyfriend Josh was there, too, as were several friends I'd presented to the Fasts through the years.

Bette was the closest person I'd ever lost. I was traumatized. So was her teenage granddaughter Molly. We bonded over our "Bette withdrawal." Molly joined my Tuesday night workshop, so I could see her every week. She penned funny first-person essays, the kind I wrote. At my readings and parties, she was the youngest in attendance, as I'd been at many Fast events. Introducing Molly to my editors, I heard myself repeating Howard's line: "Be nice to her. She's *mishpocheh*."

Molly wore a sparkly yellow mini-dress to my SoHo wedding. Howard looked gaunt and lost without his wife of half a century. As a present he gave us my favorite amber bronze torso of Bette's, today still prominently displayed in my living room. *The New York Times's* "Vows" column write-up of our reception (titled "The Bride Wore Black") pictured the bald, bow-tied Howard talking to Vivian, my twenty-nine-year-old personal trainer. Everything was off balance without Bette, but it was amusing that Howard was caught chatting up the hottest female figure in the joint.

He was soon dating one of Bette's seventy-five-year-old white-haired cronies, which creeped me out. A year later, the dapper seventy-nine-year-old Howard hired as his assistant Mercedes O'Connor, a.k.a. Mimi, a pretty, friendly, smart, fast-talking, forty-five-year-old New Orleans gal with an exuberant smile and pixie-brown hair. He was still publishing a book a year, and Mimi helped him proofread, copyedit, and get his manuscripts on the computer. Within weeks of their meeting, he seduced her.

Since I'd been so close to Bette, I didn't want to like Mimi, but I couldn't help it. She was incredibly nice to me and extremely gentle with Howard. When they flew to Detroit for the Jewish Book Fair and met my parents, I worried it would be awkward. Mom had idolized Bette, and Mimi was her opposite (a younger, Irish Catholic, divorced business brain). But my folks found Mimi dear. "She adores him," my mother said. "She'll take care of him." My father agreed. "Howard can't be alone. He needs constant attention. Plus, she's an MBA who'll help him with business. I bet he'll marry her."

Mimi and Howard wed in 1999. If their age difference created doubts about her motives, they disappeared for me when I visited Howard in the hospital after his hip-replacement surgery. Mimi held his hand and talked to his doctors, playing wife, friend, confidant, and nursemaid, the way Bette had, only sweeter. (She had reason to be sweeter; he'd never screwed around on Mimi or taken off for month-long Russian sojourns.) When he came home, I fell for the illusion that he was better. Then he had a stroke. On the phone, the doctor answered Mimi's questions, saying Howard would probably keep having small strokes until he died. She called me, mortified, after learning that Howard had been listening on the other line.

Molly was going to Connecticut with her editor friend Ryan in January 2003, so Aaron and I invited ourselves along. We had dinner with everyone at Jonathan's house in Cos Cob. Molly, who now had her own car, drove us.

If there was any tension between Howard's original clan and his new wife, I didn't notice it at all that night. Mimi spoke about her childhood as a convent girl from New Orleans. She, like Howard, had the gift of gab. Her story segued into her move East and her horrible divorce. Her first husband, father of her sons, was hell on her self-esteem, and she confided that Howard was the first man who'd ever made her feel loved and protected. He flattered her constantly, calling her beautiful and brilliant. She called him "sweetie" and "baby." Their trust seemed implicit so I trusted her, too.

Howard looked thinner and frail, and he was slurring his words since the stroke. I missed the angry egomaniac. As always, Aaron and Howard barely spoke. Dinner was strained. It was hard watching Mimi cut her husband's food and help him eat. Over dessert, the usually quiet Aaron said he'd just finished Joseph McBride's biography of the film director John Ford. In the section on Ford's film *Cheyenne Autumn,* which took a rare sympathetic view of Indians, the author wrote that Ford had stolen the structure, many incidents, and the main character from Howard's 1941 novel *The Last Frontier.* Aaron wanted to know if this was true. Everyone stared at Howard.

Howard looked at Aaron, shakily poured himself wine, sipped it, sat up straighter, and said, "Yes, it's true. Ford came to me himself and said he wanted to make the movie with just the dialogue from my book and 'no fucking screenwriter,' his words. But that son of a bitch J. Edgar Hoover threatened Columbia Pictures. Ford had contempt for Hoover. So he slipped my book to a screenwriter and told him to go ahead and use it as an uncredited source. Instead of facing a huge plagiarism suit, there was an out-of-court settlement." He spoke with perfect elocution like he used to, miraculously restored to his former glory. He took a cigar from his pocket. Mimi went to light it for him, but he took the matches from her and lit it on his own. Puffing away, he added, "Ford wanted to make a movie of my book *April Morning* and almost stole that, too. He was neither an honest nor decent man, but he was a great director."

Basking in the spotlight, he drank more, puffed more, put his arm around his girl. Then he launched into the *Spartacus*-Kirk-Douglas-scum-of-the-earth tale, one of his finest, about the cowardly actors and producers who named names and tried to ruin his career and didn't have the balls to stand up to McCarthy. Spitting with rage and sarcasm, he chronicled the royal screwing a brave man gets in Hollywood. Then he brought up Aaron's friend's father, Ladislas Farago, suddenly well versed in Farago and his Patton biography, which was made into a George C. Scott film. Odd that Howard recalled it now, when his memory was half shot from his stroke.

As Mimi and I cleared the table, someone mentioned Amherst College. When we came out of the kitchen, Howard and Aaron were singing the Amherst fight song: "Lord Jeffrey Amherst was a soldier of the king / And he came from across the sea, / To the Frenchman and the Indians he didn't do a thing / In the wilds of this wild country." Mimi poured Howard more wine. I poured more for Aaron. The two of them crooned an old Italian communist song – in Italian! *"Una mattina mi sono svegliato / O bella ciao, bella ciao, bella ciao, ciao, ciao."* Howard had learned it in his old commie days. But Aaron?

"I had an insane Italian girlfriend who taught me," he admitted proudly. I lit a cigarette and tried not to cry watching two essential men in my world finally connect.

"So, are you going to come to your senses and switch to the

East Coast Writers Guild to vote for me?" my husband asked my cousin, pressing his luck.

"I'm too old to switch East. What are you running for? President?" Howard asked.

"No, just a seat on the council."

"Susie, you married a big union man. So you're the family communist now," Howard said with a smile, hitting Aaron's shoulder.

A week later I called Howard to share the news that my agent had sold my first memoir. Howard had introduced us two decades before, at the first Fast party I'd attended, when she was his agent's assistant. "You told her, 'Susie's a brilliant new writer in town. Be nice to her, she's *mishpocheh*,'" I reminded him. "Do you remember? After twenty-two years, I finally sold a hardcover and it's because of you."

"I'm not feeling so hot today, Susie," he said, hanging up. I worried that he was fading, and I felt sad that he didn't understand what I was trying to tell him, which underscored how important he was in my life. The next day he called back, sounding more chipper, asking, "How did you get your agent again, Susie? When did you meet her?" I repeated the story, with Howard as the hero, which he always was to me.

Calling that February to talk business, he said Sterling had sold an old novel of his. He asked about my memoir deal and my advance. When I divulged the sum, he admitted he'd been paid the exact same amount.

I was thrilled to have gone up to that five-figure number! Howard was depressed that his once-million-dollar advances had come down so low. I was tickled to be in the same ballpark figure as my famous cousin, even if his smallest payment coincided with my finest hour.

"I'm sorry they're not paying you enough," I told him.

"I'm an old man. I'm lucky they're still buying my books at all," he said. "Just remember, Susie, it's the worst profession there is."

"I'll remember, Howie," I said, thinking it his biggest lie, to me and to himself. Writing was the best profession in the universe; it had elevated a poor, motherless Lower East Side kid to the front page of *The New York Times Book Review*. His words were translated into eighty languages, performed in the theater and on small and big screens, putting him on top of the world. At least for a few decades.

"I'm happy for you, Susie," he said. "You did good." I thought he meant by finally selling a hardcover, like him. But he added, "Bette was right. You married a good man."

Howard Melvin Fast died on March 12, 2003, at age eighty-eight. During his funeral service, at the Reform temple in Greenwich where they'd held Bette's ceremony nine years before, I saw his son, daughter, brother, loyal agent Sterling, Charles the toy tycoon, Erica Jong and her husband, and Molly. Mimi gave a short speech acknowledging that well-known men tended to be very hard on the people they loved.

Sitting shivah at Howard's last residence in Old Greenwich, Molly talked about her engagement to Matt, a Shakespeare professor fourteen years her senior. They planned to wed on Valentine's Day. Oh no! That was the date my memoir was coming out and I'd scheduled a big literary bash for 6:00 PM. I was worried that Molly would have to miss my publication fête or I'd have to miss her wedding. If Molly gave out my memoir to all her guests in their goody bags, someone suggested, I should switch my launch party to the next night. It seemed bizarrely appropriate to be arguing about the date of a book event at Howard's shivah.

I kept staring at the pictures, artwork, and hardbounds on the shelves, not wanting to leave. I knew I'd never return to this house, where I'd felt more comfortable than in my own home. Eventually Molly chauffeured me back to Manhattan, dropping me off in front of my building and waving, the way I used to, making sure she got back safely.

The scheduling dilemma was solved when she learned she was pregnant and moved up her wedding date. The next slew of Fast events I attended were for Molly – her Manhattan engagement party, bridal showers, wedding, and multiple baby showers. I didn't necessarily agree with her *New York Times* "Style" section essay about the benefits of marrying and having children in your twenties. I hoped I wasn't one of the older feminists she chided for telling her to get an abortion. I certainly hadn't been that tactless, though I did wonder if she were rushing into motherhood before she could handle it. I feared that if babies – not books – were taking center stage in her life, she'd no longer need me as a role model.

With Howard and Bette gone, I found that I was actually the one leaning on Molly, and not vice versa. When I complained about editors who wouldn't run my author's photo, insisting on sending their own photographers, Molly said, "I say yes to all requests. You should be happy they want to take your picture." When I was ambivalent about a book I was asked to endorse, she shared her theory: "Always give blurbs, because it's a free advertisement for your title on someone else's back cover." When I worried that an editor wouldn't like my new manuscript, she and her husband, Matt, said, "Even if it doesn't sell, look at it this way: You'll always be an author with a bunch of books out." That made me feel better, as if I'd already accomplished something no one could take away.

Molly was wise and perceptive about the emotional ins and outs of our trade. I wondered whether it was genetic, by osmosis, or from the agony she'd lived through growing up with so many neurotic scribes. I'd greatly benefited from Howard's age and experience, yet it was also illuminating to get a perspective on publishing from someone younger. Though eighteen years my junior, Molly became a compassionate, helpful sounding board and adviser I could confide everything to. Sometimes it felt like she'd picked up where Howard had left off.

Feeling close to all the remaining Fasts, I naively saw it as a nice gesture when Mimi gave Molly a few of Bette's sculptures. But Molly really wanted Howard's 1974 Emmy from his CBS Benjamin Franklin miniseries, *The Ambassadors.* She was disappointed Howard hadn't left the statue to her and her two brothers, the older one currently in TV/film grad school.

"Why would you want the Emmy?" I asked.

"We want to share it."

"With three people?" I was miffed that out of all the first edition tomes and impressive artwork, she'd focused on the glitzy prize.

"No young writer needs somebody else's award staring at them," Aaron joked. "It'll block you forever."

Molly didn't find this funny. She felt that Howard left too much to Mimi. I didn't quite understand the problem, since Molly's mother, stepfather, and her husband's family were well off, and she earned high book advances herself. When I asked further, she admitted she was upset for her father, who was depressed by his dad's death, and disappointed with what Howard had left him. I sympathized but felt torn. Not between the living people in the conflict, but between the ghosts of Howard and Bette. Bette would have insisted he take care of their two children foremost, leaving them everything. But I bet Howard felt that giving his kids houses and half of his royalties was enough. He'd chosen to also reward the woman who'd taken care of him in his last years. When I suggested that he and Mimi really did seem to love each other, Molly was outraged.

"Howard's will created an ugly circus. Why are you getting in the middle of it?" Molly said. "Everybody's pissed off at you."

"Really?" I was floored. When had I become the bad guy? I'd had nice talks with everyone at the hospital when Molly gave birth to the ten-pound Max, Howard's first great-grandchild, whom he never got to meet.

"Explain to me what I did wrong," I asked Molly, completely perplexed.

"Everyone thinks you're taking Mimi's side," she tipped me off.

"Since when?"

"Since you started helping her kids."

I recalled that after I'd handed Molly a basket of baby toys at the hospital, I'd mentioned that one of Mimi's sons had gotten into a fight with a gang of Westchester kids and needed a lawyer. Aaron's father was a judge from Rye, so we made some calls and recommended a good attorney. Apparently this gesture had crossed the line.

"The woman just lost her husband, and her son was in trouble with the law. Of course we'd make a few phone calls to help her," I argued. "Nobody can be mad at us for that."

"Sure they can," said Molly.

I couldn't bear having the Fasts angry at me. Not long later, I called her back. "What if I placed an article in the *Daily News* saying Mel Gibson wants to option one of your grandfather's books?" I blurted the secret news she didn't yet know, flinging myself right into the heart of the family's financial controversy that was – literally and figuratively – none of my business. "Gibson made $200 million from his Christ movie. If he'd pay good money to option Howard's book, wouldn't that solve some problems?"

"Mel Gibson? A movie?" Molly sounded suddenly buoyed. "Really? That would be amazing. Which one of his books?"

With *my* career finally coming to life in the fall of 2005, why was I still promoting my richer and much better known dead cousin? Idiotically, I felt affection for all the parties involved in what turned out to be an ugly scuffle to divide Howard's estate. But I certainly didn't need to be stuck in the center of a family crisis – especially when I wouldn't see a cent either way and it wasn't even my immediate family!

Over a nice recent lunch, Mimi and I had exchanged books. I'd given her a signed copy of my hardcover memoir, then feared I'd committed a faux pas, since my acknowledgments cited Howard and Bette, as if they were still together a decade after her death. If Mimi noticed, she never mentioned it. She'd given me the new paperback of *My Glorious Brothers,* Howard's 1948 historical Hanukkah novel on the Maccabees, a handful of Jewish farmers in Judea who rose against the Syrian-Greek conquerors of their land. Then she'd shared the good news: After it was reissued by Simon & Schuster's iBooks, Mel Gibson had inquired about optioning it for his next film.

"People say Gibson's an anti-Semite. How could he do justice to a historical novel about the origins of Hanukkah?" Mimi asked. "I should tell him no. I can't let the integrity of the work be compromised."

"I wouldn't say no so quickly," I stunned myself by saying. "Maybe you could get final okay of the script."

"I think it would be too controversial," she said.

"It would put Howard back on the front pages of the newspapers. He'd love that. He courted controversy," I argued. "He enraged the Socialists, the Communists, the Republicans, and the Liberals. Come to think of it, were there any political parties in the world Howard didn't piss off? He was this eighty-year-old Jewish Buddhist writing op-eds in the white-bread Connecticut paper, arguing that O. J. was innocent, remember?"

I talked her into considering it, offering to see if any of my journalist colleagues could get press on the potential movie deal. I had no love for Mel Gibson and no desire to see *The Passion of the Christ;* my passion for this project was fueled by emotion. I had the fantasy that Gibson's interest in Howard's Hanukkah story could return his byline to the screen in a splash of glory. Even better, a big film deal could quell all the money quarrels by getting lots of gelt to Howard's heirs. That included his two kids, Molly, and his other two grandkids, who were splitting the posthumous royalties with Mimi, who was watching out for her own three sons. The behind-the-scenes chaos among Howard's survivors mirrored one of Howard's soapy, intergenerational sagas.

This latest version of *My Glorious Brothers* had a short intro by Mimi, who lauded the author as "a champion of the divine right of every human being to freedom, equality, and dignity." Yet her preface only fueled the brewing storm Howard had left behind. How could Mimi's new pages not be dicey when Howard's brother, son, daughter, granddaughter, and ex-daughter-in-law were all professional authors who might have penned it differently? Ironically, Mimi, a Southern-born Irish Catholic MBA, was the only one with the time and ardor to preserve Howard's pro-Jewish epic and his legacy.

After quitting my twenty-seven-year cigarette habit (as Bette had begged me to) and having three books come out in one twelve-month period, I was pushing my former students working as interns and editorial assistants to write about my projects, in the annoying, pushy way Howard had nudged me. The sharp ones who had luck were badgered most. It was amazing how obsessed one could get with promoting one's book, especially when press influenced sales and whether you'd be able to publish again. Meanwhile, wasn't that what protégés were for? You help them get into the game, they help you stay there. And why weren't those newspaper editors assigning more space to my books, anyway?

"You're so incredibly prolific," Mimi said. "Just like Howard."

I'd had one great year. He'd kept up that rate of productivity for seven decades. I pondered why I'd finally taken his advice about expanding to books just as he'd passed away. My addictions had been a smoke screen keeping me from attaining what scared me – like financial success. It was easier to stay small potatoes and behind the scenes than to be seen as a threat. Was I apologizing for becoming more powerful by continuing to plug Howard's projects? He definitely would have been pleased with the *Daily News*'s "Fast Reaction to Mel," a piece based on the information I'd passed on about Gibson's interest in *My Glorious Brothers*. Howard had trained me well. I was still getting him press two years after his death, on a novel he'd published in 1948.

"Howie's smoking a cigar up in heaven," Mimi said. "He's saying, 'Way to go, girls.'"

Molly called to say she and her dad also liked the article, along with the prospect of a movie paycheck. I was so relieved that domestic peace was finally a possibility. Alas, the illusion was short lived. Gibson went on to another film project, a DWI, and more anti-Semitic slurs. And Howard's heirs weren't done throwing dirt yet.

An unabashed fan of Molly's, I'd coerced her to join me as a contributor to the anthologies *The Barbie Chronicles* (along with Erica) and *The Modern Jewish Girl's Guide to Guilt*, where her witty essay riffed on being the daughter of the Queen of Sex. But I was taken aback by Molly's humorous collection, *The Sex Doctors in the Basement: True Stories from a Semi-Celebrity Childhood*. She used to show me her early drafts to get my take. This time she didn't.

The section "I Caught the Bouquet at My Grandfather's Wedding" was a sarcastic send-up of Howard's second wedding, focusing on eighty-three-year-old Howard marrying a bride who was forty-nine. Portraying her new step-grandmother as Anna Nicole Smith, Molly quipped: "The bride wore a white suit. The groom wore Depends."

Howard's voice echoed in my mind, asking, *Will you keep an eye out for my beautiful little granddaughter?* I couldn't help but feel heartbroken that my twenty-six-year-old cousin was mocking her grandfather in print. Then again, it was easy to trace the roots of her hurt and anger. She'd always hated the cold way Howard had treated his only son. Did she feel that a lifetime of Howard's neglect and antagonism had ultimately deprived her of the dad she'd wanted? I finally saw the subtext of the war over the will: It was never too late to want your father to take care of you.

I recalled how much I'd resented my Grandpa Harry for the competitive, castrating way he'd treated my dad. (Who wouldn't wind up aloof and withdrawn with such a nasty, emotionally abusive father?) I was so enraged, I'd boycotted Harry's funeral and published an angry poem exposing the negativity and condescension he'd shown my dad, even when my grandfather was near death. "My father gave his father blood / then held the silver disk / to his heart and listened closely. 'You're no good, you're trying to kill me.' / My father played his father a rare / recording of *Meine Yiddishe Mama*. / Grandpa sang until the end, turned, / and said, "The other version was better."

I was stunned to learn that for a guy who'd had a small window shade store, Harry was worth six figures. As if to stick it to my father one last time, Harry left everything to my mother. She divided the money between her kids, giving each of us part of the down payment for our homes. So who was I to judge Molly? Her grandfather was more wealthy and famous than mine, but I wasn't denied my inheritance. I'd actually benefited because Harry was a misanthropic widower who'd never remarried, while Howard loved women and found a second wife to care for him.

Not surprisingly, Mimi was hurt by Molly's book. So were my parents, Howard's agent, and some of the old guard, not to mention the *Dynasty* vixen Joan Collins. A former friend of Erica's, the actress had once called Molly fat as a kid. Molly had retaliated by implying in print that Joan was bald and wore a wig. There was a full-page picture in one of the tabloids of Joan with a huge bald head. Collins was threatening to sue. Nobody could accuse the Fasts of being boring.

Amid the turmoil, a package came in the mail. Inside was Howard's posthumous memoir. It felt like he'd rushed back from the grave to argue his side. *Being Jewish* started: "My last name, Fast, is not a Jewish name. It originated from the small town of Fastov in the Ukraine." It ended with his second marriage to a Christian. Mimi, who'd sent me the rough manuscript, asked if I'd help edit and contribute a foreword. Now that I was becoming known as a memoirist, she hoped my name on the cover might help. I was honored and told her I'd give it a shot.

Within a week, Rachel and Jonathan both voiced disapproval of my involvement, as did Molly and Erica. Then two agents (mine, Elizabeth Kaplan, and her ex-boss, Sterling Lord) said it would be too hard to sell, anyway. I certainly didn't want to proceed with a project that everyone I cared about had vetoed or perpetuate a feud with people who'd been so important to me. I soon heard that Jonathan had an upcoming hardcover and blog, Rachel was trying a new book, Erica's latest essay collection discussed the Fasts, and Molly sold TV rights to her memoir. I decided that I'd stolen Howard from his family for long enough. I'd benefited from having the best of him for more than two decades. Now his name, royalties, memory, and legacy were theirs − not mine. So I bowed out of writing anything about Howard − except for this remembrance.

Institution Within an Institution

HELEN

STARK

"You look great. Very glamorous. You're such a fashion plate," said Peter, kissing me hello as he walked into my party in the winter of 2003.

"I am not!" I said, staring at him, fascinated to hear the words of my beloved late boss, Helen, coming from the mouth of her only son. It took me back twenty years, to my first real job, which ruined me for any other full-time job for the rest of my life.

It was the end of January 1983, days after my twenty-second

birthday, when I'd sent my resume to *The New Yorker*. A week later I received a response to my query. The letter was typed neatly on little yellow stationery and signed by Wolcott Gibbs Jr. "I'm afraid the job prospects at *The New Yorker* are very slight," it said. "But I'll certainly keep you in mind in case the situation changes." I liked getting such a personal rejection note and attributed its polite tone and promptness to my professor's recommendation. I slipped the cute mini-envelope into my purse, carrying it around with me as if it would bring good luck. It did. The very next morning, a Wednesday, the situation changed. Apparently an editorial assistant had been offered a better job at another magazine and resigned. Thus, I was pleasantly shocked to get a call from a woman named Helen Stark, asking me if I could come in for an interview at the magazine at one o'clock that Friday afternoon. "Yes! I'll be there Friday!" I said, jumping up and down.

The position was titled "research assistant" and paid only $13,000 a year, but I would have swept floors to hang out at *The New Yorker*. Since I'd completed my course work for my master's degree, my father expected me to move back to the Midwest after graduation. Although I had no intention of ever again living in Michigan and planned to die in glorious Greenwich Village, a prestigious publishing gig would provide the perfect excuse to convince my parents I had to stay East.

For the past two years in the big city, I'd prided myself on being a downtown hippie poet in torn jeans, black cowboy boots, and a motorcycle jacket. Yet, at the prospect of landing an assistant position at the sharpest magazine in the country, my Jewish princess instincts kicked in and I placed an emergency call to my mother in West Bloomfield. Now she was the fashion plate – a dishy redhead who gracefully donned designer suits in exotic colors with matching hose, shoes, and jewelry that highlighted her short puffy hair. She'd waited twenty-two years to hear her only daughter, a notorious tomboy, say, "Mommy, you have to help me figure out what to wear." She was quite surprised that, instead of reciting my Plath-inspired confessional poetry on the insidiousness of suburbia, I was now begging her to help me look like Working Barbie.

Within twenty-four hours, a chic interview outfit from Saks arrived: a size 6, navy blue Armani skirt and blazer, a beige silk blouse, and navy blue pumps with three-inch heels. I was two inches taller than my mother, but we wore the same size clothes and shoes, so she knew exactly what would fit me. She included a new navy blue briefcase and a bottle of Giorgio perfume, which I sprayed on my wrist. It smelled fake and sugary (I preferred musk oil or my ex-boyfriend's Old Spice). Inside the briefcase she put navy Givenchy pantyhose. Three packets – just in case, out of impatience, I ripped the first two pairs. ("A delicate flower you're not," my mom used to tease.) I put on the elaborate costume, blew my hair dry, and applied lipstick and blush. Before I left the house, I doubled my long strand of small white pearls into a two-tiered choker and hung it around my neck. The necklace had been my mother's, but she had given it to me the year before for my twenty-first birthday, even though I liked to proclaim that I hated jewelry.

At that time *The New Yorker* office was at 25 West 43rd Street, between Fifth and Sixth Avenues. The proximity to my home was important, because I could not walk very far in my mother's high heels and I still hadn't quite mastered the subway, where I felt especially self-conscious this done up. I was living in an illegally subletted one-bedroom apartment with a Michigan girlfriend at 15th Street and Fifth Avenue. (Sleeping on a futon on the living room floor seemed romantic and suffering artist–like, despite the fact that my father was paying my $450 monthly share of the rent so I could afford a doorman building.) I decided to take the Sixth Avenue bus uptown, and the Fifth Avenue bus back downtown. When I found the midtown office building, I took the elevator to the eighteenth floor, where the receptionist was wearing jeans and a sweater, as were the two people standing by the elevator. Boy, did I feel overdressed. Especially when I walked into the library.

The magazine itself, which I read weekly, looked so clean and classy that I'd pictured the modern decor of a Condé Nast or Hearst type company. I was thus taken aback to find that the four-hundred-square-foot room was old and hoary, filled with dilapidated desks and chairs that looked like they hadn't been replaced in half a century.

The space was overpowered by thousands of dust-laden, oversize, bulging black scrapbooks filed alphabetically in the floor-to-ceiling shelves. There was a poster of a unicorn on a unicycle under the words KEEP TRYING taped to the wall, a tacky orange paper turkey obviously left over from Thanksgiving, and open boxes of Oreo cookies and graham crackers on top of the radiator. A morbid section of files and books toward the back was labeled DEAD CONTRIBUTORS. It was the dingiest office I had ever seen. I immediately wanted to move in and never leave.

Sitting at the wooden desk in the center was a woman in her sixties with brown beauty-parlor hair and large round glasses. She was wearing a below-the-knee, pleated gray wool skirt and a beige silk blouse buttoned to the neck with a bow on it. She had a no-time-for-nonsense aura, like a high school principal. When she saw me she stood up.

"You must be Susan," she said, coming over to greet me, shaking my hand. She had a firm grip and regal bearing, as if she'd been taught the importance of good posture and looking someone in the eye. In my high heels, I was taller than she was. I noticed she wore flat, sensible black shoes and guessed she was five foot seven, my height.

"Yes, you must be Ms. Stark." I returned her solid handshake. "It is so nice to meet you."

"Ms. – in my day it was just 'Mrs.' or 'old maid.'" She laughed, a deep, throaty laugh at odds with her formal appearance. "What a beautiful suit you have on." She looked me up and down, nodding in approval at my matching navy briefcase and shoes. "Very elegant."

"My mother sent it from Michigan. It's Armani," I blurted, feeling stupid the minute it spilled from my mouth, as if I were four years old and still needed my mommy to pick out my clothes. As if someone at such an intellectual magazine would care about silly fashion.

But Helen did. "Everyone dresses so tacky here, in dirty dungarees and blazers ripped at the elbow. It's simply disgraceful." She spun me around. "I love Armani's clean lines. Finally, I found a fashion plate." She smiled. "So tell me about your family in Michigan."

"My dad's a doctor, mom's a housewife, three younger brothers are science-brain Republicans who love the Midwest, so I'm the black sheep." I feared I had revealed too much, and that the condescension in my voice would make her dislike – and thus not hire – me. But she was still preoccupied by my outfit.

"Such pretty freshwater pearls," she commented. "Is that Giorgio perfume you have on?"

I nodded sheepishly. "Also from my mom."

"Well, I must say your mother has very good taste."

"She's originally from New York," I offered, as if that explained it.

"Oh really?" Helen asked. "What neighborhood?"

"The Lower East Side shtetl," I answered quickly. "She was poor, and an orphan. When she was sixteen, she got a secretary job 'cause she typed one hundred words a minute. She put my father through medical school." I wanted Helen to know that I wasn't the frivolous prima donna I was dressed like. Rather, I was from solid Russian Hebrew stock, as my mother used to say. Every member of my clan was a hard worker not afraid to get dirty hands, what they called in Yiddish *shrara arbiters*. "Where are you from?" I asked her.

"My father was German. My mother is from Manhattan," she told me. "I grew up here, in the West 90s."

It interested me that she didn't say her father was a German Jew, though I sensed our families were the same religion. "So you're an uptown girl," I said.

"In my time the Upper West Side was not chichi or expensive like it is today," she clarified. "We were Depression kids, taught to be frugal. My brother was my mother's favorite, too; they always favor the boys."

Having established that neither of us grew up all that privileged or happy, we switched to small talk as Helen showed me around. The library was created to link the magazine's fact-checkers, writers, editors, cartoonists, the business and advertising departments, the readers, and the outside publishing world, she explained. She and her two assistants were responsible for indexing the entire early drafts every week, including all the cartoons and those glitches dotting the edges of the pages, which I was amused to learn had an official name: newsbreaks. They checked everything going into the magazine to make sure it had not run before, kept scrapbooks and files on everything that did run, and dealt with copyright info on articles that came out in book form, along with answering in- and out-of-house queries.

As if on cue, the phone on her desk rang. She picked it up. "Yes. James Thurber's first piece ran February 26, 1927," she said off the top of her head. "Yes, I can get you a copy." She turned to me. "Excuse me for a second. Mr. Shawn needs this right away." She searched for a card in one of the standing metal index drawers, filling out some sort of order slip and walking it to another office.

I felt like I had just walked into the 1957 Katharine Hepburn movie *Desk Set*.

When she returned, she asked more questions about my background, degrees, and skills. Then I sat down to take a typing test on one of the three IBM Selectric typewriters stationed on the desks. Helen handed me that week's mock-up of the magazine and pointed to a piece by Jonathan Schell. I typed for five minutes straight. Helen calculated my speed. Like my mother, I typed one hundred words a minute. Only two mistakes. I told Helen that my oldest brother, Brian, joked that my typing got me more jobs than my two degrees.

"What do you think of Schell's article?" she asked.

"Brilliant politics but the prose was a bit dry," I commented.

"Yes, but he's so adorable. Blond hair, blue eyes. One of my special friends. You'll have to meet him. Here, look at his book-jacket photo." Helen pulled out his last book and pointed with a discreet leer. I felt like we were in high school, two nerdy girls whispering about the basketball star.

When the other assistant came back from lunch, Helen introduced us. Her name was Katrina, a cute, slender prep in khaki pants and a blue blouse. I was immediately wary of her. (Sibling rivalry already?) Helen led me to a tiny office down the hall to finish our interview, mentioning that Katrina had a BA from Yale, had spent her junior year of college in Spain, earned her MFA from Columbia University, and spoke Spanish fluently. I feared my lost Hebrew, NYU and University of Michigan diplomas, and fast typing paled in comparison. There was just a chair and a couch in the weird little room. It appeared to be slanted, like the jagged set design in the 1919 German expressionist horror film *The Cabinet of Dr. Caligari*. Helen sat down on the couch, so I sat down on the chair facing her and said, "So now vee may perhaps to begin, yes?"

I wasn't sure if she'd get that I was quoting one of my favorite Philip Roth lines, but she laughed out loud, that great robust laugh again.

"I hated that book, with the hideous liver scene," she told me. She paused and then raised her eyebrow. "You know, even though Mr. Shawn ran part of *Goodbye, Columbus*, he wouldn't touch *Portnoy*. Too dirty for him."

Wow! *The New Yorker*'s editor in chief, William Shawn, had rejected one of the best books of the century? What great inside literary gossip! "Really? Mr. Shawn wouldn't publish anything from *Portnoy's Complaint?*"

"Not a single line. He left it to *Partisan Review* and *Esquire*. He is a prude, you know."

"Mr. Shawn is a prude? What about Pauline Kael's criticism?" I asked. "She's pretty racy." I thought she was the funniest, spiciest film writer in the world. Just following her work in the magazine taught me that criticism could be as thrilling to read as the best fiction or poetry.

"You should see her first drafts. Every review she puts in the F-word, and every week he deletes it from the final copy," Helen said.

Oh my god! It was such a juicy Pauline Kael secret! I couldn't wait to tell everyone I knew. Helen was forty years older than me, the age of my grandmother, but she seemed way hipper than my mom and her well-dressed West Bloomfield cronies. I'd never met anyone like her. Helen was in the same age, brains, and coolness range as my cousin Bette Fast, but Bette seemed more in the mold of a rich, chic Connecticut wife and mother. Helen was a down-to-earth New Yorker who rode the subways and preferred working full time. Also, Bette's talent was visual art, whereas Helen was a serious reader who knew the inside scoop on what I hoped would soon be my realm – the loony urban literati.

"Did you ever meet James Thurber?" I needed to know.

"Sure." She smiled wryly. "He used to call me and say, 'It's the blind old man of the mountain.'"

"Was he really a womanizer?" I couldn't help but ask.

"There was only one woman I ever saw him with – his mother. She was this dear, elderly Midwestern woman who wanted to see her son's scrapbooks. I took them out. 'Do you mean to say you wrote all of this yourself, Jamie?' she asked him."

Helen was conscious of her delivery, like a stand-up comic performing surefire material that always killed. I was a rapt audience; I could listen to her stories forever.

"I really want to be a writer," I confided.

"Pretend you don't and you can start Monday," she said, and we shook on it.

Every member of my family was a control freak who didn't play well with others, and I assumed that a nine-to-five office job at any company would kill me. Yet if there were a position crafted to fit the limitations and excesses of my compulsive personality, being one of Helen's library assistants was it. The hours were ten o'clock to six, but she whispered that everybody got to the office late, which was a godsend for an insomniac night owl. Within weeks my outfits degenerated to comfortable jeans and Gap sweaters, but she never said a word. The library was the most social area, since all the writers and editors came by daily to see

Helen. They wanted to pick the brain of the friendliest person at the magazine — who was a walking storehouse of idiosyncratic facts and behind-the-scenes secrets she enjoyed sharing. Sensing how starstruck I was, Helen made a point of introducing me to everyone on staff, and I fell in love daily. She was a funny combination of bodyguard and literary critic, and luckily, she had a blunt way of reining in my impulsive adoration.

Sid, a young "Talk of the Town" reporter, came in to do research one afternoon when I was alone in the office. He saw me writing and asked if he could read my work.

"This guy Sid is really cute and smart," I told Helen when she returned from lunch. "He offered to help me get into the *Daily News!*"

"He wants to get into your pants," she said out of the side of her mouth. "He goes for all the library girls. Watch out for him." Then, more earnestly, she added, "But he is an excellent writer." She handed me his "Talk" story about a shoeshine guy in Grand Central, which she clearly approved of. (I did wind up going out with him, with predictably disastrous results.)

When I completed a round of research on Montana for Ian Frazier, he wrote me a sweet thank-you note, which I showed to Helen. "He is a dear. But you're too late. He just married Jay, the nineteenth-floor receptionist. She's a writer too. Short stories, I think. If he leaves her, he's all mine," Helen said, winking.

Frank Modell, a dapper cartoonist in his sixties, took me out to lunch to brush up on current slang. When I mentioned my off-and-on long-distance romance with my L.A. boyfriend, Frank said, "Sounds crazy." I said, "It's not crazy crazy. It's healthy crazy." The next issue of the magazine sported a cartoon in which a hip chick was telling her (equally young, hip) boyfriend, "It's not crazy crazy. It's healthy crazy."

"Tell him he has to give you the original," Helen insisted.

I found Frank and told him what Helen said. His office looked as if it had been hit by a hurricane, but he said when he located the cartoon, it was mine. Sure enough, three years later, he sent me the original, signed! (It still hangs on the wall in my living room.)

One morning I went into the library and happily announced to Helen that I had ridden up in the elevator with Mr. Shawn, the staff writer Lillian Ross, and their poodle.

"Oh, no, you're not allowed to ride up with them! Mr. Shawn is afraid of elevators and always rides up alone." She looked horrified by my faux pas but then whispered, "Mr. Shawn has been frolicking with her for decades. Everybody at the magazine knows. That's why she gets so many plum assignments and we have to deal with that silly little dog." (I later reviewed the tell-all memoir that Ross published after Mr. Shawn's death, which confirmed Helen's gossip and then some.)

Within a week of my arrival, Penelope Gilliatt noticed how fast I typed and asked me to type up her handwritten stories before work.

While doing so, I caught mistakes and fixed them. She gave me signed copies of her books to thank me. I thought it was generous and felt awed to be working for the writer of the politically savvy and still-controversial movie *Sunday Bloody Sunday*, not to mention her highly acclaimed novels and short story collections. But when Helen got wind of the arrangement, she didn't like it. "Being Penelope's private secretary is not part of your job description. Tell her to pay you," Helen instructed. "Your price is ten dollars an hour. She can afford it."

"It's odd how she keeps switching the names of her characters," I confided.

"She drinks, so she can't keep track. She doesn't want Shawn to see the early drafts because they're too much of a mess," Helen guessed.

"But I've been meeting her here at 9:00 AM. She can't be drinking that early in the morning," I argued.

"Sure she can," Helen said. "I bet that's the reason she plagiarized Graham Greene. She was sauced up and probably thought something she read by him was hers. I wonder if she ever slept with him. She was quite the beauty in her day and he was known to be a lecher."

"Who? Graham Greene? Really? Penelope plagiarized him?" I'd never heard this tale before.

"Oh yes, that was a great scandal," Helen nodded. "That's why she stopped sharing the movie reviews with Pauline, and now Shawn just publishes her fiction."

"I wonder why she drinks," I said. "She's so smart and successful."

"She's going through a rough divorce and custody case over her daughter."

"I didn't know she was married."

"Oh yes," Helen nodded. "To the British playwright John Osborne."

"The guy who wrote *Look Back in Anger?* Really?"

"Yes. And *The Entertainer,* which I saw on the London stage with Laurence Olivier," Helen added.

The next day Penelope asked if I would help her with something important at her Central Park West apartment after work. When I arrived, she introduced Vincent, a very nice older gentleman. She never mentioned any typing or editing. Instead we sat around drinking wine, eating peanuts, and talking about Michigan, where he liked to go camping. The next morning, when I told Helen, she said, "That was the *New York Times* movie critic Vincent Canby. We think they're an item."

Penelope asked if I wanted to sublet the extra bedroom in her apartment, which had a wraparound terrace, for $400 a month, noting that she was in England six months out of the year. It was cheaper than what I was paying for twice as much space at a better address, an offer I couldn't refuse. Helen thought otherwise. "I love Penelope," she said. "But she's a sot who swings both ways, and when she falls down the stairs and breaks her hip in the middle of the night, you'll be the one taking her to the hospital." I stayed where I was.

Helen smoked one cigarette every afternoon with the window opened. But since I smoked a pack a day and Katrina hated the smell, they insisted I puff away on the ugly, beat-up beige couch outside the library. "Your father is a cancer specialist and he lets you smoke?" Helen was incredulous. "He smokes too," I argued, inanely.

The idea of being banished to the hall couch bothered me. But the first day on my smoking break out there, Jackie O. walked by. I tried not to stare. The next day I saw John Updike. It turned out that this corner, right by the stairway, was an upscale Grand Central Station. For a young wannabe, it was the people-watching spot of the century. Everybody I had not already met in the library for some reason wanted to check out the young girl on the couch who was chain-smoking and scrawling intently into her notebook. I soon met the acclaimed writers Garrison Keillor, Mark Singer, Alex Shoumatoff, Alec Wilkinson, Bill McKibben, Calvin Trillin, Gerry Jonas, and Jamaica Kincaid on their way in or out. "Whatcha writing?" was the most common way they'd start a conversation.

"They're so nice to care," I told Helen.

"They're not nice, they're nosy," she said. "They think you're writing an exposé about them."

Although another *New Yorker* assistant, Alison Rose, later

did just that, I was in fact quite seriously absorbed in my own mediocre poetry.

I took to sitting on the ratty couch, editing poems and puffing four or five cigarettes in a row, checking out which luminaries were in the office that day. Part of my job was to read the magazine religiously (to index and cross-reference all the pieces), so – on Helen's advice – I took to complimenting the writers walking by on their latest work, often before it was published.

"They're so well known. Won't I be bothering them or being a kiss-ass?" I asked her, afraid I would come to be seen as a sycophant or stalker.

"No. It's paying homage to your elders, and it shows you're humble and perceptive. They became writers because they have a pathological need for the attention they never got," Helen said offhandedly, as if it were a rule that everybody already knew. "Tell them the lines of their piece you liked best," she insisted. "Just make damn sure you get the quote right."

To my astonishment, she was correct. None of them were ever offended when I recited from their words, and I soon became pretty popular for a peon. I received offers to do freelance typing and editing, was given many signed books, and was invited to book parties, literary award dinners, readings, and screenings. It was an important lesson Helen taught me: Never be afraid to tell an author you admired their work, especially if you were sincere and could quote from it verbatim. She said that the bigwig editors also wrote for the magazine and suggested I look them up and start my cover letters by expressing how much I enjoyed their latest piece, before asking them to read mine. So I told the editor Dan Menaker how much I loved his Old Left stories, since I had a cherished Uncle Sol like he did, along with a relative who was a big communist. After that Dan carefully read, critiqued, and promptly responded to all my submissions. (Perhaps he would have been just as kind without the flattery. But I now call my students lazy and self-involved if they don't first Google editors and pay respect before launching into their own first-person pitches and needs.)

Former employees often came back to see Helen, and one day Monica Yates, a former library assistant, stopped by to visit. The daughter of novelist Richard Yates, Monica confided she'd also been rejected romantically by staff writer Sid. I confided that I was more hurt by rejections from *New Yorker* editors. Monica said to send my latest humor essay to her editor friend Laura at *Cosmopolitan*. Laura bought it for $500 and then hooked me up at *Glamour* and *New Woman*. Perhaps feeling sorry for me, other more successful colleagues referred me to editors at other publications, offering their names to get me in the door.

I pitched a story on Ann, a trailblazing seventy-year-old reporter, to *Folio* magazine. The profile lauded her as one of the first female *New Yorker* reporters, who was hired during World War II after several male writers were drafted into the army. The morning the *Folio* photographer came, Ann posed in a pretty pink sweater. (She normally wore brown and beige.) We went over the final version of the article, which she said was "terrific." (I hadn't yet learned that you weren't supposed to let your subject see your piece prepublication.) When it ran, I was so excited that I got to work two hours early, xeroxed it, and left two copies on top of Ann's office chair. I planned to ask her to lunch to celebrate. But at ten o'clock, Ann marched into the library, screaming that my piece was awful because I'd made a huge mistake that ruined everything. I was crestfallen and asked, "Where? What did I get wrong?"

She showed me the line that said, "They have three children" and stormed out. I was confused, sure she'd told me that she had three kids. When Helen came in a few minutes later, she found me reading over my notes and crying, still trying to figure out what I'd screwed up. I told Helen what happened.

"It's not your fault. One of her kids died," Helen explained. "What time did you interview her?"

"Twice after work," I answered. "And we went over the final draft together at lunch two weeks ago, before I turned it in. Why?"

"She's a great reporter, but when she drinks she forgets what she says. It's best to catch her in the morning."

Though I didn't think I'd really done anything wrong, I wrote Ann a note, not repeating what Helen had told me but apologizing for not "doing her justice." She never mentioned her child dying to me, but soon she seemed to forget she'd ever been mad. We went back to being pals. Whenever I thought about the article, it made me sad. I hoped all serious female writers didn't have to suffer when it came to addictions and their family lives.

While trying my hand at a movie critique, emulating the last review by Pauline Kael, she rushed past me, another smart, hyper women I admired. She wore blue pants, an untucked button-down shirt, and sneakers. She asked what I was working on. "I'm trying a film review," I told her. She plopped down next to me, read it fast, and said, "Don't write about movies. You don't love them enough. Write about books." Then she jumped up and was gone. How did she know I loved books more than movies? The next day she fixed me up with an adorable, skinny, redheaded minion of hers named Henry. Helen informed me that a group of her protégés, who were called "The Paulettes," were legendary, and indeed Henry later became the film critic for *The Washington Post*.

Sometimes the phones in the library rang constantly and I couldn't keep up with all the factoids flying around. "Let me go into a trance," Helen would say. "The first issue date was February 21, 1925," she'd continue, without having to look it up. "Harold Ross died on December 6, 1951."

Helen often talked about her husband, Ira, a chemical engineer, and her son, Peter, who worked in computer graphics. He was a little older than I was. She implied that he was politically conservative and she didn't agree with his views. It was the reverse of my family, where I was the only liberal Democrat amid right-wingers. She described Peter as single, living at home, and a bit of a loner, which seemed to worry her. "Want me to invite him to my next party?" I asked her. "I can fix him up."

"Yes, Monica tells me you're a great fixer-upper," Helen said and then added, "But Peter doesn't like girls."

We were alone in the library when she said it, and she was speaking quietly. I wondered if it was hard for her to talk about.

"I live in Greenwich Village. Half my friends are gay. Though I'm not sure if we can handle a Republican," I joked.

"Well, yes, then you can invite him," she said. "I'll tell him to keep his politics to himself."

I gave her a flyer to give to Peter, but he ended up being busy that night. A few months later, he came by to pick her up for lunch. I stared at him, amazed at how much my boss and her son looked alike. They were about the same height and weight. Like her, he was dressed in quiet earth tones, wearing gray pants and a tweedy coat. He also had a warm, expressive face with dark hair and dark eyes hidden behind large framed glasses.

"Where are you going? China Grill?" I asked him while she was getting her coat.

"No, today it's the Teheran restaurant. The food is absolutely terrible, but the martinis are strong," he smiled. Did they have the same dry sense of humor? "Thanks for inviting me to that party. Try me again sometime," he said.

"I will," I promised.

I invited him to a few more events, but he never came.

Helen met my relatives too. When my mother visited New York for the weekend, she picked me up at the magazine one Friday afternoon. I introduced her to my boss.

"What a beautiful outfit," Helen gushed. "I loved that navy suit of Sue's."

"She should wear it more," my mother said. "What's with the torn jeans she always wears, like she's a poor kid?"

"Even the sixty-year-old kids wear them here," Helen lamented. "It's like a circus for lost gifted children."

It intrigued me that she called the *New Yorker* staff "gifted children," like those who attended my private school in Michigan. I only felt comfortable in places that made allowances for overly sensitive artists and other garden-variety eccentrics. Although I definitely possessed kooky traits, I feared I'd never live up to my supposed gift.

"What are you doing while you're in town?" Helen asked my mother.

Mom mentioned an uptown French restaurant she and my father were trying, relatives we had to visit, the theater. "We have an extra ticket tonight. Do you want to come?" I heard my mother ask. I loved my mom but sometimes found her a bit too friendly. When I'd brought her in for a joint appointment with my therapist and me, she shook my shrink's hand, said, "It's so great to meet you," and complimented her on her sweater, as if they were old friends. I wasn't into all this small talk about clothes.

"Thanks so much for asking," Helen said. "But I have plans with my husband tonight."

My mother took me to lunch at the Algonquin across the street, where James Thurber, Dorothy Parker, and the "Round Table" regulars used to hang out in the 1920s. Mr. Shawn was dining alone at the next table, so I introduced them. He nodded several times but barely said anything.

"What an odd duck that little guy is," she said of my revered editor in chief. "But I like Helen. Now, she's a hoot. Too bad she can't join us tonight."

With a lot of downtime to kill in that miniscule office, we learned everything about each other. Helen spoke German, French, Spanish, and Italian and had traveled widely through Europe, Scandinavia, South America, and the Orient. After her father died, her mother had remarried a Spanish count, so she and her brother had spent a lot of time in Spain. That bonded her and Katrina, who always wanted to know all the details of Helen's Spanish adventures. I preferred to hear about the magazine and would constantly switch the subject to get more saucy tidbits out of her.

"Did everybody drink in Harold Ross's day?" I inquired.

"Yes, everyone drank back then," Helen recalled. "John McCarten, our old drama and movie critic, used to joke that they had a special *New Yorker* dry-out wing at Payne Whitney. He was a naughty man. When his wife had a child, I told him he'd have to stop partying and stay home with his wife and baby. He said, 'In a pig's ass I will. . . .'"

For decades Helen kept the library to a rigid schedule. Mondays we read and typed the upcoming "Notes and Comments" and "Talk of the Town" sections on index cards. Tuesdays we slogged through the long pieces. Wednesdays we got early copies and engaged in this bizarre cut-and-paste ritual – gluing each article, column by column, into the big, thick scrapbooks, using this messy glue in big bottles and paintbrushes that Helen must have been using since before World War II. The rest of the week was devoted to indexing the cartoons, newsbreaks, and poems.

Happily, I was put in charge of the poetry. I indexed it, typed it on file cards, and checked the copyright information of each new poetry book that came into the office, noting which poems first ran in *The New Yorker*. One day my old professor Dan's impressive new poetry collection came across my desk. Though we'd broken up, he'd included a poem to me, called "To a Young Woman of Ambition." He appeared to attribute our breakup to the fact that I would rather work than get married, which was weird, since he'd recommended me for this job. I was flattered, but there was also something unsettling about his attitude. I showed the poem to Helen.

"It's as if his ambition is normal, part of being a man, but yours strikes him as bizarre and unnecessary. Like you have three arms," she said. Yes! Exactly! How did she know? (I immediately embarked on a rebuttal called "From a Young Woman of Ambition," but it took eight years to get it published in *Poetry East*.)

I'd never worked in such close proximity with a boss before, and I worried that I'd have to sneak around to write. But Helen's openness and warmth (some staffers thought she was the *only* warm presence at an otherwise snooty, hierarchical office) engendered full disclosure. I wound up telling her which piece I was working on and what my deadline was. Since I was a fast, accurate typist and indexer, she began letting me finish a week of the magazine's work in one day. If I made sure to answer the phone and look alert when visitors came, she'd let me spend the rest of my hours working on my own poems and essays. Katrina followed suit, glad to have more time to work on her boring Spain stories, which I skimmed on the sly when she was at lunch. They were all about an affair she had had her junior year abroad. She wouldn't let anybody see them. I, on the other hand, took to reading my pieces aloud or handing them to Helen the minute I was done. Helen would say, "This one is very good," and correct my grammar and punctuation. Only once did she offer specific criticism.

Brian O'Connor, an old Roeper friend, became the editor of a small free New York newspaper called *The Westsider,* and he assigned me a roundup piece on West Side bars and taverns. Helen suggested places to try, and I plodded around Amsterdam Avenue, Columbus Circle, and Central Park, interviewing bar owners, checking out happy hour menus, getting funny stories from bartenders about which famous people had been customers or who had croaked in the bar. When the piece came out I was gratified that it took up two whole pages of the paper. I proudly showed it to Helen, who read it and said, "But you didn't mention the prices of alcohol or the specials."

"What do you mean?" I asked.

"People pick bars because of the cheap beer or drink specials," she explained.

I was a smoker and an eater, not a big drinker, so that had never occurred to me. When a cute young messenger, Mike Caruso, came into the library, Helen stopped him and handed him a copy of my published piece. "Mike, you live on the Upper West Side. What do you think of Sue's article? Would this make you and your friends go to any of these bars?"

Mike skimmed it and said, "Who cares about free happy hour food? How much is a pitcher?"

They were right. I'd totally missed it. I needed to show my first drafts to a few critics *before* handing anything in — a rule I use to this day. Now I won't even send a cover letter by email until I've had my husband or a colleague take a quick look as a second pair of eyes.

Though I usually didn't collaborate with other writers, one afternoon at the office Mike and I decided to do a *Westsider* article together called "The Westies Awards." In it we gave out Academy Awards to the neighborhood, like "Best Ice Cream" and "Easiest Place to Get a Parking Ticket," as well as "Biggest Rats," "Most Prestigious Slumlord," and "Most Yuppies in One Place." It was an awful humor piece, but it was his first publication. I teased him about it for years, after he became a big-shot editor at *The Village Voice*, *Details*, *Vanity Fair*, *Los Angeles* magazine, and *Men's Journal*.

One day my *Westsider* editor came to visit me at the *New Yorker* library and became enthralled with Helen. When she mentioned that she'd lived in the West 90s for decades, he suggested that I write a profile about her. She was flattered and agreed. She took her glasses off for the photographer, who took a lovely picture of her. In March 1984, the picture and my one-thousand-word profile ran under the heading "An Institution Within an Institution." If there were any doubts whether she'd continue to let me get away with writing all day, it disappeared when "Quotes and Comment," the *New Yorker* internal employee journal, reran my profile of her. Everybody saw it, including Mr. Shawn, who dropped her a note on how much he enjoyed the piece. This pleased Helen greatly.

Planning a trip to Europe for two weeks, Helen decided that Katrina and I could be trusted enough to run the library ourselves. Harriet Walden, who was in charge of the typing-pool girls (called "Walden's Pond"), sent a sweet, petite brunette named Serena Richard downstairs to work with us. We followed the rules on Monday and Tuesday. On Wednesday, the day usually reserved for the inane, old-fashioned glue ritual, the messengers brought the big tubes of glue and paintbrushes as usual. But instead of making a mess getting the strips of *New Yorker* copy into the scrapbooks all day, I had a new idea. Maybe I didn't like to literally get my hands dirty after all, since I asked Bruce, the head messenger, for glue sticks. Katrina and Serena were afraid, but I was adamant. Using the little orange glue sticks was neater, cleaner, faster. It transformed an archaic, silly, sloppy, seven-hour ordeal into a one-hour easy ritual. When Helen came back, Katrina the tattletale told on me, which caused outrage. Yet, upon careful inspection of the scrapbooks, Helen had to admit that the glue-stick columns were much smoother and easier to read than the bumpy pages under the old glue. They seemed to remain stuck. We took a vote and the glue sticks stayed.

Most of my fellow underlings secretly wrote all the time too, and we began an underground poetry railroad, xeroxing poems and sending them to each other to critique in interoffice envelopes. One Tuesday after work I invited everyone over to my apartment. Imitating my NYU workshops, we sat around in a circle, critiquing each other's poems, stories, essays, and scenes from plays. It became a weekly event, with rotating magazine staffers and some NYU and midwest cronies dropping by to read new work and share cheap wine, popcorn, and cookies. Little did I know that this Tuesday night workshop would meet weekly for eighteen years and lead to lifelong friendships, thousands of clips, productions, many books, three marriages, and three kids (the first one named Esme Johanna, in honor of two of the group's idols, J. D. Salinger and Bob Dylan). When students ask me where to find a free writing workshop, I always say, "Start your own."

One of my greatest talents was my ability to lure greater talent to help me. I was often blown away by the brilliance that surfaced in both the criticism and the messy rough drafts, with pencil marks scrawled on the copies, that we passed around. Liz Macklin, a tall, quiet woman I didn't know well, wrote dark poems so stunning I had to read them over and over to grasp all their meanings. (I wasn't surprised when she wound up with poetry awards, grants, and acclaimed Norton collections.) Alice Phillips, another poignant and wildly original writer, a studious Princeton grad with a Georgia accent, later worked for the *Times Literary Supplement* in London. Julie Just, a shy, bespectacled girl from Walden's Pond, turned out to be both an excellent poet and an amazingly incisive critic. (And she generously gave me — and my husband — work when she went on to become a well-respected editor at *New York* magazine and *The New York Times*.) Sometimes the loudmouth show-offs were overrated and the polite, understated ones you might not even notice were the ones to watch out for.

Gerry Jonas, a *New Yorker* staffer moonlighting as *The Times Book Review*'s science fiction columnist, also shared astute literary insights in a subtle, unobtrusive way. He came up to me before he left one night and said, "You're such a good critic. Why aren't you writing for the *Book Review?*" I asked him how one would start doing that, and his editor soon called me with an assignment.

My tiny step up in publishing coincided with Mr. Shawn's famously stepping down. In April 1985 he was forced out after Samuel I. Newhouse Jr. bought *The New Yorker*. Most of the editorial staff signed a letter of protest. Jonathan Schell quit. Meetings abounded, filled with writers threatening to quit and start their own magazines. "They're creative people who don't know much about business. As if they could make this big corporation go away. Intelligent, but out of touch with reality," Helen said. Although Chip McGrath was Mr. Shawn's choice for editor, the job went to sixty-year-old Robert Gottlieb, former head of Knopf.

Although she hated his "advertorials," Helen was eventually won over. She later told me, "Shawn and Gottlieb are like night and day. Shawn was private and secretive. Gottlieb was an open window, much more accessible. He hired more minority and gay people on staff and put more women in higher places, though it was still mostly white, with an elitist edge." I was actually one of the few employees not upset by the changing of the guard. I had hoped a new regime would appreciate me more than the old regime. No such luck.

Though I loved every day of my almost four years at the magazine, I didn't love the hundreds of rejections I received from multiple editors. Since I was having better luck selling my work to other newspapers and magazines, I contemplated quitting. My parents thought I would be crazy to leave such a prestigious, steady job. Not Helen. When I told her my fantasy of becoming a full-time freelance writer, she practically shoved me out the door. "This place is a plush-lined rut," she said. "You're smart to get out of here now, before it's too late. Some people are afraid to move on and they get stuck here their whole life." But shouldn't I be playing it practical and safe for a few more years in the big bad city? "No!" she raised her voice. "You can be practical and safe when you're sixty-five, not twenty-five. If you don't go for it now, you never will."

Helen hosted a beautiful goodbye party for me in the library, where I drank whiskey straight and sneaked to a colleague's office to snort GOOD LUCK SUE spelled out in cocaine (in tribute to Jay McInerney). I kept in touch with Helen, who wasn't at all surprised that I dug freelancing and running the workshop and didn't really miss the job. When I heard that a messenger sold a "Shouts & Murmurs" column, or that a typing-pool person had been promoted to assistant editor, I'd feel a pang. It was not regret at leaving; it was hurt that the higher-ups had basically ignored me.

Even though she was seventy-three years old, I was surprised when Helen announced she was retiring at the end of February 1992. I thought she'd stay forever. She hinted she wasn't feeling well but was never more specific. After my *New Yorker* colleague Stan Mieses became the features editor of *Newsday*, he remembered my *Westsider* piece on Helen. He said to get her drunk, get more of the lowdown on the magazine (now that she was on her way out the door), and update the profile for him. So I did! And she knew it, too – and didn't resist.

Over a three-hour, three-martini lunch, I gathered the facts of Helen's life, many I hadn't heard before. Her father, Emil Lenning, was a German fabric merchant who came to the United States in 1907 and sold silk for ties. He married her mother, Alice Gardner, in 1918. Helen Louise Lennig was born in 1919 on the Upper West Side; her only brother, Martin, was born four years later. She went to Julia Richman High School, earned her undergraduate degree in French from Hunter College and a master's in library science from Columbia. In 1942, she married Ira Stark, the handsome son of her family doctor. Ira became a chemical engineer, while their only son, Peter, worked in advertising. Losing her father in 1958 sounded like a huge blow, yet Helen found the Spanish count, whom her mother married at sixty, quite dashing.

I asked questions about her *New Yorker* job, which she had originally heard about through the Special Libraries Association in 1945, after World War II ended. She was an assistant working for Ebba Jonsson, a "strict but fair Swede" who was the head librarian from 1934 to 1970. "Once there was a scrapbook missing. Miss Jonsson told me to knock on every door until it was found," Helen recalled. "I knocked on one man's door and asked if he had taken it. He seemed surprised by my informality. I later found out it was E. B. White."

At first she didn't think *New Yorker* people were friendly. Then a coworker led her to the old Il Cortile bar on 44th Street. "Mark Murphy, a well-known writer at the time, was particularly nice to me at the bar," she said. "But when I saw him at the office, he ignored me. I asked a friend why, and the friend said, 'He probably doesn't recognize you. He's sober!'" she laughed. "A. J. Liebling was one of the few who didn't drink — just wine. He was a Francophile and an eater. He had gout. Charles Addams, who got married in a pet cemetery, used to come in with a white mutt he introduced as Alice. He didn't seem so funny," she recalled. "He seemed like a serious, straight businessman."

She remembered the hot controversy over the issue of August 31, 1946. Harold Ross wasn't sure about dedicating an entire issue to a John Hersey piece on Hiroshima. William Shawn, then managing editor, argued for it and won much praise. "After that Ross said, 'If anything happens to me, Shawn takes over.'"

Shawn, who did take over after Ross died in 1951, "had great foresight," she said. "He printed early articles on the environment, safety in nuclear plants, the ills of smoking. John F. Kennedy's office used to call here all the time." She recalled an episode from the '70s when one of the magazine's messengers was caught with several packets of drugs and a list of editors and writers to whom he was about to deliver. "He was happy to resign, and no one reported it to the authorities." (Too bad the only things I'd passed around inter-office envelopes were poems.)

"We're all intellectual snobs," she told me. "I never expected to spend a lifetime in this plush-lined rut. It spoiled me for other people. But I have no regrets. None at all."

I called Robert Gottlieb and left him a message asking for a quote about Helen. The next day he called me back and read me lovely lines he'd composed. "She's a formidable link to the past," he said. "Like everyone else here, I call Helen often for help — about a piece that ran fifty years ago, about whether or not we've ever run an article on Zanzibar or wire-haired terriers or mating customs in New Guinea. The answers always come back — not only right away, but right. . . . At first Helen seems to be a prototypically efficient and generous colleague — and of course she is. But slowly one realizes there's a wonderful New Yorkish loopiness about her that makes her as lovable as she is capable."

My piece ran in *Newsday* on March 11, 1992, under the heading "A Librarian with Great Stories in Her Files: Keeping Up with the Spirits of a Famous Magazine." I sent a copy to Gottlieb, thanking him for his great quote, throwing some other clips into the envelope. He wrote back a typed note, filled with typos, saying he loved my piece on Helen, and that we should meet to discuss what I would like to write for him. Finally – after almost a decade – I had found a *New Yorker* editor who appreciated me! Elated, I spent hours putting together the exact right clip packet for Gottlieb and coming up with elaborate, original ideas to pitch. On Monday morning I woke up early and ordered a bagel, diet soda, and the newspapers to be delivered from the deli across the street. The front pages ran pictures of Tina Brown, *The New Yorker*'s newly christened editor.

Helen and the old gang from the magazine were not happy with Tina's celebrity worship. When Tina asked the actress Roseanne Barr to guest-edit an issue, Ian Frazier and Jamaica Kincaid quit, Helen told me, laughing gleefully. I didn't send any work to Tina, but I continued to send my work to Helen. We spoke on the phone often, but I saw her in person less and less. I offered to go up to West 92nd Street to take her to lunch. But she usually claimed she wasn't feeling well. When I asked what was wrong, Helen would say, "Just old age. I won't bore you with the details." I could only talk her into getting together once a year. I was jealous to learn that she lunched more often with Chris, who'd taken over for her in the library. I was also envious that he won her job and I wasn't even considered for it. By that point I'd been away from the magazine for five years and felt fairly established as a writer. Yet freelancing had its ups and downs. I assumed the library gig would be easy to do and pay fairly well.

"Did you ever consider asking me to take over the library when you retired?" I asked her over lunch at the China Grill.

"Never. Not even once," she said. "You don't want to spend your years assisting other writers; you're a writer yourself. Don't you remember how depressed being rejected by all those highbrow editors used to make you?"

I'd sort of blocked it.

"Taking over the library would have been fun and secure – I could still write but I wouldn't have to scramble so much," I argued faintly.

"If you had applied for the job, I would have shredded your application," she said. "I wouldn't allow it!"

Weren't mentors supposed to want you to follow in their footsteps? My high school teacher Jack had wanted me to be a poet, like he was. My cousin Howard told me I should be writing novels, as he did. Bette wanted me to marry and be a mom too. But Helen didn't want me to be like her. She wanted me to escape the magazine in the way she never could. Maybe some mentors tried to save you from making the mistakes they made.

On Saturday night, July 27, 1996, Helen and Ira came to my funky, late-night wedding in SoHo (where the bride wore a black dress, chain-smoked, and got drunk while boogying down in a group dance with the writing workshop). Helen mingled with my mother and our former *New Yorker* cronies. In the pictures she was beaming at the lighthearted civil ceremony, performed by Aaron's father, a judge. Although Ira appeared frail, wearing glasses with thick lenses, Helen looked exactly the same. She handed me a card with a $50 check as a wedding gift. She wrote, "Mazel tov," and signed her name. It was the only time she ever used Yiddish around me. I was touched by the sentiment and by her presence there that night.

Aaron had recently published a cover story in *New York* magazine that he was turning into a screenplay about what would happen when the big earthquake hit Manhattan. After months of hearing the details, the topic was beginning to spook me, but Ira and Aaron hit it off, discussing the subject thoroughly. Apparently Ira, an engineer who at one point had worked for the City, adamantly agreed with Aaron's argument that the city's building codes needed to be modernized to account for larger earthquakes that could happen here. It occurred to me that I'd never had a real conversation with Ira before; I had ignored everything about Helen's home life.

That December, Charles Michener, a *New Yorker* editor I'd never met, bought my "Talk of the Town" story about meteorites. It was six hundred words, and the magazine paid me $1,200 dollars for it. The check cleared and it made it to the galley stage. Alas, Michener left the magazine and it never ran. I later sold it to the *Times,* which ran it and paid me too. But I was distraught that

I had once again come so close to breaking into *The New Yorker* and then failed. I showed Helen the early copy of my typeset "Talk" story, and rambled about my disappointment over one of our rare midtown lunches. She admitted that the magazine had once bought a "Talk" story of hers, on the artist Joan Miró, in 1962. She'd been paid for it, but her piece never ran, either. She'd never admitted to me that she had wanted to be a writer before. Was that why she'd always let me write during work hours? No wonder she was so sure that I should leave the library. She wanted me to have the career she gave up for security.

As the years went by, Helen wanted to get together less and less, but I called every few months. She always sounded happy to hear from me and had all kinds of questions and gossip she wanted to catch up on. I continued to send her all of my published work. She was never critical, offering such encouraging comments as, "It's fabulous, Sue," "Boy, you're as prolific as Penelope used to be," or "I'm so proud of you." It was important to me that Helen knew my writing was improving and seeing print, as if it confirmed her faith in me.

The first week of June 2001, I phoned several times, but nobody answered at her home. That was odd. She had no answering machine, but usually she, Ira, or their housekeeper, Beth, picked up on the fourth or fifth ring. I called once more, letting the phone ring seven, eight, nine, ten times. This gave me a bad vibe, but I kept trying. Finally one afternoon Beth picked up. "Where's Helen?" I asked, fearing she was in the hospital. I wanted to go visit her.

"Helen died in April," Beth told me.

What? I was stunned. In April? Six weeks before? Why didn't I know? Why didn't somebody call to tell me? Why hadn't I seen an obit in *The New Yorker* or anywhere? I was in a panic of tears and grief. I was angry that nobody thought to let me know, but I also felt incredibly guilty that I hadn't been in better touch. Had I just imagined we were so close? We couldn't be if nobody had even thought to tell me she was gone. I was confused and hurt. Where was Ira? Where was her son, Peter? I called Chris in the library. He knew she'd passed away. "Why didn't you call to tell me?" I was outraged. It was possible that I was being irrational, since I hadn't spoken to Chris in years, and he might not have known how attached I was to Helen. But I demanded that Chris give me Peter's phone numbers. I called Peter at home and work several times and left messages. I was even more despondent when he didn't return my calls.

When he finally got back to me, Peter offered a good reason for the delay: He had been busy burying Ira, who'd passed away right after Helen died. They'd been married fifty-eight years. Although many of the colleagues Helen had worked with were no longer alive or at the magazine, Peter was also shocked that the editors didn't run an obituary, or even a paragraph, about her passing. I picked up the phone and called *New Yorker* editor Roger Angell several times.

Then I called the new editor, David Remnick. I faxed over Helen's bio and told them they owed her an obit. They both apologized for the omission, but neither offered to fix it. I was no longer intimidated by anyone at *The New Yorker*. "She devoted herself to your magazine for half a century! What the hell is wrong with you people?" I heard myself yell, slamming down the phone.

Finally, I called my friend Ian Frazier, one of Helen's favorites. I sobbed that it wasn't fair that *The New Yorker* hadn't published an obit of Helen, who had given more than half her life to the magazine. Ian quickly wrote a lovely, subtle obit himself. It ran as a "Talk of the Town" story in the August 13, 2001, issue. It started: "In the disconnected way things happen sometimes, many friends and former colleagues of Helen Stark, *The New Yorker*'s longtime librarian, learned only recently of her death in April. . . . "

I later learned that the timing of Ian's submission couldn't have been better. He had stormed out of the magazine in a moralistic outrage over Tina Brown's hiring of Roseanne Barr as a guest editor. David Remnick, now in charge, sympathized and was trying to talk Ian into returning under the new regime. So when Ian approached him with Helen's obit and yet another moral stance, saying, "This woman worked for the magazine for fifty years and deserves to be remembered," Remnick had the chance to prove he had a soul to win Frazier back, which — by both accounts — he did.

Peter was pleased with the obit, along with my fit in honor of his mom. Since he was an only child with hardly any living relatives and had basically buried both of his parents alone, he was happy to know somebody else cared. I was giving a party for my former colleague Serena's upcoming marriage. Since many former *New Yorker* staffers would be coming, I invited Peter. This time he came! When he walked in, I threw my arms around him, as if we were related, which it suddenly seemed we were.

"You look so glamorous. You're such a fashion plate," he said.

Oh my god, he sounded like Helen! He looked like Helen!

"I am not the least bit glamorous. I hate dressing up and putting on makeup," I argued.

"My mother always said you were so glamorous," he told me.

That was her big falsehood, which she told herself and her son. I was, in the words of my mother, "a schlepper." Yes, I could put on a suit and heels for a few hours. But most days I could be found in sweats. I was Helen's friend, former employee made good, and loyal fan. But sorry, Helen, I was not, and never would be, a fashion plate.

"Come on, after that first interview suit, my attire totally degenerated," I said. "Your mother saw me in torn jeans and T-shirts every day for years. She knew I was a downtown slob."

"Well, we thought you had a glamorous, interesting, clever life," Peter finally conceded. "But your mother — now, *she* was really glamorous."

"Your mother talked about my mother?" I was intrigued.

"Oh yes. She told me about the first time she came to the magazine. 'Very well turned out' was what she said. And warm. She invited my mother to go to *Chicago* and dinner with you, but my mother felt it just wasn't appropriate to let her employees' parents treat. She discussed it at dinner."

"Really?" I remembered that my mother had asked Helen to join us, but I had no idea the offer had created such a conflict. Leaving my husband to handle the other guests, I pulled Peter to a quiet corner so we could talk more privately.

He'd brought old pictures of Helen I'd never seen before – as a child with her father, as a young woman on the arm of a handsome Ira in his soldier uniform, another from college. She looked thinner, fresh faced, and was smiling. In each picture she was standing tall and looked well pulled together – even when she was five. In a few of the shots she was in matching coats, shoes, eye makeup, and red lipstick, like my mother used to wear.

"So what else did she say about me?" I was desperate to know.

If in reality I barely knew this woman who'd started my career and changed my entire outlook, he was offering a second chance. Plus, Peter and I agreed, Helen would be happy we were finally hanging out, so many years after she'd made the initial suggestion.

"Do you remember when I invited you to a few parties I was having in the '80s?" I asked him. "You didn't seem interested in being friends at all."

"I wasn't. I resented you because you took her away from me. She was gone by nine every morning and didn't come home until seven. I was raised by a German nanny. I always wanted a warm, stay-at-home mother, like yours," he said.

"I never wanted my mother's role," I admitted. "All she did was take care of her husband and children and subjugate her own needs."

"That's funny, because my mother's mother tried to be a secretary in the Depression but couldn't do it. I think that really affected my mother, because she always said, 'You have to learn how to type, just in case.'"

"Your mother's mother was Alice Gardener?" I asked, trying to get the family tree straight.

"It was originally Alice Goldberg," he said with a smile, knowing the overtly Jewish name was giving away a family secret. "And Lenning was Levy."

"Maybe seeing my mother's life was why I never had kids of my own," I continued confessing, as if I'd known Peter forever and could trust him with such intimacies. "I bet that's what so endeared me to your mother. I had never met a woman who loved work so much before. That made much more sense to me."

"I really do love my advertising job, so maybe I understand her better now," he admitted. "I've been at my company more than twenty years. I work in the archives. I've become the mascot there, like she was."

"So she was a good role model to you in some ways." I needed to think she had been.

"Well, my father kept losing jobs and getting different ones. He wasn't well for a long time, really. So her salary was essential to support the family. She had a Depression mentality. She did teach me the importance of a stable job," he said. "But she played it too safe and never took chances or made waves. So we're both stuck in middle management forever."

I kept staring at the pictures on my lap, my mind racing with this new information. I hadn't known Ira had trouble keeping jobs. I had never thought that Helen played it safe or saw her position as middle management. "She wouldn't see me much after she left the magazine," I told him.

"Well, she was so sick," he informed me. "First she had vertigo, then arthritis. Then she was so brokenhearted when her brother died. Then she had breast cancer and needed a mastectomy."

"I didn't know any of that," I said. "She never told me." Did I even know this woman at all, or had I deluded myself? Maybe she was just a nice boss I had for a short time in the '80s, and I'd been clinging to some symbolic connection or maternal fantasy all these years. "What did she die from?"

"Intestinal cancer," he said.

"I'm so sorry I wasn't at the funeral," I said. "I bet her niece came. The yuppie." I recalled a girl in a fancy suit who used to come to take Helen to lunch a few times a year.

"You didn't like her?" He egged me on.

"I didn't like that Helen made such a big deal out of her. I was jealous. Didn't she work on the business side of a magazine? Selling ad space," I said, disdainfully. "What was the big deal about that?"

"*Thank you!*" Peter said emphatically, grinning. Obviously he'd also been envious of the attention Helen had lavished on this favored niece. We'd gone from sibling rivals to comrades with a shared enemy who'd taken Helen's attention away.

"Did she ever tell you about her boss, Ebba Jonsson?" he asked.

"Yes, she told me all about her for the profile I wrote."

"So you knew Ebba was a lesbian alcoholic?"

"No, I didn't know that," I said, eating up any bit of *New Yorker* gossip I might have missed. "Tell me about Helen's funeral."

"It was quiet, no frills. It was a stark ceremony," he said, making a pun on their last name. Then he looked away. "I know that my mother loved me. But I wonder whether she respected me."

"I know she did," I reassured him. "She talked about you all the time. She wouldn't shut up about you."

"She did? Really?" He was pleased. "What did she say?"

"She mentioned the trips you took together. Spain, England. It used to bore me to tears. Oh, and about your trouble finding an apartment."

"Right. I didn't move out until 1988."

"She talked about how you were buying a place in the Village, right near me." I recalled. "Didn't they help you buy it?"

"First they didn't want me to spend the ninety thousand dollars. Now it's worth five times that much. They loaned me money but charged me 10 percent interest." He sounded still annoyed by this. "She came to your wedding downtown, but she hardly came to see me. I had to go uptown."

"I offered to go uptown to see her, but she didn't want to see me," I lamented.

"She was impressed when you and Aaron bought a two bedroom, two bath," he said, looking around. "It's very nice. Love the high ceilings and bookshelves. She thought you married well."

"She did? Really?" I asked. "What else did she say about me? Can you remember anything else?"

"You typed one hundred words a minute. That really bothered me, because I type one hundred words a minute, too, but she wasn't impressed that I did," he said.

"You type one hundred words a minute?" I asked. "So does my mother."

"Really?" he asked. "Oh, she also said you wore Giorgio perfume."

"She told you that?"

"Yes," he said. "And that your mother used to send it to you."

What funny details people retained. I never even liked Giorgio –

too loud and fruity — and hadn't worn the scent in twenty years. Now I wore Opium, which — come to think of it — my mother also sent me. Now that we were talking about perfumes, I noticed a bit of a spicy scent. "You smell like your mom," I told him.

"I wondered if you'd notice," he said. "I wore a bit of Mitsouko cologne — as an homage. You know it was always her favorite."

I'd never heard of it and shrugged.

"Mitsouko, by Guerlain. It's French." He appeared annoyed that I wasn't familiar with it.

"How old were you when you came out to her?" I wanted to know, fearing it might be too personal a question but asking anyway.

"Late," he said, matter-of-factly. "I was twenty-six."

"She seemed open about it."

"She was too open about sex — she used to tell me about these petting parties she went to before she was married. But she never talked about money," he said. "You know her thesis for her master's at Columbia was the theme of money in George Eliot's work."

I never knew that either. Did I just notice that Peter spoke as quickly as I did? We shared the same breathless excitement to uncover any hint of Helen's hidden side.

"There are a bunch of people here from the magazine who loved her. Do you want to meet them?" I asked.

"Yes, it's always nice to meet people who saw her as a hero," he said. "Because she was never a hero to me."

Wow, that was so heavy. Hearing it bummed me out. Yet I guessed that was the whole point of mentor-protégé relationships: They overcompensated for the adoring parents or children you never had. I updated Peter about my friend Monica Yates, Helen's former assistant who wound up marrying my brother Brian, the trauma surgeon in Michigan. She moved to Midwest suburbia and had four kids in seven years — three boys and a girl, just like my mother.

"Oh yes, I remember. That story always tickled my mother," Peter recalled.

"Tickled" — that was a verb Helen would use. I smiled.

Monica drove forty-five minutes with her four little kids to visit my mother every week. She got her hair done at the same salon my mother frequented, bought food at the same gourmet stores. She'd hang out at my childhood home in West Bloomfield for hours and hours, listening to my mom, watching her. When they'd first met in New York, Monica also thought my mother was very glamorous. My mom clearly became her role model, while Helen — the lifelong urban working woman — was more my type.

"I wanted parts of my mom that were always unavailable. *The New Yorker* was the love of her life," Peter said, as interested in deconstructing all the relationship dynamics as I was. He sounded astute, like he'd been in therapy too. He was an overly analytic downtowner, like me.

"The magazine wasn't always her top priority, was it?" I asked, wondering if work would be the love of my life, already knowing it was.

"Of course, definitely. It was her grand passion. I don't think she ever really wanted children. Her friend Esther told me I was an accident, which I believe. They'd already been married for twelve years. She just wasn't that maternal. Some women aren't."

I never had children; I wasn't so maternal either.

"You and my mother had an ardor for *The New Yorker* that I never shared. I've come to terms with it. I understand it now," he said. "But you know what pisses me off the most? The day after they learned she died, they canceled our free subscription to the magazine."

A Quiet Brother

IAN

FRAZIER

"I can't be on *The Today Show.* Can you do it?" I asked Sandy over the phone.

"Do I really have to?" His voice was filled with dread at the prospect. "I suck on television."

"I'm sure you don't suck," I reassured him.

"Last time I was on *The Today Show*, Jane Pauley fired quick questions I answered so slowly, I came off as learning disabled. Even my close friends said it was a disaster."

It was a Tuesday afternoon in the middle of November 2004. *The Today Show* wanted to shoot a feature at the church on Thanksgiving weekend about *Food for the Soul*, the book Ian Frazier (a.k.a. Sandy) and I had just published. It was a nonfiction anthology of stories about life on the streets from the Holy Apostles Soup Kitchen Writers' Workshop, and it was a great human-interest story.

"Why can't you do it?" he asked.

"My publicist thinks it would ruin my chances of getting on TV for my new book in December," I told him. I didn't admit that I'd feel a bit uncomfortable being seen on national TV at a church, an unsuitable setting for a racy Jewess desperate to sell books on self-destructive sex, drugs, and rock 'n' roll. "But I'm sure you'll be great, Sandy. Please."

It occurred to me that this should be the worst problem I ever had – trying to get out of a major network appearance, not to mention pawning it off on one of the writers I admired most. It was actually fairly amazing that I was even friends with Ian Frazier. Ironically, if it were up to him, our book project, the climax of an important ten-year collaboration, would never have happened in the first place.

Sandy and I spoke often when I worked at *The New Yorker* from 1983 to 1987, but he barely knew who I was. Born in 1951, he was ten years older and already a star. He'd published two well-received books, including the droll humor collection *Dating Your Mom,* which earned him comparisons to James Thurber and Robert

Benchley. As a twenty-two-year-old assistant, I mirrored my boss Helen's preferences when it came to the staff, and she just adored Sandy. It was hard not to. Many of the *New Yorker* bigwigs were pushy and condescending with the underlings. Legend had it that when a foreign-born author ordered a messenger to get his shoes shined, Mr. Shawn had to explain to the foreigner that we had no caste system in this country. When I rushed to hand-deliver clips to a senior editor, he saw me and said, "Tuna on rye." I didn't understand and asked, "What?" He raised his voice and repeated, "Tuna on rye." I realized he wanted me to get him a sandwich. "I'm not your secretary. I work in the library," I explained. "Well, go tell one of the other girls to order me lunch," he snapped.

Sandy was the opposite – friendly, soft-spoken, self-effacing, humble. He did most of his research himself, and if he needed any extra copies, data, or books, he asked nicely and always wrote us thank-you notes. In the late '70s, while writing a "Talk of the Town" story on University of Alabama football coach Bear Bryant (whom he called "the Babe Ruth of football coaches"), he'd bumped into Helen and Ira Stark at an alumni event. Ira had graduated from the University of Alabama. Sandy asked Ira all about Alabama for background information. They all bonded over drinks and Southern jokes. Ever since then, Helen had made Sandy's requests top priority.

"I moved here from Ohio and started working at *The New Yorker* when I was twenty-three. I was nervous and intimidated by everyone at the magazine," Sandy later told me. "At the first office party I went to, Helen and I both wound up getting drunk on this noxious purple punch. I think she threw up." He paused. He did speak slowly, unlike me, thinking before he answered a question, taking breaks between sentences. "Helen was this nice, attentive, warm, motherly woman. She was the only one there who made me feel at home," he recalled.

How strange that Sandy and I had seen Helen as more maternal than her own son did. I'd identified with Sandy because, like me, he was the oldest child of a big Midwestern clan. When I asked how many kids were in his family, he said five, but then he told me that his brother Fritz had died of leukemia at fifteen, when Sandy was in college. I wondered if that tragedy had made him so compassionate, but I guessed he was just born that way. He had a sister with my name, he added, but she spelled it "Suzan." He'd moved to New York right after college, as I had. But he'd attended Harvard, where his work for *The Harvard Crimson* had caught Mr. Shawn's attention and led to the offer of a staff reporter job.

With his long ponytail and schleppy clothes, he appeared to be a fellow left-wing hippie. Yet there was something noble and old fashioned about his face, like Thomas Jefferson's. I was in awe of him. It was different from a crush. I admired his manner, which was calm and filled with an unpretentiousness and humility that came across in his humor pieces and nonfiction. It made people feel at ease, like you could trust him with anything. I didn't want to date Sandy, I wanted to be him. Okay, maybe at first I wanted to date him, but he was already taken. I had many bad habits, but pursuing married men had never been one of them. (I had enough trouble with single men.)

Outside of day-to-day library business and a few encouraging pep talks, Sandy didn't pay much attention to me, and we lost touch after I left the magazine. In 1990 another *New Yorker* colleague introduced me to *Newsday*'s book editor, Abe Katz. I always told my students to look for an editor you have something in common with, and I bet the very Jewish-sounding Abe Katz would give Susan Shapiro an assignment. He did! After I did six reviews in a row for him, Abe offered me a great weekly gig reviewing paperbacks for their Sunday entertainment section for $300 a pop. He rejected my suggestion of calling the column "Paperweight" and instead named it "Soft Focus," which sounded to me like pornography. Still, *Newsday* was a smart paper, and I'd been promoted from freelancer to book columnist.

I soon figured out how to self-syndicate my column in the *St. Petersburg Times, The Detroit News, The Cleveland Plain Dealer, The Washington Times*, and other papers that paid me anywhere from $10 to $100 for each column they ran. I didn't have to be in the office; I just had to drop off my copy with Abe every Wednesday afternoon and make sure the column ran in *Newsday* first. Abe let me pick my own titles. So if I discovered a book that had been unfairly ignored in hardcover, a special paperback original, an obscure reissue by a dead author, or a new translation of a foreign novel or memoir, my rave could run across the country. Because few critics ever gave paperbacks any press, I'd inadvertently stumbled upon a tiny seat of power. Publicists sent me thousands of books, in both paper and hardcover. The first year, I made $8,000 selling the extra copies back to the Strand Book Store.

The nights I didn't stay home to read, I drank wine and ate shrimp at uptown book parties. In September, I attended a soiree for an impressive Washington Square Press paperback original by Bernard Gotfryd called *Anton the Dove Fancier and Other Tales of the Holocaust*. Walking into the swanky apartment, I bumped right into Sandy.

"Sue. Hi. How are you? What are you doing here?" he asked. He looked stunned to see me, as if away from the *New Yorker* library, I was out of context. Although I'd sent him a few clips and phoned to invite him to parties he never came to, I hadn't seen him in person in almost three years.

"I reviewed his memoir for *Newsday*," I said.

"Really? You reviewed *Anton the Dove Fancier* for *Newsday*?" He seemed confused by this news.

"I write *Newsday*'s Sunday paperback column now. It's syndicated around the country, so my review ran in several outlets." I showed off, not quite getting what the big shock was. He could be a staff writer, but I couldn't? I saw the old work gang at uptown book parties all the time; most of them knew about my new title. In fact, since I could choose which books I reviewed each week, I'd intentionally picked paperbacks I thought worthy by *New Yorker* writers Mark Singer, Alex Shoumatoff, Lawrence Weschler, Jane Kramer, Roger Angell, and Ward Just, my old colleague Julie Just's brilliant novelist father. Of course I hoped that the *New Yorker* bigwigs who'd never recognized my work would notice my column if their books were in it. So this was my way of licking my wounds, empowering myself, showing off, and kissing ass all at the same time. I was also being lazy. I'd already read most of those books, first in the magazine and then in hardcover, so it was way less work to read them a third time.

At twenty-nine years old, I'd finally fully recovered from my disappointing stint at the magazine. My Tuesday workshop was so popular, I was turning down new members daily. My studio apartment was overstuffed with the free books I was sent, as if every day were Hanukkah. Quotes from my *New York Times, Washington Post,* and *Newsday* reviews were reprinted on many book jackets and book ads. Sometimes they even used my name, which semi-thrilled me. Had Sandy expected me to stay a broke and frustrated editorial assistant forever?

"That's great, Sue. Really great." He nodded, paused, and then asked, "Well, did you like the book?"

"Of course. I loved it." I laughed. "I wouldn't come to the party if I didn't like the book." Did he think I was still a hick?

When I raved about an author in print before the press party, I found I was treated like a VIP. Publicists fawned over me, pitching me more of their books to review, inviting me to all their other events. *The New York Times* book critics might not want to fraternize with authors they reviewed, but they trashed way more books than I did. And full-timers with good salaries and benefits could afford to be more picky than low-level freelancers like me.

Even with the syndication checks my salary started to bother me, since Abe had insisted I review five books a week – twenty books a month – probably more than any reviewer in the country. I'd taken to reading everywhere – on buses, subways, cab rides, and planes, during doctor's appointments, doing leg lifts at my exercise class. On our first date, one man I was fixed up with assumed I had little children. "No kids. Why did you think so?" I asked. He pointed to my chicken, which I'd cut in tiny squares. I explained that I was so used to reading during meals that I sliced up all my food first. That way I could eat with my right hand while holding the book with my left and turning pages with my thumb.

When George, the athletic theater professor I fell for, wanted to spend weekends in the Hamptons, I sometimes said no because I was spending the weekend writing my column. (I didn't yet have a laptop, and my IBM Selectric wasn't portable.) When we took a vacation to Jamaica for ten days, I took ten books with me. They took up more room than my clothes. He wanted to snorkel, water ski, parasail, mountain climb. I wanted to sit on the beach and read. "Sunscreen," the poem I later published about that trip, interwove the books I was reviewing as a metaphor for our lack of intimacy. " . . . I'll join you under the water / after essays by an Asian feminist / or maybe I'll lend you a slow book / of sadness set in Ecuador / so we can share the same journey . . . "

My social life was compromised, I still couldn't pay my rent without my father's help, and my eyes were strained. Yet what a thrill to be paid for reading and getting smarter and more literate by the minute. Despite my fatigue, I'd been getting more confident, full of knowledge, and full of myself. At this book party I felt like a sophisticate, so I was annoyed that Sandy was so shocked by my presence there.

"Really? You raved about *Anton the Dove Fancier* and it ran in different newspapers?" He wanted me to explain it again; he was try-ing to wrap his head around the concept.

"I'll show you a copy of the reviews," I said, pulling out two xeroxes of my latest *Newsday* and *St. Petersburg Times* columns that I just happened to have in my briefcase. "I have extras. You can keep them."

Because the entire column was only one thousand words (plus artwork), each of the five books had to be encapsulated in two hundred words, one long paragraph. Though I was verbose and long winded in conversation, studying and composing poetry — the most concise, condensed art form in the world — was good preparation for the task. (When my journalism students have trouble cutting extra words, I recommend they study poetry.) In this brief review, I'd woven in that Gotfryd was a Polish Jew who had survived six different Nazi concentration camps during World War II, came to the United States in 1945, and was working as a *Newsweek* photographer when *Anton the Dove Fancier* was published. I had called the twenty-one autobiographical pieces that made up his literary debut "beautifully rendered," "heartbreaking," "ironic," and "all the more chilling because they are true." I'd also highly recommended the book to Jewish editors I knew.

"So what are *you* doing here?" I asked Sandy. After his two *New Yorker* collections, his nonfiction book about traveling out West, *Great Plains*, had been a national bestseller. I'd heard from Helen that Sandy and his wife, Jay, were living in Brooklyn and had a baby girl named Cora. He hardly ever went to parties anymore, Helen said. He never reviewed books or wrote about authors. He wasn't Jewish — like the rest of the crowd. Sandy was Protestant. I didn't see any other *New Yorker* people in attendance. What was his connection?

"Bernie is the *Newsweek* photographer who took my picture for this feature they did on *Great Plains*," he said quietly. "He showed me an early draft of his book, which I thought was poignant, really astounding. It just blew me away. I tried to help him get it published."

Sandy put the emphasis on Gotfryd's talent and not the fact that he'd selflessly shared his connections. Knowing Sandy, he'd probably shown the book to agents and editors personally.

Okay, a well-known WASP author's championing a Holocaust survivor's unpublished manuscript trumped my two-hundred-word, post-publication Jew-on-Jew review, which suddenly appeared to be a peripheral link. But why was I feeling competitive with Sandy, anyway? He wasn't one of the snobs at the magazine who'd made me feel like a junior high school nerd. He was the cool kid who let me hang out with him. He'd been generous with his time and advice. When I used to show him my rejection slips, he'd say, "Keep trying. You're really good. You'll break into *The New Yorker* one day soon. I'm sure of it." He confided that one of the cartoonists used to submit the same cartoon that had been rejected over and over, until the art director forgot he'd already said no and finally took it. I believed Sandy, and between my column and other assignments, I still sometimes submitted work to *The New Yorker* (and had it rejected).

I realized that I'd misread Sandy's surprised look and his social awkwardness. He wasn't acting so stunned because I'd done something with myself careerwise in the last three years. After all, he was one of the few higher-ups who'd always been on my side. Rather, he was happily startled that our paths had crossed again in such a wonderful way – both helping a Holocaust survivor's inspiring tale get the attention it deserved. He introduced me to the author, his agent, editor, and publicist, handing them my rave review and adding, "Sue and I used to work together at *The New Yorker*." (Not adding, "I was a staff writer while she was a glorified typist.")

We kept in touch over the next few years, as Sandy and his wife had a son named Thomas and moved to Montana. Then they wound up back East. He kept cranking out jewels for the best publications in the country and landing high-paying book deals from Farrar, Straus, and Giroux, the Mercedes-Benz of the book biz. Jay was also published in *The New Yorker* and sold her first novel. Meanwhile, my career and love life took a downward spiral.

I relished the little acclaim my paperback column brought me, but reading and reviewing five books a week, for $300, was becoming too difficult, even with the added $20 to $100 weekly syndication checks. Instead of the thick novels, biographies, Tom Wolfe and Camille Paglia treatises that Abe preferred, I chose 160-page novellas, essay, and short story collections. I threw in art and photography books that were mostly pictures with little text and gravitated toward slender poetry volumes. Abe started to complain about my choices and minor mistakes he noticed in my copy. I'd been going through a rough time after my boyfriend, George, dumped me — for a young wannabe actress who could barely read a script.

Abe wanted me to apologize for my errors and say I'd shape up, get my facts right, and go back to real books. Instead I lost it, complaining that critiquing more than 250 books in one year had burned me out. I pointed out that most reviewers handled one book a week — two at the most — and insisted he be fair and reduce my load to four books a week instead of five. He'd been a nice, nurturing boss. I expected compassion. His response was to say, "This isn't working out" and fire me. As if that weren't hurtful enough, the next day he hired someone to replace me who included only *three* books a week in *my* column. When I tearfully asked another *Newsday* editor what the story was, she said the new critic tried to review five books but couldn't handle it. When she told Abe three books was her limit, instead of admitting he'd been wrong, he saved face by pretending the switch was his idea. I calculated that she was being paid the same amount as I'd been — to review a hundred fewer books a year!

George had dumped me for another woman; now Abe had too. I looked up the bio of my book-reviewer rival, like a literary stalker. This pseudo-intellectual thief who'd swooped in and stolen my beloved weekly newspaper space had an MFA in poetry from Columbia (Abe had obviously figured out that poets could review books and worked cheap). She'd published poetry in highbrow journals — and worse, her poems weren't bad. I don't know which was more agonizing — seeing my ex-boyfriend with a younger, thinner girl, or seeing a shorter version of my column written by a better poet.

I wanted to wreak revenge on George, his new idiot actress, my ex-editor Abe, and his new wussy poet/critic who could handle only three books a week. But my shrink promised, "They'll dig their own graves," and suggested I refocus my energy. Some of the newspapers who'd syndicated me offered to keep running my column. Thus, I could stay on all the reviewers' lists and still praise books I wanted to champion. My kind buddy Stan, *Newsday's* features editor, began printing long features of mine right next to Abe's book column. I did more work for *The New York Times*, which I sent to Abe with nice notes that said, "Just wanted to keep you posted," but that really meant *Somebody better is publishing me – you jerk.*

In 1993, I started teaching writing at the New School. Scrambling for freelance work led to my idea for the instant-gratification-takes-too-long method of journalism. I'd only assign specific pieces in the same length, voice, and style that were easy to sell. The head of my program allowed me to pay speakers a small stipend, so I'd bring in professional editors and writers to share the tricks of the trade. The experiment worked. In my first ten-week class, eight out of twelve students got published; three earned $1,000 for one-thousand-word pieces. Touché!

I made a rule that in the future, any student who earned $1,000 on one of the assignments I edited owed me dinner. Many dinners ensued, as well as excellent student evaluations, and word of mouth grew. This led to the newly invented, soon-filled-to-the-brim classes "Reviewing," "The Secrets of Selling to Newspapers," "Breaking into the Women's Magazine," and "Writing for NYC Newspapers and Magazines." (Everybody else just called their journalism courses

"Feature Writing.") I saved the love letters from pupils whom I helped see print. Living well was the best revenge. So what if teaching was Plan B, C, or D? Fuck George and Abe.

When my "Art of Writing Humor" students spoke about their influences and idols, several said *Dating Your Mom* was their favorite humor collection. I called its illustrious author, my old friend Sandy Frazier, asking him to be a guest speaker. What a terrific idea. Unfortunately, he didn't think so. In the fall of 1994 he was doing publicity for his new book, *Family*, a multigenerational account of his white Protestant family tree, which retraced his ancestry during the past three centuries. He'd reconstructed the stories of his distant Midwestern relatives, who were colonial governors, slave-ship captains, Civil War soldiers, ministers of the First German Reform Church, and school teachers paid in whiskey. In the most poignant parts he chronicled his kid brother Fritz's battle with leukemia, his grief after his Alzheimer's-stricken father died of pneumonia in 1987, and his mother's death from cancer a year later. I wanted to ask him whether it was easier for a guy so normally reserved to write a "family history" or an "intergenerational American genealogy" rather than a "memoir," but he seemed too busy.

He was past due for two magazine articles and a new book. (Like Aaron, he'd never met a deadline he couldn't miss.) His wife and their two kids weren't thrilled that he'd spent so much time on the road for research. So my timing sucked. Disappointed, I said I understood, and I was actually embarrassed to even ask him to come to my class at West 12th Street at nine o'clock at night for a $75 stipend. He laughed and recalled that once he and Jay were totally broke, and a $75 New School stipend he'd forgotten about wound up paying for their dinner.

Knowing he was a big softie, I relayed the pathetic story of my *Newsday* ousting, bad breakup, and latest *New Yorker* rejections. Remembering Helen Stark's insight that there was never a limit to how much one should praise a writer, I told him how much I loved *Family*. (It was my favorite book of his, perhaps because it was the most revealing.) I threw in how much my students adored his work, and how, if he ever had an hour, meeting him and having him sign his books for them would make their lives. Hemming and hawing, he finally changed his mind and said yes. His hour-long talk was quirky and inspiring, and it made my students think I was very hip and well connected. Since no good deed goes unpunished, I asked Sandy back the next term. And the next. He always said yes.

Almost all the guests on my growing roster of speakers let me buy them dinner or drinks afterward, but not Sandy. He'd rush home right after his talk ended. That changed in February 1996. When he finished speaking this time, he watched me teach until the end of the class and then let me take him out for dinner. Something was on his mind. I thought he was going to let me down gently by saying he just could not possibly keep coming to the City to give hour-long lectures for barely any money. Instead he said, "I want you to teach with me."

"Teach what with you?" I asked, not even aware he was a teacher.

It turned out he had just received a $30,000 Lila Wallace Foundation grant that required the recipient to start a social welfare program. He was a supporter of Holy Apostles, an Episcopal church in Chelsea that housed Manhattan's largest soup kitchen, feeding 1,300 people a day. Sandy had started a twelve-week writers' workshop the spring before. It met on Wednesdays after lunch at the soup kitchen. It had gone well the first year, and to extend the class for a second year, he wanted me to teach with him, beginning in March. Was I in or out?

I had no idea what a spring writers' class at a soup kitchen would entail, and I had no interest in working at a church. As a Jewish atheist whose essential tenets were culled from confessional poetry and psychotherapy, I didn't even feel comfortable in a temple. Committed to teach several night classes at NYU and the New School the next term, I was already overloaded. Yet I admired Sandy. I admired Sandy. I advised my students to hang out with writers doing what they wanted to do and people they wanted to be. So without asking more questions, I said, "I'd love to teach with you."

We made a plan to meet two Wednesdays later at the church to recruit members before class. Sandy said, "I'll see you there at ten."

"Ten? In the morning?" I asked. "You said we were teaching at one o'clock!" Even one o'clock was too early for me. I was a freelancer used to sleeping late, writing in sweats, and teaching and socializing at night.

"Just for a few weeks. Until we get a group together," Sandy promised.

On a cold Wednesday that March, I dragged myself out of bed. I'd planned to take the subway to the church. Yet walking to the station, I was freezing, saw a cab with his light on flying by, and flagged him down. Taking a taxi to volunteer at a soup kitchen seemed lazy and/or hypocritical. But I'd been up working until three A.M. as usual, and was too tired to feel guilty. I figured the God I didn't believe in wouldn't mind which method of transportation I used to get to a good deed.

When the driver dropped me off at 28th Street and 9th Avenue, there were more than a thousand people waiting in line around the block for the free lunch. Wearing my old jeans and sweatshirt, with no makeup or jewelry, I didn't look out of place. As I made my way to the front door, a grizzly-looking guy with long dreadlocks complained that I was cutting in line. "I'm teaching the writing class," I explained. He nodded, as if I'd said the magic words, and let me pass. I searched for Sandy and our fellow teacher, Bob Blaisdell, a handsome, soft-spoken English professor who'd started the grassroots writing group with Sandy the year before. I found them sitting on the sidelines of the dining room under a WRITERS' WORKSHOP sign, next to tables for TB testing and petitions against welfare reform.

After the free lunch, many soup kitchen regulars stopped by our table on their way out of the church. They asked questions about the program and wanted to enroll. Since a few gave no last names or addresses, Bob marked down descriptions. A big, unshaven white man named Tim said he would come. I looked over Bob's shoulder. Bob wrote down, "Tall scary guy." A man with a Spanish accent named Juan said, "Been there, done that." When we asked what he meant, he said he'd been in a prison writing group in 1975 with John Cheever. "He got the Pulitzer Prize for *Falconer*. What did I get?" Juan asked, walking away. Seventy-four signed up for the workshop. Eleven showed.

Before one o'clock we gathered in a small room called the narthex in the lobby of the church. There were two women and the rest were men. Jay and Donald, two of the guys, were old pros, having been in the group the spring before. They heartily shook hands with Sandy and Bob and caught up, like long-lost relatives. The church workers put out coffee and tea so people helped themselves. I drank my Diet Coke, hoping the caffeine would wake me up. Sitting on beige foldout chairs around an oblong table, we gave out free notebooks and pens and introduced ourselves. Wanda, a thirtyish pale woman who'd left her belongings in a shopping cart by the door, put a dozen sugar packets in her skirt pocket.

Mitch, who had dark hair and a mustache, spoke in broken English of missing his wife and son in Poland. He asked why we were doing a writing class here, at a soup kitchen. Sandy said, "Writing is a way of organizing experience and defying loss." Bob said that you don't write to gain money or fame but because you have an important story that must be told. I said that writing was a way of turning the worst things in life into the most beautiful.

When I walked outside for a cigarette break, Clarence, an older, chocolate-skinned man with glasses and a white mustache, followed. He said he was a Christian Scientist from Jamaica who'd quit smoking twenty years before "with the faith of Jesus." I told him how lovely I'd found Negril and about my poem chronicling the trip I'd taken there with my ex-boyfriend. Clarence asked if he could read it. I brought him a copy the next week.

These original eleven people showed up fairly regularly for the next eleven Wednesday afternoons. Others came and went. The group included white, black, Latino, Asian, Jewish, Muslim, Catholic, and Protestant members, ranging in age from fourteen to eighty. The first spring, when only Bob and Sandy taught, just men had showed up. Now that I was teaching, more women came, a few bringing teenage kids with them. Was that why Sandy wanted me here? He asked Alec Wilkinson, another *New Yorker* journalist, to teach some weeks, too. Someone was hired to put all the handwritten pieces on computer. Some of the writers came early to go over their work with the typist. Clarence came early to see me. Each Wednesday we'd drink our Diet Coke and tea and catch up, as if we were old friends. We were an odd couple. He was sixty-eight, a former government clerk in a suit, giving quit-smoking tips to a thirty-five-year-old Jewish journalist in torn jeans and cowboy boots.

It was safer to have at least two teachers there each session, according to Sandy. One week, when Sandy, Bob, and Alec (who all had kids) were busy, I offered to teach alone, insisting that I had handled classes with thirty or forty students before with no problem. But Sandy nixed the idea. He admitted that a few soup kitchen members had shown up drunk or high, and one guy had been so violent that they'd had to call a guard. A few of the men made sexual comments to me, but I was never scared. I was pretty out of it at 10:00 AM and refused to do any more early-morning "recruiting" duty. I made sure to pick the same weeks as Sandy, so I could watch and hang out with him.

At the start of each session, the teachers suggested two topics to write about, and everyone scrawled furiously for about an hour. Then, one at a time, the members read their work aloud. When they finished reading, fellow scribes clapped, nodded, and said, "You tell 'em, baby," or, "Amen, ain't that the truth." Sandy and the other teachers preferred such poetic topics as "A Wild Ride," "If I Hadn't

Seen It, I Wouldn't Have Believed It," "My Hidden Talent," "When One Door Closes, Another Opens," "In My Other Life," "The Rest of the Story," and "My Best Mistake." Some pieces produced were talented, unique, brave. Others were incoherent, with verses from known songs, jokes, bad puns, or biblical quotes strung together. A man named John wrote a ditty about how he liked "sea food," because whenever he would see food, he would eat it. Clarence penned vague meanderings about "divine providence and the plan of God."

The best work was first-person nonfiction. Wanda began her piece, "Abandoned by eight families: foster, step, and blood." L. M. S., a twenty-five-year-old rap star–looking guy wearing baggy pants, chains, and a backward baseball cap, wrote, "Where is my home, my true home, my twin home, my self-employed home?" Harriet, a WASPy-seeming woman in her fifties with long silver hair, wrote about being raped at gunpoint in Brooklyn and hugged me after the session. Alan, a funny, middle-aged former thespian with a cane, wrote, "From the moment Gary and I met with his famous opening words, 'I know what you want,' until his death twenty years later from lymphoma cancer, there wasn't anything we wouldn't do for each other." Tom, a forty-ish white man from Connecticut, wrote about receiving second- and third-degree burns on his face and having to wear a Jobst garment for six weeks. It looked like a silk stocking, and Tom was afraid the bank guard would think he was a robber. So he called the bank first to explain, because "I didn't want him panicking and shooting me."

When Sandy asked me to come up with ideas, I intentionally chose the heavy, timely subjects "The Saddest Mother's Day," "The Loneliest Christmas," "The Worst Night of My Life," "The Hardest Loss," "What Really Pisses Me Off," "Lost Family," "The Worst Advice I Ever Got." The difference in topics reflected our personalities. I was literal minded, impatient, practical. Sandy had a more expansive, philosophical, tolerant outlook. Although I was known as an upbeat cheerleader type of teacher, my topics were darker and harsher. The worst criticism everyone from my own Tuesday night writing workshop imparted was, "There's no blood here." I wanted the blood.

Sandy was more creative than I was. He let participants ignore the weekly topics and attempt to tackle fiction, light verse, and fairy stories, or come up with their own language or science fiction universes. I argued that encouraging silliness or bloodlessness was a mistake. The more rope the writers had, the more juvenile their work became. I didn't want to promote gibberish, incoherence, illiteracy, or trite song lyrics. I enjoyed the poetry, but I knew it could take years to develop the skills to complete a decent short story or novella or fantasy fable. Journalism, which was called "literature in a hurry," was easier to write well quickly, not to mention teach and publish.

Despite Sandy's doubts, I gave the soup kitchen group rigid parameters, corrected their punctuation and grammar, and suggested newsy leads, the way I did with my paying students. I explained the difference between being an amateur dabbler versus a professional journalist, brought in clips of my work, and showed them the essay and op-ed sections in the newspapers that were open to new contributors. As a teacher known for helping scribes first see print, I had no doubt that topical, dramatic tales about life on the streets had a better shot at interesting city editors. Sandy didn't think mentioning the possibility of publication was a good idea.

"You don't want to exploit their pain," he said one Wednesday.

"You don't want to patronize them by letting them scrawl fictional junk when they could be crafting publishable essays," said I.

"Don't get their hopes up," he pleaded. "It's amazing enough that they show up each week and trust us with their stories. These people don't need pie-in-the-sky dreams. It's like encouraging them to buy lottery tickets."

"This is the opposite of buying a lottery ticket," I argued. "Journalism isn't luck; it's a skill you can teach. It's not so hard to get a short piece printed in the dailies. You know my students get in all the time, at least ten students each term. I'm editing their work and helping with cover letters, so it's a very educated guess. Nothing will get a writer working harder than getting a yes from an editor and seeing their first byline."

"They can't handle any more disappointment," he said.

"But what if they're successful?" I asked.

"They might not be able to handle success. That's why some of them wind up here to begin with," Sandy told me.

"The perspective the soup kitchen members offer is really unusual. Most newspaper guys are white, married, middle class. I bet editors would want to hear how homeless people or drug addicts or schizophrenics negotiate city systems," I told him. "Readers should know what they have to go through."

"It's hard enough to get the writers to open up about what they've gone through. Some of them don't even give us their real names." He crossed his arms. He never raised his voice, but it was the first time in a dozen years of knowing him that he was annoyed with me.

I was pissed off too. I thought Sandy had picked me to coteach because he admired my strong opinions and emphatic teaching methods. He knew I encouraged professionalism and brought in editors and writers to my NYU and New School classes — he was one of my regular speakers. Yet the minute I started to work with him, it was like he expected me to be some docile sycophant! It reminded me of Aaron, who'd recently become my fiancé: He'd fallen in love with me when I was a wild, chain-smoking late-night stoner. The moment I put on his engagement ring, he expected me to quit smoking, toking, and going to wild parties so we could watch TV and go to sleep together at eleven thirty every night. Aaron and Sandy were both ten years my senior. That was the problem with older men — they tried to mold you in their image.

Yet, I had to admit, Sandy did have a point. My dismal topics

had inspired the soup kitchen members to cough up pretty hor-
rific confessions about sexual abuse, life in prison, giving themselves abortions, the violent deaths of parents and children, bloody
assaults, selling their bodies for crack. I admired Sandy's earnest
and protective stance, and I loved him for it, but I still disagreed.
Having his words published regularly in prestigious places since college had completely changed his direction and career path. By this
point he'd forgotten the initial thrill of selling your first piece, what
a monumental, life-altering experience it could be. Since I hadn't
yet "made it," I continued to note how getting an editor's approval
and seeing my byline altered the color of everything. I watched students of all ages and backgrounds get their initial clips and blossom
before my eyes. They'd walk taller, get more confident, quit full-
time jobs they hated, go into therapy, enroll in graduate programs,
or take a shot at internships that led them to better jobs. There was
something about the external validation of publishing your work
that was downright transformative.

I sent a *New York Times* "City" section editor a roundup of
excerpts from the soup kitchen pieces I'd culled, and he said yes.
I told everyone at our Wednesday session. Anyone who wanted to
could be in the picture that the *Times* photographer would be taking of the group the following Wednesday, I announced. They all
applauded and said they'd be there. Only Sandy was apprehensive.

"What could possibly go wrong?" I asked.

"An ex-con wanted by the law could be recognized by their picture in the newspaper and get arrested again," he threw out. "Someone's employer who doesn't know they used to do cocaine could read the story and fire them. A guy who didn't give his permission could sue the church for printing his piece and name in the *Times*."

"Don't worry. Nothing bad will happen," I reassured him.

I was wrong. The day the *Times* photographer came, one of the members showed up screaming and foaming at the mouth, completely freaked out on crack.

"Is that what you mean by fear of success?" I asked Sandy sheepishly, as two guards led the raver out of the church.

Sandy looked at me with a weary *I told you so* expression. "You have to understand. These aren't your New School and NYU students," he said.

On the bright side, the next week the crack guy showed up smiling, clean, and mild mannered again, as if nothing out of the ordinary had happened. Everybody else had gleefully posed for the *Times* picture, which ran in May 1996, under the heading "Where Creativity Is Cooking: Soup Kitchen Writers Tell the Stories of Their Struggles." Michael Molyneux, the nicest editor in the history of newspapers, handled the story with utmost sensitivity. He had the foresight to mention that we were going to be giving a public reading the next Wednesday night at the church. That evening, more than a hundred people showed up. Sandy, Bob, and the typist had gone to Kinko's, xeroxed everyone's work, and put together a yellow-covered book, which they gave out to everyone as a keepsake. My other students who came were touched by the evening and made donations. One artist in my NYU class, who'd just published her first piece in the *Times,* was so moved she donated $1,000 to the program. (Turned out her husband worked on Wall Street. Who knew?)

Reverend Elizabeth Maxwell, who oversaw the soup kitchen, was pleased with the turnout and press and thought it would help get grants to keep the workshop going another year.

I was elated. News of the *New York Times* story drew more soup kitchen regulars to the workshop, and Rev. Liz (as I took to calling her) said the church had received more donations from it as well. Still, I didn't want to teach there again. I was getting married, I had already signed up for three paying classes the following term, and this workshop had wound up taking up way more hours than I'd expected. During the reception Rev. Liz pulled me aside and handed me an envelope. When I opened it, I was surprised to find a check for $1,200. Sandy had never mentioned a teaching salary, so I assumed I'd been volunteering. I learned that he signed back his check to the church. But since I was broke, I took it. I rationalized that he was giving money to his people the way I donated money to Israeli charities. The reverend, social workers, shrinks, and teachers all did good work they were paid for. But even with the payment, it didn't seem worth it to do the workshop again. It was a fascinating experience but too time-consuming and draining.

Before we left the reading, everyone posed for group pictures. Several members asked me about screenplays, agents, and book deals. I gave out my business cards and told everyone they could call me, email me, or attend my summer classes. The next night, at my NYU lecture hall, Harriet and Clarence were there. Then Alan showed up, saying, "I just schlepped forty blocks with my cane in the rain. This better be good." Clarence handed me a piece of paper. After I'd showed him my Jamaica poem "Sunscreen," he'd written less religious dogma and started writing poems, too. The one he gave me ended: "The wise patient old owl / rests on one leg, one owlish eye peeping, the other closed." I analyzed it, trying to figure it out like a hidden code. Was it about hope? Was Clarence the wise old owl?

I invited Sandy and Jay to my wedding that July, but they were out of town and couldn't come. After the *New York Times* "Vows" column ran, I received lots of unexpected mail. My least favorite was from my former *Newsday* editor, Abe, who wrote, "I was so happy and relieved to read about your marriage." Why relieved? Because it got me off of the streets? My favorite card was from Clarence, who congratulated me on my marriage and my teaching. "I think I've detected the revival of something dear. . . . I am inspired. . . . Please be prepared for more poems," he wrote. "Thank you so much! And I love you!" I'd known Clarence only a short time, but I loved him too, like a favorite student. Maybe he saw me as the daughter or granddaughter he didn't have.

Like many of the soup kitchen writers, Clarence didn't have a home where I could write him, or a phone where I could call. I hoped he'd write, phone, or sit in on my class again. But a few weeks later, somebody from Bellevue Morgue called to say that Clarence had died of a heart attack. He had my card in his wallet. Was I next of kin?

In the group picture we took after the May reading, Clarence was standing in the front row, wearing a blue jacket, gray pants, and a red tie, proudly holding the yellow anthology of everyone's work that Sandy had prepared. Sandy was sad to hear the news and said the population who came to the soup kitchen had rough lives, with no access to health care or decent hospitals, and thus often died young. With no money or estates, they were buried at Potter's Field. I asked if the church could help. He asked the reverend to include a prayer for Clarence in the next service and said we could dedicate the next year's anthology to his memory. I carried his last poem in my purse and reread it often. Once I thought I saw Clarence on the subway, but the guy in his coat turned out to be someone else.

"You're teaching with us again, aren't you?" Sandy asked.

"Of course," I said.

Our clientele didn't have calendars, computers, or Filofaxes to jot down class dates. Sandy felt that if they saw us sitting there while they were eating lunch, they'd remember to come to class. So the next March he once again talked me into showing up in the freezing cold at the ungodly hour of 10:00 AM. To retaliate, I suggested negative, twisted, depressing, newsy topics. One of the members who'd been featured in the *New York Times* roundup piece was Donald, a sixty-year-old New Jersey black man with a salt-and-pepper beard. He wanted help getting published again. When I threw out "The Worst Job I Ever Had," Donald came up with an excellent essay about the problems he was having with workfare, the new program the City was using to make welfare recipients work for their checks. I'd never read anything about it from the perspective of someone who wanted to work for his welfare but was stifled by bureaucracy.

"If you want to flesh this out with me, I'll send it to an editor I know. I bet he'll buy it and print it right away," I said, to Sandy's chagrin. But Donald couldn't wait to fix it and send it out. I emailed it to a *Times* editor who'd recently spoken to my class. The next week, on April 24, 1997, the op-ed page ran Donald's essay, "Working for My Welfare." Donald received $150 and major applause from the group. We reprinted the piece in the end-of-the-session anthology, noting that it had been first published in *The New York Times*.

At the soup kitchen's next final reading in May, Donald stood up at the podium. "Before I read my piece, I'd like to introduce you all to someone important who came tonight — my daughter and grandson. Please stand up," he said, pointing to them. A woman dressed in a light blue dress stood up, holding the hand of her adorable young son. "When I started this workshop, I was not clean and not in touch with my family," Donald said. "I didn't talk to them because I had nothing good to tell them. But now I'm clean, and two weeks ago I called my daughter to tell her, 'Go get *The New York Times* to read the piece written by your father that they published.'" He then took out a magnifying glass, since his eyes were bad, and proceeded to slowly read his published article. I noticed several tears and sniffles, including my own.

Twenty of my NYU and New School students came; it was becoming an annual event. A pretty, vivacious woman who enjoyed the night was Connie Kirk, who'd just had her first piece printed in *Funny Times*. (A benefit of helping students get published was that they saw you as a hero and always showed up to your readings.) Connie was so moved to hear the struggles of the soup kitchen regulars that she donated her laser printer to the church workshop.

While my paying students were intrigued with Holy Apostles and begging to sit in on Wednesdays, the soup kitchen writers were excitedly asking which editors were coming to my night classes. I wrote down the info and invited anyone who was interested to attend. It was hard to find engaging editors from top newspapers and magazines willing to come downtown, lecture, and offer to read new work. I started requesting larger rooms and often let as many as sixty students from all of my classes take advantage of the speakers.

Eight different members of the soup kitchen group showed up that term. They dressed and behaved better than my other students, who were often raggedy eighteen-year-old undergraduates who swore, whispered to classmates, and forgot to turn off their cell phones. Aaron called my soup kitchen visitors the "Sue Shapiro Scholarship." I called it a pleasure to see people of all ages and backgrounds so open to learning a new craft, and anyway, I had a right to invite whatever special guests I wanted to sit in on my classes. Didn't I?

Inspired by Donald, other Holy Apostles members began officially submitting their work. A suave, hulking Latino writer had his piece on homelessness printed in *Street News*, which was picked up in *Harper's*. Nelson, a tall, soft-spoken, thirtyish African American man, wanted to be a professional photographer. At the New School, Nelson met the editor of a small rag called *Cover* who wound up printing his photographs. *Cover* didn't have money, but I suggested Nelson just get some clips. Then he went on to do regular work for Bronx and Brooklyn newspapers that did pay. We announced these successes every Wednesday at the church and passed around the clips. Rather than set up unrealistic expectations, as Sandy had worried, each little triumph galvanized the group to try harder.

Carol, a sardonic redhead in her fifties, who had an amazingly piercing, honest way with words, let me know she was "ready for her fifteen minutes of fame." She charmed the editor of *Cover*, who printed her reviews. Then she took a part-time job working in his East Village office. Unfortunately, after two years he went out of business. Bit by the publishing bug, she wanted to branch out. Enjoying a speaker from *Wine Spectator,* Carol followed the editor's directions on the kind of pieces they wanted. She earned $400 for her delightful piece "That Cheeky American Wine." It chronicled her buying a bottle of cabernet sauvignon that her ex-husband, a British wine snob, found "unacceptable." Then *Time* magazine ran a cover story on California wines that listed her cabernet. (When I expressed surprise to Sandy that Carol knew so much about wine, he implied that too much of it had perhaps been her initial problem.) An editor from *The Forward,* a Jewish newspaper, explained that its contributors did not have to be Jewish; they just needed to come up with a topic of interest to Jews. Carol penned "Passed Over for Passover," about how, despite her best efforts, nobody ever invited her to a seder. After the piece ran, she received many offers and finally got to go.

I thought the steady work she was getting would provide a stabilizing force. Carol now had a place to live, a typewriter, and contacts with editors, and I was trying to hook her up with a computer. She was well on her way to a real career. But a week later she called me, screaming into the phone, "The editor changed seven of my lines without asking me! How the hell can he do that? That's not what I wrote!" The next call, she sounded frantic. "She said she would pay me in April. It's been three months! Every day I look for the check,"

Carol yelled. "It's not fair! Why don't they do what they say they're going to do?" I realized she couldn't handle it.

"It's worse than being homeless. You've sentenced her to the life of a freelance writer," said Sandy, and we both laughed in recognition.

Thinking that two happily married couples, all witty scribes, would make a hilarious foursome, I asked Sandy and Jay on a double date after the final soup kitchen reading that year. Jay and I had a lot in common. Although she was a little older than I, already had books out, and was a mom in New Jersey, she'd also been a one-time *New Yorker* peon and a smoker. She was sexy and hip looking, wore black jeans and big glasses and kept her dark hair really long, like mine. I was sure we'd make fabulous friends. Yet over the cheap Italian meal, somehow Aaron and Jay's cynical banter was effortless, while I couldn't help deconstructing the Holy Apostles event with Sandy ad nauseam. He assured me that, despite the three-page limit, the guy who read thirteen pages of his Scotland opus had not marred the night. Nor had Wanda's switching to fake French in the middle of her piece.

I didn't mean to be a bore. So I turned to Jay. "My friend Nicole, from my writing group, lives in Montclair with her two kids," I said. "She's a fan of your last book."

"I hate writing groups," said Jay. "There's too many writers. They should ban any more from popping up."

"Or tell them to keep it to themselves," added Aaron, who was antisocial and hated being asked what he was working on. He and Jay's personalities were meshing – they were both private people, with dark, nonlinear sensibilities. I was too literal minded, hyper, and eager to please, operating on a different frequency.

We all seemed to like each other, but somehow the magic only happened between Sandy and me at the soup kitchen. Did Jay ever resent all the time he spent there? The rest of the year, Sandy was often researching books in Montana, Ohio, or Siberia. I resented when Aaron went on business trips to Korea, Japan, and Toronto, (where they did the animation for a few TV comedies he worked on.) I guessed it wasn't easy for Jay to raise kids and write books in the burbs while her husband was traveling the world and then doing good deeds for strangers for free in his spare time.

One year a younger, perky blond girl affiliated with the church sat in on the writers' group. Each Wednesday she'd pay no atten-tion to me but held on to Sandy's every word. "Oh, I'm from New Jersey too," she told him. "Can I read my piece? I would love to hear what you think." She was so obvious and gushy. I felt out-protégéd. I wasn't crazy about Aaron's female students fawning over him. I feared Jay wasn't crazy about how much I looked up to her husband and how needy and demanding of his attention I could be. Even if you were happily wed and monogamous, having a married mentor of the opposite sex could be complicated.

I enjoyed the soup kitchen class, but I had to admit I kept teaching there year after year to please Sandy and spend time with him. As if he weren't busy enough, I handed him rough drafts I was working on and asked for his opinion. Once he wrote me a letter I saved that said, "Sue, thanks for showing me your latest work. You got off some excellent funny lines. I have a sense that you are moving to a whole new category of fame and success. You're inspiring. Sandy." Another time I asked him to read something new about meeting up with my ex-boyfriends.

"This is really amazing. Very funny," he responded the next week.

"You mean it?" I asked.

"Sue, you're one of the funniest writers about love and marriage and family that I know."

"Wow! Can I quote you on that?" I asked.

"Sure," he said.

I made him write it down and sign it. Whenever I'd get a rejection slip, I'd take out Sandy's praise and reread it, for hope, luck, and good energy. I didn't think it was fake — he really believed in me, which made me believe in myself more. I'd become an expert at encouraging and inspiring so many students. Sandy encouraged and inspired me.

As a Freudian, I assessed the world in terms of family dynamics. My high school teacher Jack was a substitute father. My cousin Howard was the age of my grandfather. Helen was a feminist role model and fantasy maternal figure. Sandy was closer to my age, a contemporary, like a sibling. When I was growing up, my three younger brothers had been aggressive and rambunctious, tackling me on the lawn, teasing me constantly, letting their pet rats out in my room and taking pictures of my shocked reaction. Although they'd become generous and supportive as we got older, all the Shapiros had strong, argumentative personalities. Sandy was the gentle, low-key older brother I'd never had. The word "brother" also applied to a male in a religious order. I adhered to no theocracy, but Sandy was so nonjudgmental and willing to listen, he became like my confessor or priest.

By the spring of 2001, the soup kitchen group was on such a roll that it seemed to run itself. Janice and Thyatira, a vibrant, charming black mother-daughter team from the Bronx, shared soulful pieces about homelessness, their fourteen-month ordeal getting through Manhattan's shelter system, and their psychic abilities. Jay, a bespectacled white guy in his thirties who walked with a cane, had been disabled by a car accident as a teenager. It was hard for him to get around, but he volunteered at the soup kitchen and wrote about his tribulations with both manual and motorized wheelchairs and with trying to get decent medically ordered shoes.

Though he had twenty years' sobriety, Pierce McLoughlin, a gray-haired, Irish Catholic former navy man in his sixties, kept reliving his bouts with alcoholism. "The Worst Night" chronicled his suicide attempt, when he leapt into the East River but was rescued by the police. Most of Pierce's pieces began with the fact that his mother wanted him to be a priest, but he wound up hearing more confessions in Alcoholics Anonymous. They all ended with "one day at a time." Norman, a wise-cracking, blond, mustached guy in his fifties who reminded me of the Norm character on the TV show *Cheers*, focused on his gambling problem and dealing with his bipolar disorder. He sent me notes and a daily haiku by email, and his work was filled with lovely, piercingly honest, intriguing lines, like, "I am mentally ill, so it is sometimes nice to be on the ground in sunlight."

At this point, I was working on conquering my own demons. Right after 9/11, I quit smoking, toking, and drinking. The withdrawal and deprivation overload made me feel frail. As a result, I overidentified with the Holy Apostles members dealing with addiction. Without my smoke screen, I felt closer to my students and more sympathetic to their vulnerabilities. I was only comfortable writing and teaching and became shy and nervous in the outside world. When I heard that Pierce had died of a heart attack, I called Sandy, distraught. He talked me down, suggesting we dedicate that year's anthology to Pierce's memory, as we'd done for Clarence.

I was distracted and out of it when Michael, the head of my NYU program, asked me to participate in a reading. A novelist professor had backed out of the event at the Torch Club, a nearby university space. It would be a favor to him if I filled in. Usually a social butterfly and a ham, I was apprehensive. The nonfiction I'd been scrawling about my old lovers was too rough and raw.

"All I have is part of this new raunchy memoir about remeeting ex-boyfriends," I told him. "It probably sucks. It's not appropriate to read."

"I'm sure it's great," Michael said.

I recalled that Sandy had liked it and reconsidered. "Well, maybe I could try. But I want to read last," I said, thinking the audience would have thinned out by the end.

"Thanks. You're really doing me a solid," he said. "Plus, I can pay you $200."

At the Torch Club, I was disturbed by the bios, which showed that the fiction readers' work had appeared in *The New Yorker* and *The Atlantic,* and that they had books coming out from Farrar, Straus, and Giroux and Knopf. I worried that the crowd of a hundred would like the highbrow work better than mine. Everyone was drinking, eating cheese, crackers, and finger sandwiches on the tables, fidgeting. When my turn came, I went up to the microphone. I hadn't given a reading in a while, and my hand was shaking. As I started my piece about reconnecting with an ex who made me realize I'd wasted my life, the vibe of the room changed. It was silent. The audience stopped shuffling around and eating. There wasn't any other sound but my voice. Then there was laughter at all the subtle jokes. When I finished my six pages, there was loud applause. A bunch of twenty- to twenty-two-year-old girls ran up to meet me, shaking my hand, asking me to sign their programs, telling me about their exes. I felt like a rock star. In the swarm I saw my former student Connie Kirk, the one who'd donated her printer to the soup kitchen. She congratulated me and then introduced her new fiancé, Ken Arnold.

"Are you a writer too?" I asked Ken.

"No, I'm ordained in the Episcopal Church," he said.

"Hey! I know another Episcopalian priest!" Since I knew nothing of Protestant denominations, and in my head divided the world into two religious categories, Jews and non-Jews, I was pleased with myself for knowing two Episcopal big shots. "Do you know Elizabeth Maxwell at Holy Apostles?" It was probably a dumb question, like asking someone from Tel Aviv if he knew your Israeli cousin Steve Schwartz.

"I do know Elizabeth Maxwell," Ken said. "She does great work at the soup kitchen."

"Yes, I told Ken about your workshop," Connie said. "By the way, what you just read was terrific."

I worried the pages were too blue for a clergyman, but Ken said, "It was funny. And poignant too. You really got something there."

I used Sandy's advance praise when I sent the manuscript to

agents and editors. After it sold, I called him to see if I could officially use his endorsement as a blurb. He said yes. Before it even came out, I finished and sold a second memoir about my addiction therapy. After the withdrawal symptoms died down, I was clean and feeling hyped up, optimistic, and lucky. I had bubbling energy for my classes and loved everybody that season.

In the spring of 2003, Connie called. She and Ken had married and moved to Boston, but now they were back in Manhattan. She sounded a little frustrated about work, a feeling I knew too well. "I'll buy you lunch. I have some ideas for you," I said. "Come meet me downtown." (Another benefit of students who first got published in my class: They'd happily travel to Cozy's, my favorite neighborhood diner.)

"I'm so glad you're back in New York," I told her. "Is Ken still working as an Episcopal priest?" I was still patting myself on the back for knowing his denomination.

"Actually he just took a job running Church Publishing, the publishing arm of the Episcopalian Church," Connie said.

"Really?" I asked. "Hey, I got a book for him."

It was the least sophisticated book pitch ever. But after lunch I handed Connie a copy of the past year's Holy Apostles anthology, which Sandy had put together and xeroxed at Kinko's. I was sure it could be used as the proposal. She remembered the Holy Apostles reading she'd loved, and thought it was a marvelous idea. So did

Ken. What a dream! I called Sandy, out of my mind with glee, and told him we had to coedit this anthology. Both of our names would be on the cover! We could work it out so that each writer would get $100 of the advance and two copies of the book! The royalties we earned could go back to the soup kitchen! We could do a reading together! Or a joint TV appearance! We'd be brilliant!

He wasn't into it.

"Sue, I have to finish doing research in Siberia," he said, using even slower diction than usual. "I'm late for two of my own books. I barely have time to teach at the soup kitchen on Wednesdays. I can't take on another project now."

"But it's your program," I said, feeling dejected. "You started it. You'd have to be involved." Since I didn't have kids, I became emotionally involved with my books; they'd become my children. This was our baby. But he didn't want it.

"The timing is just off," he said. "Are you sure this would be a good idea?"

His voice sounded negative and weary, as if he thought there were a chance this wasn't going to happen. It was already happening! I held back tears. I felt like I had just told my lover I was pregnant and he was acting like I was faking it, or unsure he was really the father.

"Are you serious?" I raised my voice. "Of course it's a good idea."

"Can we do it another time?" he wanted to know.

Now he was asking me to abandon our child. Or put it up for adoption. But there was no way I wasn't keeping it now – with or without him. "No! We have an editor interested this week," I said.

"You know you'll have to get all the writers to sign permission slips. How are you going to find them? I don't think anybody's work should be reprinted unless they give their written permission."

"Sandy, of course I'll find them, and they'll give permission!" I told him. "What writer wouldn't want to be published in a book?"

"They confide painful personal stories to us in a secure, trusting, limited atmosphere," he said. "They're not shouting out their humiliating problems to the world at large."

Unlike I did, I bet he was thinking. I was the one who spilled my sordid past in memoirs. He wrote respectable humor and family histories. "Don't you remember when Donald and Carol got paid for publishing their work?" I shouted. "Do you know that they've both been clean since then? They have places to live, and their writing keeps getting better. It's not a coincidence. Validation and success are good. It helps them!"

"Listen." He paused, in the Sandy way that meant he disagreed, my neediness made him nervous, and I was exhausting him. "I have to go meet my kids. We'll debate this more later. Do me a favor. Please don't mention it to the group on Wednesday. Don't get your hopes up, because they might not be interested. Let's talk about it more before we get everyone upset."

Nothing like pouring a bucket of ice on my blazing book passion. I ignored him and called Bob, our fellow Holy Apostles teacher, and said, "Hey, Bob, I have incredible news. Want to edit a book with me? I have a small religious publisher interested in doing an anthology of the soup kitchen work."

He paused too. He had Sandy's slow, mellow manner. I was the only one with fast and furious energy around here. "When?" he asked.

"I'm thinking we could get them two hundred pages by July."

"July? This July?" He sounded alarmed. "Sue, it's May. I'm finishing two classes and a book this semester." Also, he had two kids, his wife was out of town on business, he was late with deadlines, and not very gung ho about my project either. "I'm sorry, I just can't take on something else right now."

Never one to think no really meant no, I called Reverend Liz to ask if she wanted to edit a Holy Apostles soup kitchen anthology with me. "Yes, of course!" she said. "What a fabulous idea!"

Finally someone with a brain! She was as nuts about the idea as I was. I told Ken yes and made an appointment for Liz and me to meet with the Church Publishing staff to iron out the details right away. Liz and I named the book *Food for the Soul,* after a line she'd used to explain why a soup kitchen needed a writing class. The title sounded a bit like the uplifting book *Chicken Soup for the Soul,* and that had been a bestseller, so what the hell.

"What about Sandy?" Liz asked. "Does he like the idea? Will he be involved?"

"Sandy loves the idea. He's all for it. He's just on deadline for two books right now, so he doesn't have time to edit. But he offered to write the intro, so we can use his name on the cover," I said. An atheist Jew's lying to a female reverend seemed to count as more mixed metaphor than sacrilege. Especially if it were in pursuit of a mitzvah that would make my fellow Holy Apostles friends very happy. Plus, I was sure Sandy the Grinch would come around.

On Wednesday at one o'clock, I didn't say a word to the writers' group. I kept my promise to Sandy and didn't plan to bring up the idea of an anthology — at least, not until the end of the session. After everyone straggled in, we handed out the notebooks, pens, and typed work from the week before. "I thought of a few topics for you today," Sandy said, not even asking if I had any ideas for subjects this time.

"Is it true we're all going to be in a book that's being published?" Carol asked excitedly.

"Yeah? Is it true?" the Spanish poet John wanted to know. "Can I be in it?"

"Can I put my fairy story in it?" Leucio asked.

"When is our deadline?" Jay asked.

"Will I have a chance to edit my work?" asked Tory.

Sandy looked at me, but I was innocent. I hadn't told a soul. Had Rev. Liz?

"So, you would want your work to be in a book?" Sandy asked, looking surprised.

What writer in history wouldn't want their work in a book? There was a rousing chorus of "Yes!" "Sure!" "When?" "Of course!" and "Hurrah!"

"I knew you guys would be into this. It'll be so cool," I jumped in. "Here are some permission slips I just happen to have with me that you all should sign. Liz and I are going to make sure that each writer who gives us permission to use their work gets $100," I threw out, handing out the slips Church Publishing had faxed.

"Can I have the money now?" a new member named Dave asked.

"No, we haven't signed the contract yet," I said. "Rev. Liz and I are meeting the editors Friday."

"Can we get the money on Saturday?" Dave asked.

"When are you signing the contract?" asked Norman, the poet.

"What about film rights?" Luecia asked.

"Are you using all my pieces, or do I get choose which ones?" asked Tory.

They were so hyped up, they could barely write new pieces that week.

I looked at the permission slips. Some had signed two or three of them. Sandy shook his head.

"I didn't bring it up," I protested. "It wasn't me."

"Can we get back to the topics now?" Sandy asked, looking at me skeptically.

Liz and I hammered out the details with the publisher. Since they didn't have estates, we could only use the work of dead members (Clarence Clark and Pierce McLoughlin) and those who signed permission slips (so far, only thirteen). They'd pay a $5,000 advance to cover $100 for each contributor (they'd each also get two free books and more if the book had a second printing). It would come out before Thanksgiving under the not-too-religious-sounding imprint Seabury Books.

"I have some ideas for the cover," I emailed the editor, Joan, before our big meeting. I hoped we could use one of Nelson's photographs of the church.

"Oh, we already have the cover," she emailed me back. "We'll show you when you get here."

Uh oh. I hadn't liked the first − or second − stabs at covers that my publishers had come up with for my latest memoir − and they had a whole staff of designers and professionals. Indeed, arguing about the artwork had been protracted agony. I pictured a *Food for the Soul* cover that showed Jesus holding a tray. That would be horrible, because every Jewish friend, relative, and journalist I knew would love the anthology, but my people had an unwritten, subconscious rule to never buy a book with Jesus on the cover. Oy. This could be a problem.

The next week, when I arrived at Church Publishing, Joan handed me the upcoming catalog. I intended to turn to the page that featured our book, already rehearsing my argument for a different, non-Jesus-with-tray cover. When I looked down, I froze. It turned out that the cover of the catalog had a picture of Jesus holding a tray. The image wasn't dredged up from my imagination; it was a famous Michelangelo painting I must have seen before.

Happily, when I opened the catalog, I found that the cover they'd chosen for *Food for the Soul* showed a bowl of soup on a plate with the title in classy handwriting. Leaning on the plate was a pencil instead of a fork. In small letters it said, *Selections from the Holy Apostles Soup Kitchen Writers Workshop.* It was perfect, nonreligious, and subtle. The only change I requested was an apostrophe after *"Writers."*

They needed pictures and short bios of us for the book cover, as well as public relations material. Rev. Liz gave them a picture of herself wearing her clerical collar and a paragraph saying she was "associate rector of the Church of the Holy Apostles and the program director of their soup kitchen for fifteen years." I assumed that would suffice, but they asked for my bio and picture, too. I thought they'd want to suppress my Jewish name listed as the editor, my overly made-up, sexy author's picture, and my provocative titles and subtitles. But a Church Publishing person informed me that its books sold at most five thousand copies, while my books sold more than that and had landed me a movie deal, foreign editions, a spot on *The Today Show*, and good press in three sections of *The New York Times*, *Jane*, *Elle*, *Glamour*, and *O, The Oprah Magazine*. The Jew with cleavage and risqué titles stayed. I loved Episcopalians.

With a tight summer deadline, I got to work. Rev. Liz found me copies of the last ten years' worth of Kinko's anthologies and I pored over them, xeroxing all the work I liked. Unfortunately, I hadn't stayed in touch with more than half of the former members. The biggest hurdle would be getting the missing contributors to sign permission slips. I tried the last phone numbers and email addresses I had, but they were all disconnected or changed. I sent letters to homeless shelters and residential group homes. I went to the church one afternoon and stared at the sea of hungry faces, looking for my lost writers, to no avail. Finally I enlisted Carol to be my assistant, offering her $25 for each signature she could get. Hey, it was a legitimate (albeit original) business expense.

Every day during the summer, Carol called me from the church, or the street, or the subway. "I'm narrowing in on Bill," she would say. "I found his corner, and the florist down the street keeps his mail." Or, "Ronnie's here! Having lunch at the temple! I got her on the phone! She said yes!" If it would help, I would run to my ATM and get the found writer his or her $100 cash advance from my own bank account. Then I would send Rev. Liz an invoice and the church would pay me back out of the book advance. Carol bumped into one former workshopper who was drunk and didn't recall ever writing anything. But for $100 he'd sign the slip anyway. "Go for it!" I instructed.

"Who is on top on your wish list?" Carol asked me one Monday in July, when I took her to lunch at Cozy's to go over which of her powerful pieces we'd be using.

"I really want to find Janice and Thyatira English," I said. "I tried their old email address, but it's not working. I called their number in the Bronx, but they must have moved."

This mother-daughter team were the stars of the workshop for a few years. They had gotten up, one after the other, to share their work at one of the annual readings, beaming at each other with support and pride. Janice English was a big, bubbly woman in her fifties who looked a bit like Aretha Franklin. Although she'd had an extremely difficult life, Janice's warm smile was charismatic, and her wit, irreverent attitude, and hard-won wisdom came through in her essays. She was coming to my NYU night classes at one point. She wanted to be there so badly she brought her kids and grandkids a few times and I let them color on the floor. I was sure if she stuck with it, she could get published. I sent a gut-wrenching essay she wrote about the death of her disabled son to several women's magazines. Unfortunately, the editors found it a bit too harrowing to handle. Then Janice changed her email address and stopped coming to the church. "They both wrote so many amazing pieces I would love to use for the book," I told Carol.

"Okay," Carol said. "How about $25 for a real signature, $5 for a forgery?"

"Very funny," I said, and then considered it. Though I was a solid citizen who tried not to break the law, I never liked to play by the rules. I wasn't afraid of exploiting writers, like Sandy was. I believed most writers would gladly exploit themselves — or their families and friends — to get published any chance they got. I just feared that I'd get the church sued or somehow get the printing of the anthology halted. Okay, and maybe I feared Sandy's wrath — just a little. He'd reluctantly agreed to pen an intro and let us use his name and photo, which I didn't want to chance.

"Let's keep trying. We have another month before our deadline," I told Carol.

On Tuesday Carol left me a buoyant message. "I got a phone number for Janice English and Thyatira! It's Brooklyn, not the Bronx!"

I called the number and heard Janice's voice on the answering machine. Yes! I left a message. Janice called me right back. She was happy to hear from me and flattered that I wanted to use her work in a book. She said it was fine, that she'd ask her daughter and sign the permission slip. She asked about my classes; I reminded her she could come back whenever she wanted. I mentioned the advance and told her that if she could come to Manhattan, I could give her $200 cash for her and her daughter. I offered to take her to lunch to go over all her work with her, in case she wanted to edit, add, or take out anything. She said she'd meet me at my apartment on Friday at one o'clock. I emailed Sandy a note with the subject heading "I found Janice and Thyatira!" Although he found my obsessive search for former members a bit unsavory, he emailed back to say, "That's great, tell Janice and Thyatira I say hi. I love their work." The first draft of the manuscript and pictures was due. Since I had their verbal approval, I included Janice and Thyatira's pieces and photographs, figuring I'd have the official permission slips soon.

On Friday it was very hot and muggy out, ninety degrees, and I wondered if it would be too hard for Janice to ride over on the sweltering subway. I had the cash, with the permission slips and all her xeroxed pages ready to review. But Janice never showed. I left messages for her, asking if she wanted to reschedule, or needed me to come to Brooklyn, or would prefer to meet at the church. No response. This was not the first time somebody from Holy Apostles had stood me up. Yet it was unsettling because Janice had always kept her appointments and her word. I hoped she wasn't in trouble. Could she have just forgotten?

Two weeks later a message from Thyatira said that her mother had unexpectedly had a heart attack and died. Oh my god. Another soup kitchen writer dead from a heart attack? I couldn't believe it. Thyatira said she would have returned my messages sooner, but that she had to take care of the funeral arrangements. I called Sandy crying. Janice was the third member who'd passed away whose death was listed as "cardiac arrest." What a metaphor – these poor people with such hard lives, dying early of broken hearts. I called Rev. Liz, who agreed to send Janice's daughter a card from the church. I also mailed Thyatira the $200 cash, which I knew she could use, especially now, with a sympathy card, one permission slip (I didn't need one signed by Janice now), and a copy of the *Food for the Soul* galley. I included a self-addressed envelope, hoping to get word back from Thyatira that she liked the book. When my envelope came back it was just her signed permission slip, nothing else, no note. I felt horrible, as if Sandy were right – I'd exploited her and her mother for my book – but not horrible enough to stop.

All in all, working with Rev. Liz was a breeze. She was an easygoing, pretty woman who was five years older and stood about my height. I'd spent time with her every spring for nine years, but now I finally got a chance to ask her personal questions. She was originally from Texas, had an undergraduate degree in European history from Duke and a master's in divinity from Princeton. Her grandfather, a Methodist minister, had been her role model. Though she'd never married, I was interested to learn that she'd dated a Jewish guy for a few years.

When Sandy had first approached her with the idea for the workshop, she'd never guessed there'd be much interest. She certainly never anticipated anyone getting published. But she loved doing the book and called me a "force of nature." We were both strong women.

Although I didn't lead a religious group, I wondered if, in some ways, being a writing teacher was similar to being a spiritual leader. You had to be consistently inspirational and uplifting, answer tons of questions, offer rules to live by, and give people faith in themselves.

Yet Rev. Liz's external temperament was the opposite of mine. She was as calm and unobtrusive as Sandy was. They were both yin to my yang. I started confiding in her, realizing this reverend was becoming my rabbi. I questioned why I felt more comfortable in her church than in my old temple. The rabbis I knew were men, so Rev. Liz was the first female religious authority I'd befriended. I'd grown up a conservative Jew. She explained that Holy Apostles was very liberal, all inclusive, and housed the gay and lesbian synagogue. I guessed I was more at home with anything liberal than with anything conservative. After all, I'd traded West Bloomfield for the West Village.

I'd hated going to Hebrew school from grades one to twelve, where I found the principal and teachers ominously obsessed with the Holocaust. Judaism seemed extremely sexist. Teachers and rabbis at my old synagogue were moralizing and preachy. I preferred Reform services in English. The only rabbi I'd met who'd engaged and entertained me was Sherwin Wein, a brilliant, provocative, gay atheist at Michigan's Birmingham Temple. My Orthodox relatives were intrusive, all my adult life asking, "When are you getting married?" and, "When are you having children? You're not a spring chicken, you know." Sandy and Liz were so humble and unobtrusive. Then again, the comparison wasn't fair, because I wasn't a member of their families, faith, or congregation.

That May, I signed my check back over to the church's soup kitchen for the first time. I paid for the auditorium space for a benefit that earned $2,000. Then I wrote a check to an emergency Israeli charity and called the soup kitchen at the Village Temple, two blocks away. Even nontraditional Jews had to get rid of their guilt some way.

Everything about *Food for the Soul* felt like a miracle. The book's dedication read: "To all members of the Holy Apostles Writers' Workshop past and present, and in memory of Clarence Clark, Pierce McLoughlin & Janice English." We did a great reading at the church. *Publishers Weekly* raved about it, quoting work by contributors Tory, Peter, and Carol. *The New York Times's* "City" section editor who'd first run a piece about the program ran an excerpt with a picture of the cover. *The Chicago Tribune's* book editor chose it as a personal favorite, and the *New York Post* put it on its recommended reading list. Mediabistro threw us a book signing at Mannahatta, a hip downtown club on Bleecker Street and Bowery. "The Bowery's certainly an appropriate place for this book party," a friend wisecracked.

Sandy, Carol, Nelson, Tory, Mitch, Peter, and other contributors were happy to sign books for the five hundred hipsters who showed up. A cute twentyish assistant at NBC, a nice Jewish girl named Daria, said she wanted to pitch a piece on the book. The next day, the *Today Show* producer Daria worked with called. I declined to go on TV, but Carol and Tory were filmed at the church. The crew went to New Jersey to interview Sandy and Donald, who lived in South Orange. The segment that ran on Thanksgiving was extremely moving. My colleagues bet that since I wasn't getting a cent from the book, this one would be the bestseller. It wasn't, but it did shoot to position 1,100 on Amazon.com for ten minutes after *The Today Show*. (Yes, I checked.)

Next to my copy of the book, signed by all the contributors, I keep two cherished notes. After I sent her author's copies, Thyatira wrote that the anthology was "amazing" and requested more copies, which Rev. Liz sent. Sandy sent me a note that said, "Thank you for doing the book. You did a good thing. It's beautiful." He loved our baby after all!

"Hey, I have a question for you," I asked him over the phone one day. "Why did you choose me to teach with you at Holy Apostles? When you came to my New School class, did you like the way I taught?"

"Well, I liked that you taught," he said. "After I came up with the idea for the soup kitchen program, I realized I'd never been a teacher before. I needed people with teaching experience. Bob was an English professor who had me come to his class. So I asked him. Then you had me speak. I knew you taught at NYU and the New School, so I figured you probably knew what you were doing."

How ironic. I thought he'd hired me a decade before because he was so impressed with my teaching prowess and how much my students adored me. Turned out I was just the easiest coteacher around. He hadn't misled me; I'd misled myself.

But Sandy had told me one true lie, over and over. He'd promised that I would get into *The New Yorker*. Since he had no trouble getting in there, he probably thought I would eventually break in there, too. I did have another close call. When my memoir about reconnecting with my ex-lovers saw print, the publisher worked out a special deal with a full-page *New Yorker* ad contest they called "The Eat Your Heart Out Sweepstakes" around Valentine's Day. Readers wrote in five reasons why they deserved a $500 romantic dinner. People really wrote in. I let my editor determine the winner.

"See, you did finally get into *The New Yorker*," Sandy kidded me.

"I didn't know it would cost $10,000," I kidded back.

"Hey, my publishers don't buy full-page *New Yorker* ads for my books," he said.

They don't have to. Your real writing is in there, I didn't say.

"I gave the *New Yorker* editors copies of *Food for the Soul* and asked if they could write a brief review. I'm sure they will," Sandy said. But they never did.

Tory had a piece printed in another Church Publishing anthology and landed a full-time job as a bookseller at Barnes & Noble, getting two promotions in her first year. Peter broke into *New York* magazine, and Thyatira is completing both her GED and a memoir. Some accomplishments beat getting published in *The New Yorker* any day.

The Rescuer

RUTH

GRUBER

When I bumped into my editor friend
Gael McCarthy leaving a restaurant one freezing afternoon in
December 1987, she turned to her lunch companion and said, "Ruth,
you must meet Sue Shapiro. She just reviewed your book for *The
New York Times.*"

Ruth, a petite, blue-eyed, blond, seventy-seven-year-old Jewish
lady in a light blue skirt outfit with matching scarf and jewelry, stood
there frozen. My short piece on her upcoming book, *Rescue,* had not
yet run, so she had no idea whether I'd praised or panned her in the
most influential literary publication in the country.

As a struggling twenty-six-year-old freelancer, I was pleasantly shocked that anyone from the *Times Book Review* would return my phone call, let alone ask me to critique the latest project by someone as accomplished as Ruth Gruber. New to reviewing, I didn't know the protocol one followed when bumping into an author whose book you'd just been assigned. Was I supposed to remain detached, nodding hello but not speaking? Or pretend the assignment wasn't a big deal and make small talk, ignoring the elephant in the room? "I loved your book! It's a total rave!" I blurted. "Mazel tov!"

Ruth's face lit up and her body relaxed as she wrapped her arms around my waist and hugged me. I hugged her back. Not a bad introduction to an acclaimed writer.

After my piece ran, Ruth asked me to lunch. My most exciting recent adventure was using my frequent flyer miles to get to West Bloomfield, so I was impressed by *Rescue*. It chronicled her trip as the only journalist permitted on the 1985 secret airlift of Ethiopian Jews to Israel, known as Operation Moses. Looking up Ruth's biography, I was intrigued by her fifty years as a foreign correspondent for the *New York Herald Tribune*, which led to eleven other books on the Soviet Arctic, Israel, Korea, Kenya, Vietnam, and Puerto Rico. She brought me a signed copy of her 1983 memoir, *Haven*, about how President Roosevelt had dispatched her to Italy to help a thousand Jewish refugees escape Nazi Europe during World War II.

"So tell me more about you," I said.

"You already read my book, so you know all about me. Tell me about you," she said.

Compared to her international travels combined with political heroism, what I did seemed small and insignificant. "What do you want to know?" I asked.

"How did someone so young break into *The New York Times Book Review?*"

I told her about Gerry Jonas, my brainy *New Yorker* staff writer friend, who'd joined my Tuesday night group, thought I was a good critic, and introduced me to his *Book Review* editor. I figured that Ruth, like everyone else I met in the media, would ask about *The New Yorker*. Instead she asked about my workshop. Maybe she was politely feigning interest in the details of my downtown scene. How thrilling could the nitty-gritty of a young, ragtag clique be to the seasoned author of twelve books who lived on Central Park West?

I'd recently explained all the critiquing and rewriting we did to an editor who'd bought a piece from me. He'd interrupted to say, "Listen, keep this stuff to yourself. Nobody's ever gonna be interested in your process." But Ruth really was interested in my process!

"Where does your group meet? Do you go over nonfiction? How many pages a week can each writer bring in? Do you give out your pages in advance or read them aloud?" Ruth fired away questions. For a paranoid moment, I feared she could tell I was an impostor who didn't have enough credentials to review her book for *The New York Times* and was merely gathering proof to confront the editor in chief with this horrible blunder. But then she concluded, "I want to join your workshop. I just started a memoir and I need some feedback."

I laughed. "Ruth, big publishers have already bought a dozen hardcover books of yours. You're too advanced."

"Nobody else in your group is advanced?" She looked disappointed.

Actually, aside from being a *New Yorker* staff writer, Gerry had also published three nonfiction books. Lori had an award-winning poetry collection and an art book out, and Mike had won Emmys for his TV documentaries. But Ruth had a fifty-year career as a newspaper journalist and was already a best-selling author.

"Don't you already have an agent and book editor you have to listen to?" I asked.

"They say everything I show them is great," she said. "They don't really criticize me. Who needs sycophants? I need criticism."

"Listen, why don't you come sit in on the group one Tuesday night to see if you even like what we do? It's really intense," I told her. "The worst insult the group can give is, 'There's no blood here.' And when someone is too in love with a precious phrase or sentence, we use an expression that you have to 'kill your babies' and delete it. We really kill each other's babies."

"Good, I want my babies killed," she said. "I'm not afraid of blood. I'm coming this Tuesday night."

I'd started the workshop with *New Yorker* and NYU colleagues in 1985, emulating a private West Village class I'd taken with an astute poet and critic. Charging $250 for a ten-week session, he'd sit Buddhalike before everyone, offering his verdict of your latest creation, his voice the only one that counted. His perceptive yet lacerating comments initially freaked me out. I wasn't the first student to flee his apartment in tears, clutching my battered poetry to my chest. But I mustered the courage to come back and soon craved that kind of harsh word-for-word judgment on every page I wrote.

In my version of the literary cluster, I didn't charge any money because I wanted help with my own work every week. I desperately needed new mentors to tell me what mistakes I was making in several different arenas — essays, reviews, profiles, fiction, and poetry. Most good writers crossed genres. (A *New Yorker* staffer used to joke that John Updike wanted to win the contest for publishing every conceivable form in the magazine — including short fiction, scenes from novels, "Talk of the Town" stories, essays, book criticism, poetry — as well as drawing his own illustrations.) I only invited colleagues I thought were smarter and further along than I was, not hard to find at this point. I moved the furniture against the walls of my eight-hundred-square-foot studio apartment, set up folding chairs, and threw pillows on the floor, so twenty-five guests could be crammed into a circle.

I was the facilitator who organized it, called on people, and kept order, but the founding members and I together decided on bylaws: You would reserve space to bring in xeroxed, collated, and stapled copies of up to ten double-spaced pages. Everyone's convictions were equally important. It was better to first hear the painful truth from each other than to risk humiliation and business connections by sending out work too early to editors, agents, and producers. While we discussed a piece for twenty minutes, the author of that piece wasn't allowed to speak. (If you were arguing back defensively, you wouldn't hear the critique.) After we went around the room, dissecting the work, the author could ask a question or make a statement. Usually it was, "Thanks, I'm going to revise it," or, "Do you think third person is the way to go?" Once, after a guy named Jeff's story was trashed and I asked if he had any comments, he answered, "Yeah, you're all assholes." Everyone applauded.

Luckily, there was usually a consensus about which sections were strong and on target, which could be improved, and which parts should be thrown in the garbage. I was the fastest and nicest, so I'd speak first, starting with what I liked, even it was only "fabulous title" or "really good energy," before identifying problem spots. Gerry, who became the group's dad, was a journalist/poet/ science fiction genius well versed in science, history, and mythology. He often didn't like the first few paragraphs, which he'd call "throat-clearing." Common advice was, "Start in the middle," where the drama/conflict/tension tended to begin.

Marla, a sultry poet and world traveler, analyzed subtle sexual innuendoes, once famously challenging the semi-shy author of an inadequate sex scene by saying, "I just don't see the penis here. I just don't feel the penis." Bob Brown, a bald, bespectacled, no-nonsense ex-con etching out a harrowing tale of his prison days, cut through artistic pretension by adding, "Sounds pretty, but I have no idea what the hell you said." Tsipi, an Israeli novelist and poetry translator, waited until everyone else had spoken, and at the end would throw out, "You're all completely wrong." Her work was so original that we took to calling her style "Tsipian."

Several members who followed the group's advice soon infiltrated *The New York Times, The New Yorker, The Paris Review,* and *New York* magazine, and had plays produced at La Mama and Dance Theater Workshop. The external approval confirmed what we already knew — there was serious good chemistry going on. As more work improved and saw print, we added rules: If you sold an article you'd workshopped, you owed us champagne. Fiction warranted wine. A poem, which usually earned two free copies of the journal nine months later, called for a box of cookies.

Word of our success spread, bringing weekly calls from those who wanted in. It was free, after all, and no matter how broke I was, I served soda, cheap beer, cookies, and popcorn, and everyone shared joints later. It didn't hurt that many members were cute and single – or in some stage of a painful breakup or divorce. (Writers and poets were not a subset known for domestic tranquility. What would they write about?) Being satirized in an article in the *New York Observer* increased the group's cachet.

Along with poems and essays that saw print, books bound, plays produced, jobs landed, apartments subletted, and friendships and marriages formed, a few businesses thrived. Dave was a poet/carpenter and Ron was a novelist whose day gig was running a moving company. So whenever members needed to move or have shelves built cheap, they hired Dave and Ron, who became our unofficial carpenter and mover. We also shared an accountant who specialized in suffering artists and extended a workshop discount for writers desperately in need of someone to do their taxes for $100.

Every Tuesday night at seven thirty, about twenty-two regulars showed up, along with a few strangers who'd requested admission and were in essence auditioning as new candidates. This gave us the opportunity to see if they were good critics. It gave the newcomers a chance to witness how candid, competitive, or hostile we could get in the face of clichés, artsy fluff, or overwrought, self-important drivel. Once was enough to scare off many weak wannabes or midlevel luminaries expecting fawning attention. I was afraid this screening process would weed out Ruth, who was used to getting standing ovations from rich uptown Jewish audiences and had no idea what she was walking into.

"Okay, I'm bringing my first chapter this Tuesday," she told me. "I'll make copies."

Her eagerness surprised me. Usually prospective members came by to observe and listen for a week or two before jumping right into having their babies butchered. "Why don't you see if you like what we do first? Then you can bring your work the next week," I suggested.

"No, I'm bringing my chapter Tuesday. I can handle it." Ruth was emphatic and could not be dissuaded. She never took no for an answer, a philosophy that used to annoy me – until I stole it from her.

"Okay, xerox off twenty-two copies," I said. "But remember, I warned you."

She showed up Tuesday night, wearing a lovely pastel silk skirt and blazer with silver jewelry, looking twenty years younger than her age. She was the best-dressed member we'd ever had. I introduced her around. The group was a mix of male, female, Caucasian, African American, Latino, Asian, gay, straight, Muslim, Protestant, Jewish (clearly divided between left-wing and right-wing Jews), and Catholic (who'd brought in a spate of sadistic-nuns-who-haunted-my-childhood stories). We had members who were born in India, Israel, France, London, Canada, and Amsterdam. My fourteen-year-old cousin Molly Jong-Fast, Howard Fast's granddaughter, was the youngest member, while Ruth, at seventy-seven, was the oldest, with the most books out. She greeted everybody warmly, as if she were just one of the gang.

I read my new humor piece about a bad breakup, which I knew sucked. Next we did an angry, three-page political essay by Raj, a Kashmiri whose gorgeous poetry trumped his polemics. Following that was a rough draft of a seven-page short story by Jeff, a funny nerd who kept unconsciously emulating his idol, Philip Roth. Then we went over a section of Bob's searing prison memoir, in which he revealed that he'd killed someone in a robbery forty years before.

I wanted to give Ruth a chance to see how we picked pieces apart, trashed lines we didn't like as "trite," "pedestrian," or "obvious," and lingered over what was lacking, in case she wanted to back out. She didn't. Ruth explained that the chapter she'd passed out (on old computer paper, with holes on the sides), was the start of her memoir, *Ahead of Time: My Early Years as a Foreign Correspondent*. Her ten pages had tiny margins, and instead of double-spacing, she'd used space and a half, so it was more like fifteen pages – a lot to read aloud. Luckily, she read really fast, like I did.

The precocious daughter of Jewish immigrants who grew up in middle-class Brooklyn, Ruth chronicled how she'd skipped grades in school and gone to NYU early (like I had!). She earned fellowships and grants and made her way to the University of Cologne, where in 1932, at age twenty, she became the world's youngest Ph.D. Her Orthodox

Jewish family flipped out when she wound up in Germany on the eve of Hitler's reign. I was relieved that her rough draft wasn't so rough. When she finished reading, I complimented her first and then mentioned a few places where she could add more specific details. Hands shot up, and I called on people in order.

"Is there a way to verify that she's the youngest Ph.D in the world, and that she got her doctorate in Cologne?" asked Bob, the ex-con memoirist, who was cynical about everything.

"It's true," I said. "I looked it up."

"Okay, if it's true it's a good story, but the family stuff is pretty schmaltzy. Calling Williamsburg a 'shtetl' is cliché," said Gerry, who I hated to admit was usually right. "And unless it's a Hallmark After School Special, every relative can't adore every other relative so much."

"Ditto. Too schmaltzy," echoed Mike, a sardonic, burly gray-haired documentary filmmaker, a man of few words who usually agreed with Gerry. A youngster in the group started calling Mike, Bob, and Gerry "my three dads."

"Didn't Tolstoy say happy families are all boring?" asked Ron. "I have five brothers and sisters, and nobody was ever this happy. We were Catholic, but it seems like the same guilt." He was a soulful Midwest transplant whose day job, owning a moving company, had inspired his current project, *Mover's Memoirs*.

"Think about what an Orthodox Jewish family with three sons

would be like. Her mother is washing and cooking all the time. Her brother becomes a doctor, so they don't know what she needs degrees for," Lori jumped in. "And yet there's not one mention of sexism. I don't believe it."

Lori, a talented poet in her fifties who specialized in Italian history, was a left-wing Jewish WASP who wrote freely of her many wild love affairs. Her personality clashed with Ruth's more patriotic, sexually modest aura. But Lori did have a point. I had three brothers; two became doctors. Although I grew up in a less religious family than Ruth's and it was fifty years later, gender bias still abounded. Male offspring were celebrated with bris and bar mitzvah ceremonies.

"Right. The main character is this strong trailblazer, so getting scholarships and degrees is her rebellion, her way to escape her mother's domestic slavery. And her mother's chastity belt," added Marla, "which is a different kind of chain."

"You feminists are getting carried away with the slavery metaphors," teased Hal, a tall, handsome black playwright I was developing a crush on. "But I agree — the parents and brothers are too perfect. They don't seem real."

"I want the characters to be more quirky, like Isaac Singer. Or Salman Rushdie," said Raj, who often found a way to bring Rushdie into the conversation. "Warts and all."

"Right, don't airbrush," instructed Mike.

"You're all wrong," piped in Tsipi. "She should take out the family altogether. That's the mistake – it's not about her relatives. It's about her alone."

It went on like this for twenty minutes, honing in on the holes in Ruth's narrative. Had I been too impressed by her credentials? Or too blinded by our superficial similarities to see that, like all writers, her early drafts needed work? As she furiously scribbled down notes, Ruth looked tiny and fragile. I was excruciatingly uncomfortable. First I'd raved about her book in the best place to rave about a book and gave her a huge hug. Now it felt as if my gang were beating up my fantasy bubbe. After the group was over, Ruth shared the "Upper West Side express" cab with the three dads, leaving abruptly. I felt guilty and conflicted. I knew it was risky to let her jump in so soon, but she'd insisted. I went to bed worried that she was hurt and offended.

The next morning the phone rang at eight o'clock. Nobody ever called me so early. I picked it up, fearing an emergency.

"Sue, it's Ruth," she said.

I bolted up in bed. "Ruth. Hi. Are you okay?"

"I've been up all night," she told me. "Couldn't sleep a wink."

I was about to apologize for the way the workshop had slaughtered her pages, but she didn't give me a chance.

"They were absolutely on target. Gerry was right. It was too schmaltzy! What a great critic he is," she said. "Bob, the ex-con, is pretty sharp too. I added dialogue and tons of specifics to flesh it out. Of course my degrees were in rebellion, like that clever girl Marla said. Who wanted to cook or clean? They were all sexist. They just wanted me to get married and have babies and thought I was crazy. But I wanted to travel and be a foreign correspondent and change the world. I rewrote the whole thing. You wouldn't believe how much better it is. You have to hear it!"

Thankfully, she wasn't hurt at all! What I'd taken for anxiety was glee. It was the same rush I'd felt after the group diagnosed the problems with my pages and showed me exactly how to rectify my writing sins. Often I'd stay up revising all night – cutting extra words, adding idiosyncratic details – until I broke through. Ruth read me her entire rewrite over the phone. It was too early for me to really focus. But even in my half-asleep fog, I could tell that in twenty-four hours, Ruth's first chapter had been fixed.

"What a wonderful group," she said. "In my day they didn't have writing workshops or MFAs or what they now call creative nonfiction. I've learned so much from you, Gerry, Bob, and the others in just one session. I'll bring in the second chapter next week. I can't wait to hear what you think."

I hung up the phone, pleased with her praise. But I also found it ironic that instead of my becoming Ruth's protégé, she wanted my workshop to become her mentor. I thought of the Mark Strand poem about how you become what's missing. Yet Ruth had already taught me something essential. There were so many award-winning authors whose later books stumbled because they thought they were above criticism. So they no longer asked for, or listened to, any serious dissection of their work. That someone of Ruth's age and background would be open for an honest assessment, and so willing to take our opinions into account and rewrite, made a deep impression. No matter how smart or talented you are, it's too hard to see your story when you're in the middle of it. You're never too old to learn more and get better, she told me. If people in your life tell you how great your work is, find someone who isn't afraid to be more candid and critical. I made a mental note to always be like that.

The next workshop, Ruth again arrived dressed to the nines, with her pages xeroxed and ready to go, patiently waiting for her turn. She read her second chapter as quickly as the first. Although she liked that nobody gave her a pass because she was older, or semi-famous, I was not yet convinced that Ruth really belonged in the Tuesday night crew. Did she really want us scrutinizing every word she wrote through such an intense, young, and modern filter? It was especially itchy because her project was a memoir, so she was the lead character we were obsessively questioning.

"Your story is really engaging," I said, speaking first, as I usually did. "I'd just say be more specific."

"Well, something's not right here," Marla jumped in. "You make a point of saying that you never slept with the German boyfriend, Johann. Then you write that you married when you were thirty-nine. You repeat twice that you didn't believe in sex before marriage, but I have a hard time believing this brave, globe-trotting woman not afraid to argue with Harold Ickes and President Roosevelt was a virgin until she was thirty-nine."

"Yeah," Bob leapt in. "Calls up more questions than it answers."

"Too bad she can't sleep with Johann the Nazi," Lori suggested.

Uh oh, this discussion was putting me on edge. I feared that our intrusive psychoanalytic and sexually frank nature would weird Ruth out.

"She can't sleep with the Nazi! It's not fiction!" said Jeff, defending Ruth's honor. "It's nonfiction!"

At the end of each critique, the author was allowed to answer the questions raised. Ruth repeated that she had not slept with Johann the Nazi. In fact, she made clear, they'd barely held hands. Then she admitted she'd had a brief early marriage a few years later, when she was twenty-five, which ended badly.

"Put it in there! You have to be honest!" Gerry urged.

"I don't want to put it in there," Ruth argued. "It was a mistake."

"But that makes your narrator more human and interesting," I argued back, using the third person as if it were a novel, which made it easier for me to criticize. "Here she is, a genius, getting her Ph.D. at twenty, meeting Virginia Woolf, working for *The New York Times* and the *New York Herald Tribune* by the time she's twenty-six. Yet she still picks the wrong guy." As a single journalist with several psychotic relationships in my recent past and a staid Michigan clan wondering what was wrong with me, I could totally identify.

"Okay, okay. I get it," Ruth said. The next week her rewrite had an added sentence, hidden so you could barely catch it, about "an early relationship that didn't work out."

"Too vague," Mike complained.

"It's like Hester Prynne's scarlet letter. But it's not even clear that it was consummated," Marla seconded the thought.

"Half of the people in this room had brief early marriages that didn't work out," Raj said. "All the best writers are divorced – Bellow, Updike, Roth, Rushdie."

"But in an Orthodox family, it was a *shanda*," Tsipi explained, using the Yiddish word for "big shame."

"Maybe he was married to someone else?" Lori asked. "Or cheating on her?"

Not allowed to speak during the critique, Ruth nevertheless vigorously shook her head no.

"Well, a divorce is nothing to hide or be ashamed of," I threw in, quickly counting eight members who'd mentioned first unions that didn't pan out. I'd lived with a few losers myself but couldn't even manage to get to the stage with the ring.

"I lived through it too and survived. We call them 'trainer marriages,'" Gerry said, confirming it was okay to admit divorce in public. Sometimes I thought we were really doing group therapy.

"It's my life. The book is about my work!" Ruth raised her voice. "Why does an early bad relationship matter?"

"You called it an autobiography," Bob replied. "So don't give a false account. If you're deceptive about when you first wed, readers will wonder if you're playing fast and loose with other facts, too." He was writing a prison memoir; he should know.

"Maybe the guy turned out to be gay and Ruth doesn't want to out him," said Jeff protectively. One of the other conservative Jews in the group, he'd become very attached to Ruth and always took her side.

"Or he could have been physically abusive," Marla guessed.

Like dogs with a bone, we didn't let this one go. Ruth kept shaking her head no, annoyed with our guessing game. To shut us up, the next week her rewrite included the line, "An early, disappointing marriage to a gambler ended badly."

In much longer sections, she chronicled her joyous union with her husband Phillip Michaels, with whom she had two children when she was forty and forty-two. Since she'd given birth in the early 1950s, we questioned what her family thought of her having kids so late. She added the line, "My brother the doctor warned me that my child would have Down syndrome and told me to get an abortion." The group was pleased to be the catalyst that made her cough up idiosyncratic dialogue and darker data about her personal life.

I tended to spill intimate details of my affairs, conflicts, and therapy without provocation, so it was the place where Ruth and I diverged. I guessed it was our different generations. Or it could have been the difference in our chosen genres. My first love was confessional poetry, though it was easier to make a living publishing opinionated reviews, op-ed pieces, and first-person essays. As a Jewish feminist born in 1961, I believed the personal was political and made my private life public. As a Jewish feminist born in 1912, Ruth started out as an academic, writing her third-person thesis on Virginia Woolf. Then the need to make a living – and her rage at the European anti-Semitism she witnessed – turned her into a journalist. She wrote first-person accounts of her experiences, making the political personal, but viewed herself more as an activist than as a poet. "Fortunately, I never took a course in journalism, so I never knew you were supposed to be objective," she once told a reporter. "All I knew was that I had to live the story to write it. If it was a story of injustice, I had to fight it."

Her memoir *Ahead of Time*, published in 1991 by Wynwood Press, was the first of many books the workshop had fully critiqued, from prologue to last page. It received the best reviews of her career, Ruth said. Think of that – to be writing better than ever as you were turning eighty. In her acknowledgments, she thanked "my good friend Susan Shapiro and her writer's workshop" and invited the group to her book party. She looked radiant in a long blue-and-orange gown, with a corsage pinned to her lapel. We all gave her a group hug. Then she introduced us to the crowd – famous editors, best-selling uptown nonfiction writers, heads of state.

The mixture of guests at the party made me long to know more about her past. A few weeks later, working on a freelance article about why it was better for women to marry late than early, I asked Ruth for an interview. She opened up, reminiscing about her blissful love for Phillip Michaels, whom she met in Puerto Rico at age thirty-nine, when she was covering the inauguration of the first elected governor in 450 years. Phillip was a forty-five-year-old popular lawyer and Jewish community organizer from the Bronx. "Everyone took credit for introducing us – the mayor of San Juan, an official in the labor department, the governor," she recalled. When they wed at her huge Manhattan apartment, one thousand people came. Someone said, "If there was a bomb, you'd wipe out the Jewish leadership of New York," she told me, chuckling.

She traveled with Phillip and their two kids, Celia and David, published books on Puerto Rico and Vietnam, and penned a regular "Diary of an American Housewife" column in a monthly magazine for Hadassah, the women's Zionist group. She was married to Phillip for seventeen and a half years when he died in 1968. The kids were thirteen and fifteen, teenagers who didn't like it when she began dating again. If she brought someone home, they'd say, "You're not going to marry that creep, are you?" Since she was a single parent and their sole provider, she instead focused on her career.

Six years later, at a book party in 1974, she bumped into an old acquaintance, Henry Rosner. He was New York's deputy commissioner of human resources who ran the welfare department in New York City. He was divorced, with three girls, and his daughter Barbara pointed to Ruth and told him, "Now, *that's* a woman you should date," Ruth told me. Her children loved Henry too. Four months later he was going to give a speech at the Concord Hotel in the Catskills. He was old fashioned and wouldn't take Ruth along unless they were married, so he proposed. After he retired in 1976, they spent a year in Israel, where Ruth wrote *Raquela,* the history of Israel seen through the eyes of a ninth-generation Jerusalem midwife, which became a bestseller. They were married eight years before Henry passed away in 1982.

Ruth said both of her husbands were proud of her and not threatened by her work, even when she made more money, or when they were called "Mr. Gruber." She spoke glowingly of her kids. Her daughter, Celia, was a TV newswoman who followed in Ruth's footsteps by marrying and having two children in her forties. Ruth's son, David, an assistant secretary at the Department of Energy in Washington, also had two kids. Her favorite times were when they all came to New York, crashing at her apartment. With such an imposing professional dossier, it was impressive that Ruth also had such fulfilling family ties. She made it sound so ideal and effortless. But then I recalled her early speed bump.

"What about your first husband?" I asked. "Whatever happened to him?"

"Who?"

"The guy you married when you were twenty-five."

"What are you talking about?" she asked.

"The gambler guy you married and divorced in your twenties."

"Never happened," she insisted.

"You told me about him. You told the whole writing group."

"That's not so."

How fascinating that she'd forgotten she'd told us. "Come on, Ruth. You wrote about him in *Ahead of Time*."

"I did not," she argued.

"Wait, I have a copy right here on my shelf." I opened the chapter in her book where the reference had been, stunned to see the lines about him were gone. "Why did you take him out?" I asked.

"Look, it's my book, my life, and my tragedy," she said. "I can delete him if I feel like it."

I questioned why she was so reticent to reveal anything about him. So what if he was a gambler? That wasn't her fault. I told her the whole point of my article was to help young women not feel pressure to wed in their twenties. Instead they should get their careers, heads, and homes in order first. This bit of social good convinced Ruth to finally open up and tell me the rest of the story.

It seemed this guy lied to her, took money from her, and wouldn't come home for days at a time. When he'd eventually show up, he'd beg for more money. After they divorced, he was involved with a scheme to rip off soldiers in World War II and went to jail. He remarried and had a son. Ruth met and liked his second wife, who also divorced him when she learned what he was really like. She'd called not long ago to tell Ruth that the gambler had died in New Zealand. Miraculously, his son became a doctor.

"This is so fascinating," I told her.

"You don't have to mention any of this in your article, do you?" she asked.

"Of course I want to mention it. My whole theme is about why it's better not to rush into marriage," I explained. "Wouldn't you advise young women that it's better to wait?"

"Yes. When you're older, you know who you are and have more wisdom," she said. "I'd tell young women to first get your career together, travel, take risks, and work with all the passion you have. Then it'll be easier to get married because you'll be putting out all that good energy. You're busy; you don't look like you're sitting home waiting, like you're man-hungry. You have more important things to do." As a journalist, she knew the importance of good quotes and always came through for me. "I was lucky to find two wonderful men who weren't jealous of my work." As usual, she changed the subject back to her successful marriages.

"Ruth, the fact that the first one was a bad guy wasn't your fault. You did nothing wrong. You only believed what someone you loved told you." I echoed the kind words my shrink had once told me after a horrible breakup with a loser.

"If he's still there, then he has the power to stain or bring me down. So I'm not giving him the power. I just put all the bad things out of my mind," she explained. "I get rid of what I don't want to remember."

This omission typified our quintessential disagreement. Growing up, I'd hated the conservative, Midwest Jewish mentality that everything ugly, weird, or antisocial should remain hidden or glossed over. Where others saw the American dream, I felt stuck in a suburban nightmare. Repression seemed a fearful trait that my parents, the children of Russian and Polish immigrants, had inherited from their troubled families. Whenever my mom told me to keep something negative to myself, I'd whisper, "We have to be quiet. The Cossacks are coming." I preferred psychoanalysis and confessional poetry, where you dig up your demons and face them down, constantly quoting W. H. Auden's line "Believe your pain" and my therapist's adage "Lead the least secretive life that you can." I argued with Ruth about it, but she wouldn't budge in her overall opinion on this issue. Eventually we agreed to disagree.

Like shrinks and most NYU classes, the workshop took off in August. Planning the potluck dinner party for the final workshop of the year at the end of July 1992, Ruth invited us to her place. Nobody had ever asked to have a workshop party at their home before. I warned her that friends of friends could push the number of guests to fifty – not to mention increase the amount of smoking, drinking, and dancing. She insisted that she host the soiree, where smokers could puff away on her terrace. What the hell. I was broke and overworked, so it eased the burden of shopping, hostessing, and mass cleanup. She could be queen for the night.

Thus the workshop trekked uptown to her Central Park West apartment, with ten rooms and a wraparound terrace, where she'd lived for more than fifty years. It was stuffed with books, artwork, and scrapbooks, and artifacts from her travels were displayed in cases in her foyer, making it look like a museum. Lining the hallway were photographs of Ruth with Moshe Dayan, Golda Meir, President and Eleanor Roosevelt, Winston Churchill, Charles de Gaulle, Harold Ickes, David Ben-Gurion, Mario Cuomo, and Bill and Hillary Clinton. Many were inscribed with personal notes, thanking Ruth.

In the roll of pictures we took, Ruth wore a long yellow-and-pink gown with turquoise jewelry. Looming over her petite frame on one side was Hal, the handsome six-foot-four playwright I'd recently started dating. On the other side was Raj, smoking a pipe. Behind Ruth were Ron, Marla, and Tsipi, along with Sally, a frizzy-haired documentary filmmaker who'd recently joined the group. Everyone else was stuffed to the sides, arms raised, waving to the camera, smiling and laughing, with little Ruth right in the middle. She looked ladylike, genteel, and serene standing there, as if she were most relaxed surrounded by chaos.

I asked if it bothered her that I was dating a black guy. She said she thought Hal was "a mensch." That was how she classified people – you were either an honorable human being, or not. A year later, after Hal and I switched back to friendship and I was dating a Catholic guy, Ruth said, "I hope you're not rejecting all Jewish men just for the sake of rebellion. We all know you're not going to be your mother. It's not an original story. If you're happy, she'll be proud of you."

For someone not into therapy, Ruth was very perceptive. She never said "I told you so" when I announced my engagement to Aaron, a TV/film writer from my tribe. His father was a judge in Westchester, which seemed similar to growing up in a doctor's home in West Bloomfield, and we joked we were from the same family. Of course Ruth came to our wedding. Despite the funky loft setting, she was instrumental in initiating a workshop members' horah.

In the two decades I'd known Ruth, the only time I saw her lose her Zenlike calm concerned Sally, the independent filmmaker. "What's her story?" Ruth asked, picking up my colloquialism. Sally was the child of Holocaust survivors, I reported, which was why she knew Ruth's work and wanted to meet her. I admired Sally's films but didn't know her that well. "How long has she been in the workshop?"

"Sally intermittently shows up for a while, then disappears," I told her.

"She sure does disappear," Ruth said, sounding disgusted.

"What happened?" I wanted to know.

It seemed that Sally and a known director had approached Ruth about making a film of her life. After interviewing her, Sally borrowed eight hours of tapes of the Holocaust documentary *Shoah*, in which Ruth was featured. Ruth didn't want to part with her only copy of the tapes. Sally talked her into lending them to her by promising she'd view the tapes quickly and make Ruth another copy, for safekeeping, that weekend. But Sally never did. Ruth called to get her tapes back. When Sally finally returned them a month later, she hadn't made a copy for Ruth; she'd made a copy only for herself.

"I've been featured in many documentaries," Ruth said. "Several have won Academy Awards. But I've never been treated like this before. What's wrong with that girl? She wasn't honest with me. Is she self-destructive?"

"I'm sorry," I told Ruth. "What Sally did wasn't nice. In fact, it sucks."

I'd never seen Ruth pissed off before. Since she was literal minded like I was and had hit it off with most everyone we knew in common, I believed her side of the story. Sally had recently suffered two deaths in her family, so I assumed grief had clouded her judgment. Regardless, Ruth and I had little patience for flakes. I confronted Sally, who admitted that she was in mourning and was thus distracted. She couldn't remember if she'd told Ruth she'd make her a copy of the *Shoah* tapes, she claimed to not recall their conversation. She promised she'd write Ruth to apologize, but she never did. I asked why she'd ruined her connection to such an important subject for a film.

"I admire Ruth and everything she's done," Sally said. "But after our interview, I realized I could never make a documentary about her. She sugarcoats everything. She can't say anything negative or admit failure. She has an inability to see darkness. Everything with her is black and white. I see the world as gray."

I knew what Sally meant – it had also been my first impression of Ruth. But was it a superficial judgment? As I'd become older and happier, I'd revised my assessment, personally experiencing the benefits of selective retention. Ruth minimized or deleted her difficulties, while all good news became more prominent. I'd grown sick of self-destructive artists I barely knew spilling bitter tirades about their troubles. I came to believe that Ruth's ability to focus on the bright side was a conscious struggle and the trick to her longevity.

At one session I was trying to quit smoking, Dr. Winters, my addiction specialist, accused me of having an inability to see darkness and stay with negative, uncomfortable emotions. I didn't agree, but I heard myself arguing, "What's so bad about having an upbeat outlook, like my friend Ruth? That's why she's so healthy and productive, publishing books into her nineties."

Or maybe I'd inherited my optimism from my mother, who shared the trait. One winter when Ruth was speaking at the Jewish Book Fair in my hometown, my mom went to hear her talk. Later my mother called me from our house, where a bunch of her friends were having lunch. Ruth got on the phone and said, "Your mother is such a warm, generous host. Now I know where you get it from."

The connections kept overlapping. My childhood friend Lisa went on a mission to Poland with her friend Rosa, a Holocaust survivor. Ruth was also on that trip, with Doris Schechter, one of the thousand Jewish refugees Ruth had saved from the Holocaust in 1944. Doris, who was five years old when Ruth escorted her on the ship across the Atlantic from Europe to the refugee camp in Oswego, New York, considered Ruth "a second mother and national treasure." I subsequently bumped into Lisa, Rosa, and Doris at many Ruth events. At my bridal shower, Ruth sat with Lisa, Lisa's mother, my mom, and my aunts and cousins. She had joined my family. I spent time with her kids and grandkids when they were in town and with Ruth's young researcher, Isabel, a Columbia University freshman who'd studied in Israel. Isabel wound up joining the workshop, too. Everyone I was close to adopted Ruth, and vice versa.

When Ruth and I were in L.A. at the same time in 1993, I saw a theatrical version of her book *Haven*. I hadn't driven a car in years, I hated L.A.'s big highways, and it was three hours from my hotel to the theater. Luckily Leah, a poet from the writing group who'd moved

West, came to get me. We made it to the play in time to hug Ruth before the curtain went up. The musical was written by Gerry Coopersmith, my husband's Writers Guild colleague, who used to work on the series *Hawaii Five-O*.

Ruth later sold the TV rights to *Haven*. Back in New York that fall, she spent half an hour excitedly relaying details of the *Haven* miniseries CBS was making, with Natasha Richardson in the role of Ruth and Anne Bancroft as her mother. When she mentioned her kids were in town, I asked if they were just there for the Jewish holidays. Ruth mumbled that she'd had an operation. But she was out of the hospital, everything was fine, and the movie was about to air.

"Wait. You were in the hospital?" I asked, worried. Talk about burying the lead. "When? What's wrong? Why didn't you tell me?" I wasn't sure if she was being private or was afraid to be seen as weak, even to one of her closest allies.

"They wanted me to stay, but I'm fine," she reassured me. "Guess what? In the movie version, I have an affair with Johann the Nazi! I'll have to call my relatives and make sure they know it isn't true."

I thought of Beatrice, an acquaintance twenty years Ruth's junior, who complained of her illnesses so endlessly I'd stopped asking how she was. Conversely, here was my dear confidant Ruth, ignoring serious surgery I wanted to know about. Her ability to downplay any trouble fascinated me. Of course, not many ninety-year-olds had new books and movie deals to schmooze about.

Then again, Ruth made her own luck and had clearly made a decision to minimize her problems and slights through the years. When *New York* magazine stole one of my story ideas in 1995, I wanted to call a gossip columnist to make a stink about it. Ruth talked me out of it. She told me about the time she'd bumped into the film director Otto Preminger when he was making the movie *Exodus*. Ruth had heard that Leon Uris, author of the best-selling novel that Preminger's movie was based on, had been very influenced by Ruth's book *Exodus 1947: The Ship That Launched a Nation*. Ruth asked Preminger if it was true.

"If I'd read your book first, I would never have bought his," the director told her. She asked about the rumor that Preminger had used material from her book that was not even mentioned in Uris's pages. Preminger admitted it was true to her face. Then he asked, "You know what I'm going to do for you?" She thought he was going to officially option her book, or at least give her the credit she deserved. Instead he offered her two tickets to the movie opening, which she already had tickets to.

"Weren't you mad?" I asked. "Didn't you want to sue?"

"No. I wasn't interested in litigation or money," she said.

For Ruth, the movie served a higher purpose, telling a crucial story of the Jews she wanted to publicize. Plus, at this point Uris and Preminger were both dead, and she was alive and getting her due late in life. It was the best time to get acclaim, after you'd struggled hard, accomplished your goals, and deserved it (another lesson she taught me). The TV movie *Haven* won an Emmy award and inspired a laudatory five-thousand-word profile on Ruth in *Vanity Fair* – the only fawning piece I'd ever read by the journalist Maureen Orth.

Indeed, whenever I was frustrated with work, Ruth advised: "Just keep doing it. Someone will notice." She often spoke of the "power of the press" and promised, "If you keep going, your work will make a difference one day. You'll see. You're going to wake up the world." I didn't think that was true. It wasn't that she meant to deceive me – it was just her idealistic desire, her projecting herself onto me. She could change the world. My ambitions were more selfish and my canvas smaller.

In 1996, when a tiny publisher put out my poetry collection *Internal Medicine*, I complained it was being ignored. A month later Ruth sent me a beautiful piece on my book that she'd penned for *Hadassah* magazine. "With wit and wisdom, Shapiro reaches out to young Jewish women who think they must leave their families to find themselves," she'd written. Even though she was in the middle of a new book, she made the effort to praise my poetry in print. None of the other journalists from the writers' group – whom I'd hooked up with jobs, clips, and connections – attempted to get me press. Only Ruth, the busiest and most prolific member, understood how hard it was to get ink on a small book, and how much it meant to me. The one other person I knew who wrote about my poems was

Ruth's young researcher, Isabel. At Ruth's suggestion, her assistant did a profile of me for a national Jewish magazine in which she'd also interviewed Ruth.

Ten years after I'd raved about her book *Rescue*, Ruth rescued my poetry book from obscurity.

Although I'd begun to view workshop members as relatives, my husband wasn't thrilled to have fake in-laws, siblings, or cousins around. He didn't want to compete for my attention, often feeling like I was a mom with twenty-two children. His resentment started at our wedding, when we got up for the first dance. He was annoyed when everybody in the group joined us. I thought it was sweet. It wasn't as if we were slow-dancing to a sentimental ballad. For "our song," I'd jokingly chosen Dion's "Runaround Sue."

Then Dan, the carpenter/poet I hired to build bookshelves in our new apartment, took two months instead of the two weeks he'd promised. Aaron made cracks that Dan wanted to saw my husband's head off so he could move in with me. Aaron hated that I made him stay out of the apartment every Tuesday night from seven to eleven, and he resented when I moved his jackets in the closet to make room for workshop members' coats. An avid science fiction reader, Aaron enjoyed talking aliens and intergalactic wars with Gerry and my ex, Hal. Yet he didn't appreciate other male workshoppers who'd call me late at night to ask advice, or brought me flowers, or wrote me cards ending with "love and kisses" or "love and miss you."

Aaron shared his theory that the secret pact of my workshop was "We'll all help each other become almost successful." I attributed this barb to his jealousy, and to the difference between writing for the page versus the screen. None of the poets, playwrights, or fiction writers I knew wrote for big money, whereas screenwriter pals of his earned $400,000 for a 120-page action script that would never get made. While my poetry- and prose-writing fellow members of PEN American Center fought for world freedom, Aaron's TV/film colleagues at the Writers Guild had battled to ensure they got first-class airline tickets to L.A. In my mind they were materialistic hotshots, while we were politically minded artists and truth-seekers.

Yet after I sold my second hardcover, I liked earning real money too. As I rushed to get the manuscript to my editor, the writing group became hostile. An essayist called me self-involved, claiming I was more into sexy confessionals than literary fiction. A poet accused me of hogging the group, bringing in too many pages. A short-story writer implied I was too intense, hurrying through everyone else's weekly submissions. They acted as if I'd joined the enemy camp. I cherished ardent scrutiny of my work, but I was thin skinned when my personality was being critiqued.

When Ruth was on her final lap of *Ahead of Time*, we'd gone over the equivalent of two chapters each week to help. When screenplays or three-acts for the theater had an interested producer, we'd spend an entire evening reading the projects out loud. I'd led the troops on field trips to everyone's opening nights, lectures, readings, and panels, getting comps or paying for anyone broke. I'd read five-hundred-page novels, edited poetry and story collections line by line, thrown book parties for members' chapbooks and tiny press publications that were being ignored. Now, on the biggest deadline of my life, I felt a little abandoned.

Lighting Up, the project I was finishing, chronicled how I'd quit cigarettes and alcohol. I wondered if my smoke-free sobriety had made me self-righteous. The book's hero, Dr. Winters, said that after almost two decades, changing everything was hard on my mentors and colleagues. It was as if I were leaving them. I was putting myself first, which appeared selfish in relation to my past compliance and need to please. The group identified with me, so I was holding up a mirror to issues that were hard to deal with. In fact, the members most annoyed at me were smokers, tokers, and drinkers who felt I was intrusively judging their habits. If I blamed my compulsions for blocking my career, I was implying that their addictions were linked to their inabilities to finish projects and nail book deals themselves.

The group had changed too. It had taken a downturn when Bob died suddenly in his early sixties. (Twenty years in jail had taken their toll on his heart.) We gave a benefit reading to help pay for his funeral costs and emotionally bonded with his daughter, but his absence left a gaping hole. Then Mike, Ron, Dan, and Jeff moved away. I let in more former students, until it was like another class I wasn't getting paid for. Then Gerry and Marla – the most incisive, essential critics of the group – stopped coming regularly.

In July 2003, after eighteen years, I ended the Tuesday night workshop. It was as if I'd graduated, grown up, and needed to go off on my own. A well-known theater director said, "All creative groups should end after ten years. They start out counterculture, rebelling against the establishment. But then they become the establishment." Some found my announcement upsetting. A poet feared I was getting rid of the old crew to start another group with only published memoirists. I said no, but crafting books was different from the art of essays and poems. I mainly listened to my agent and book editor, who'd become my bosses. A novelist who couldn't finish his rewrite asked, "So after you sold two hardcovers, you don't need us anymore?"

I'd believed the saying "A true friend walks in when everybody else walks out" and had judged friendships by noting who'd be there for you when you were down. But it turned out that sharing editors, lending money, and offering consolation and popcorn during 3:00 AM bouts of depression were only part of the equation. When my dreams materialized, I considered other criteria: Who'd be there for you when you were up?

I recalled how hard it was to celebrate girlfriends' weddings and baby showers when I was miserably single. I tried to be honest or humorous about my envy, blurting out, "I'm happy for you, but I feel jealous and totally deserted." When my friend Rachel, an MBA, made a mint on a best-selling self-help book, I dropped her the note, "Mazel tov on having a mega-hit on your first try. I'll try to forgive you."

But my comrades weren't acting open or funny. One kept inviting me to parties where she'd hand me joints and drinks, no matter how many times I said I'd quit. Others dropped off novels and memoirs for me to edit without asking, expecting me to pass their work on to my agent and editor. When I said no, they blew up or blew me off. I wasn't used to being resented. In my twenties, workshop cohorts had built me up and hooked me up, helping me get into the game. By middle age, I needed permission to compete in the big leagues, colleagues to celebrate with me and show me how to keep up the pace. After working so hard for so long, I wasn't going to feel guilty for finally getting what I wanted, and I penned a piece for an anthology called *Quitting Guilt*.

Ruth, who'd always been smoke- drug- and alcohol-free, was the most proud of my penchant for clean living and the tiny acclaim my memoirs received. She had a busy, joyful life and lots of memoirs of her own, so she didn't begrudge me a few hard-won hardcovers or five minutes on *The Today Show*. She wasn't conflicted or ambivalent; she was simply thrilled for me. She said to ignore any negative or mixed reactions. It wasn't the least bit personal, she said. It was just that work difficulties and financial frustrations made it hard for some colleagues to act generous. She'd been there before and had a better perspective. Fifteen years after we met, Ruth turned out to be my ideal mentor, after all.

On her suggestion, I invited everyone who'd been important to the group from the start to return for the final Tuesday night session. Everybody showed up. Reporters and photographers from *The New York Times* and *Forward* came to cover the last workshop, a historic-seeming occasion. Yet the press coverage exacerbated the conflicts. Someone was mad that one of the papers ran a picture of me and not the group. I didn't appreciate the member who said, "I thought Sue would keep it going until she was on her deathbed," and another who told a reporter, "Sue is a cult of personality," making me sound like a moonie. Some were annoyed that the *Times* reporter cited young Molly's first novel as one of the books the workshop had nurtured, but not Ruth's historical memoir. I didn't like the quote Ruth gave, about how her book editor forbade her to workshop her fourteenth book, worried that the group would have time-consuming suggestions that would lead to a missed deadline. Especially because Ruth wound up joining one of the four spin-off workshops, the one led by Gerry, where she was going over her next project.

I never joined any of the spin-offs, but I wished them well. I was relieved to not have to rush around, xeroxing, cleaning up, and making popcorn every Tuesday. I kept in touch with everyone, and Isabel and I planned a dinner to celebrate Ruth's ninety-second birthday. When word got around, more people wanted to attend – as was often the case with Ruth's events. She was amazingly popular. Everybody felt like they were her best friend. Soon we had twenty-five people, including a few of my students who barely knew Ruth but wanted to get close to her.

"I thought it was going to be an intimate little dinner," complained Mary, one of her contemporaries. "Now it's all these strangers. Ruth won't like it."

"Oh, Ruth will love it. She likes being around young people," I argued.

"The more, the merrier! Bring your students! Bring everyone!" Ruth confirmed.

It was another lesson Ruth taught me: Befriending younger people keeps you hipper, in the loop, up on everything from pop culture to current slang. I made a point of inviting more of my protégés to accompany me to book parties and readings, and I tried to show up to events they'd invited me to. I found their hopeful, hyper energy invigorating. My pupils got off on my acclaim, which they expected and welcomed; the uneven dynamic was what they were paying for. It was different from my workshop colleagues. Contemporaries who were on my level or further along had felt jolted when I'd started publishing books and changed the status quo.

After a fun dinner at an Italian café in Ruth's neighborhood, she invited us back to her place. The twenty-year-olds walked around, asking about the artifacts and photo gallery of Ruth with Golda Meir, Moshe Dayan, President Roosevelt, and the Clintons. Ruth answered their questions as they sat at her feet in awe.

"She needs fresh blood. They're the only ones who haven't heard these stories before," Mary joked.

Isabel and I sat in the corner, watching Ruth in action. While Isabel had worked as Ruth's assistant, she'd also questioned Ruth's practice of editing out the negative. As a truth-seeking poet with a difficult, divorced family, Isabel didn't share Ruth's sunny take on everything. But instead of looking at it as denial, Isabel concluded, "Ruth is a diplomat, very aware and protective of her legacy. If she's the one to write the official record of her life, then she controls her own story."

That was something else Ruth and I had in common — we were control freaks. Was that why we preferred first person? We'd both grown up with three opinionated brothers and had trouble getting the floor at family dinners. Becoming writers was a way to insist we were heard, and that our words counted. I understood censoring out dark secrets, but it still seemed odd to deny facts that were public knowledge.

"Ruth's family, friends, colleagues, and the writing group already know about her first marriage. Aren't marriage certificates part of official records?" I asked. "Any biographer would have access to the facts."

"If she keeps writing memoirs, there won't be the need for a biography," Isabel said with a laugh.

We agreed the self-portrait of a brave working woman with flaws would be more helpful and inspiring than the image of a female Jewish saint. But were Isabel and I imposing our modern confessional bias on our illustrious – yet conservative – mentor?

Just then my friend Ilya complimented Ruth on the bright pillows decorating her round living room couches. They looked familiar. When Ruth said they were handmade by the Ethiopian Israeli friends she met when she'd written *Rescue*, I recalled that the same colorful figures had graced the cover of her 1987 book, the one I'd reviewed for *The New York Times*, the reason Ruth and I had met. She was displaying so many pillows because she was selling them for a good cause for $30 each. It seemed sweet and frugal that on her ninety-second birthday, she was doing charity work for Israel.

To thank me for introducing them to this Jewish journalism goddess, my students pitched in to buy me one with a dark-skinned Joseph wearing an amazing coat of bright orange, blue, red, green, purple, and yellow. Ruth's dress that night had the same colors. I went to take my pillow, but Ruth pulled out the inside. "Just the pillowcase," she said, going to another room to replace the handmade cover. Man, she had a whole pillow factory for the Holy Land happening here!

At home I tried to slip the Ethiopian art over my other pillows, but they were the wrong size. What good was an artistic pillowcase without a pillow? The next day I ran to Kmart, buying one in the right size. Aaron took a shine to Ruth's *Joseph and the Amazing*

Technicolor Dreamcoat design, so the Falasha biblical pillow art now resides on the couch in his den.

Ruth's book *Inside of Time*, published in 2003 and subtitled "A Memoir with Eleanor Roosevelt, Harold L. Ickes, Golda Meir, and Other Friends," told of her experiences with these notables. It provided the inspiration for my book about my own mentors. I called Ruth, who was flattered I wanted to write about her. She gave me a long interview over the phone, confirming dates and quotes. When she asked me my title, I made the mistake of sharing my tentative moniker, *Lies My Mentors Told Me*.

"What a terrible title!" she said. "You have to change it."

Former workshop people felt forever entitled to critique your projects, whether you asked for their opinion or not. I didn't want comments on my title; I liked it. "It's a play off the old movie *Lies My Father Told Me*," I told her.

"I don't want to be in a book about lies," Ruth snapped.

I explained that my book, like her book, would pay tribute to my teachers, role models, and heroes. The title was just a conceit so it wouldn't come off syrupy sweet.

She told me that she didn't want her book about meeting her idol, Virginia Woolf, to be syrupy sweet either. She'd first told the juicy story in *Ahead of Time* about how she'd written her Ph.D. thesis on Virginia Woolf, then met her, and then – half a century later – found comments Woolf had written about Ruth in her diary. Woolf had called Ruth a "German Jewess" and a "pure have yer," which turned out to be disparaging and anti-Semitic. Interestingly, the slurs didn't ruin Ruth's admiration of Woolf's work.

"I'm calling the book *Virginia Woolf: Her Will to Create as a Woman*," Ruth said.

"I remember that story and love it. But I don't love your title," I confessed, though she hadn't asked for my opinion, either.

In April 2007, I joined five hundred people to celebrate the 95-year-old Ruth's 19th book, *Witness*. She asked about my mentor project, which I'd sold to Seal Press. The imprint was owned by the same company as Carol & Graf, who'd published her Virginia Woolf book, a coincidence I saw as a good omen.

"Did you get rid of your old title? It sucks," she told me.

"It doesn't suck," I said, amused she'd picked up my vernacular.

"You have to change it. You can't use the word 'lies,' because I'm not a liar. And don't use *Tricks My Mentors Taught Me*, 'cause I'm not a trickster.... I came up with a better title for you. You should call it *Friends and Mentors I Love*."

Asinine

MICHAEL
ANDERSON

"This is Michael Anderson from *The New York Times Book Review*," the serious-sounding male voice told my answering machine that Thursday afternoon in August 1989. "Are you available for a rush assignment over the weekend?" He left his phone number.

I'd written several three-hundred-word "In Short" critiques for different editors at the *Book Review* but didn't recognize his name. How many editors were there? Like *The New Yorker*, it had no masthead, a choice that kept the public at bay and gave the impression that its staff was an elitist secret society only insiders understood. Editors there seemed to pass around freelancers the way high school football players passed around easy cheerleaders. But his cold call thrilled me; it meant that somebody must have told him I was good!

I called him back to say yes, even though I had plans to spend the weekend in the Hamptons with my then-boyfriend, George. I realized that I'd rather stay in the sweltering city to read a book and write a three-hundred-word *Times* review by Monday morning than spend a randy weekend at the beach. Hell, I'd even cancel my upcoming three-week vacation for this byline. (I'd once read that the definition of an intellectual was someone who'd found something more exciting in life than sex.) For a young Manhattanite with literary aspirations, the *Book Review* was God.

"I'm free and available. I would be honored to do a rush assignment for you, Mr. Anderson," I told him.

"Good, because we're really under the gun here. This Little, Brown hardcover just showed up without warning, with a pub date in two and a half weeks."

He was telling me more than the other assigning editors usually did, acting as if I'd know what this info meant. Was saying it was a Little, Brown hardcover a code that meant it had a prestigious pedigree, so treat it well? Did sending me a book with a publication date in two and a half weeks mean that the publisher had submitted it to the *Book Review* late? Why? Wasn't that a faux pas? He sounded as if he knew me.

"Have we met before?" I asked.

"No, I just started here in July," he said.

"Really? Welcome!" I said. Good, he wouldn't know I was a *Times* neophyte, since he was even greener than I was. "Are you from New York?"

"Originally from Chicago," he answered.

"Did you get my name from Mr. Levitas?" He was the *Book Review* editor who'd called last time, the one my colleague Gerry had given my name to.

"No, from Becky," he said.

Becky? It took me a minute to get that he was referring to Rebecca Sinkler, the *Book Review*'s editor in chief, though for some reason the staff just called the person in their top spot "the editor," which confused me because there were a dozen editors there. Since I was fairly new to book reviewing and to the *Times*, I was thrilled that "Becky" even knew my name. Had she noticed the other short reviews of mine they'd published? How cool was that? Getting back to business, Mr. Anderson assigned me a review of Harrison E. Salisbury's new book, *Tiananmen Diary*. Could I get him a thousand words by Monday morning?

"Of course. Thank you, sir," I said, completely stunned. Harrison Salisbury was not only a Pulitzer Prize–winning journalist, but he wrote for *The New York Times!* So they were trusting me with a *Times* icon — one who was chronicling an important political tragedy. The massacre of Chinese students had taken place three months before. That explained Little, Brown's rush to publish the first book on the subject. But why was *The Times* giving a girl who described herself as an expert on Jewish topics, feminism, and poetry a long review of a prominent book on China?

I'd written three-thousand-word pieces for *Cosmopolitan* and *Glamour*. But the most words I'd ever been assigned by the *Times* was three hundred (about one double-spaced typed page), so a thousand words was triple my normal length. Mr. Anderson got the book to me within the hour. They'd never paid a messenger to get me a book before. I should have suggested that I could go up to 43rd Street and get it, but I was so nervous I forgot to offer.

Since working eighty-hour weeks was bringing in less than $20,000 a year, and 90 percent of my submissions to editors were still being rejected, I'd been worried that I'd chosen the wrong profession and didn't have thick-enough skin to make it as a writer in New York. I feared that I should have listened to my father, who said it wasn't too late to apply to law school and learn how to make a real living. Hungry for any sign of hope, I viewed this call from this new man I'd never met to be a major promotion, a surprise vote of confidence, an incredible omen from the writing gods. I felt like I'd finally made it, like my life now justified the LOCAL GIRL MAKES GOOD T-shirt my Michigan pal Andrea had sent. Did Mr. Anderson, a Chicago native, know I was also from the Midwest? My beloved little brother's name was Michael, so his name had good karma. Whoever this editor with a deep, serious voice who was saving my career was, I felt eternally grateful. It was a good way to meet a new mentor.

I remember his call came on August 10, 1989, on my father's birthday. I'd already phoned my dad to wish him a happy fifty-seventh year that morning. The minute after I hung up the phone with Mr. Anderson, I called my parents in Michigan again.

"This new editor at the *Times Book Review* just gave me a rush assignment for a major book!" I shrieked into the receiver.

"That's wonderful, dear," my mother said. "Jack, a new editor just gave your daughter a rush assignment for the *Times Book Review*."

"Which book are you reviewing?" my dad asked, picking up the line.

"He just assigned me *Tiananmen Square*, the new book from the Pulitzer Prize-winning journalist Harrison Salisbury! Can you believe it?"

There was silence. "Do you even know where China is?" my father asked.

"Jack! That's not a nice thing to say to your daughter! What the hell's wrong with you?" my mother yelled at him.

"Why would they give her a book on China?" he asked.

I guessed it was jealousy on the part of my father — a history buff who'd practically memorized Salisbury's *The Long March*, *The 900 Days*, and *The Great Black Dragon Fire* and tried to get me to read them, to no avail. In fact we'd had arguments over what he judged as my horrible taste, since I preferred such literary genres as confessional poetry, memoirs, essay collections, magic realism, and great, bawdy, in-your-face novels like *Herzog, Portnoy's Complaint,* and *Fear of Flying.*

I admit that I'd also been asking myself why *The Times* gave me a book on China, but I guessed that most Manhattan critics were out of town on August weekends. And of the few freelancers left in the sweltering city, they'd chosen me because I'd done a terrific job on Ruth Gruber's book on Ethiopia and Israel, so the editors probably assumed I was an expert on international nonfiction. Plus, I'd handed in my other reviews within twenty-four hours, so they knew I could turn around copy fast. (I wasn't the smartest, so I figured I'd stand out as the quickest.) I handed in pages with perfect grammar and no spelling or punctuation mistakes. That was because I brought my rough drafts to the writing group, where Gerry Jonas would edit my assignments before I turned them in.

I nixed the Hamptons jaunt with George, who wasn't pleased. He decided to go anyway, but I didn't care. I had a higher calling. I rushed out to get supplies for a few all-nighters in a row: six-packs of Tab, packs of menthol cigarettes, and extra paper, typewriter ribbons, and erasers, since I was still using my trusty IBM Selectric. At my desk, I gently caressed my Holy Grail — a skinny, tacky-looking little book with *Tiananmen Diary* in red lettering and

Thirteen Days in June in yellow, the picture of four tanks on the cover above the name Harrison E. Salisbury.

Luckily the book was very short, 178 pages. I read it in a few hours. Though I sucked at math, science, and history, I had strong reading and comprehension skills. I'd helped my schoolmate Nicole translate her academic thesis into colloquial English to get her book published, and I had recently edited my friend Terry's article on leverage buyouts and helped him sell it to *The Wall Street Journal*, though I had no idea what LBOs were. But I just wasn't understanding this day-to-day diary by Salisbury. He explained that through an astonishing coincidence, he'd been in China, along with a camera crew, to make a television documentary about the fortieth anniversary of the People's Republic of China. He'd witnessed the slaughter of Tiananmen Square students from his window at the Beijing Hotel, where his room overlooked Changan Avenue, a major boulevard leading into the square. I read his account again. Aside from describing the military action he could see out his window, he interwove interviews he'd conducted later with local workers, plus newscasts, historical analysis, maps, and diary jottings. It was terribly confusing. I tried to draw a timeline of the events, but contradictions abounded. I feared I was stupid and not getting it, that the subject and author were way over my head.

Friday at 7:00 PM, I rushed to the library to look up Salisbury's previous books *Orbit of China, Behind the Lines – Hanoi, China: One*

Hundred Years of Revolution, The Great Black Dragon Fire. They were much more lucid. I xeroxed pages from the relevant chapters, along with encyclopedia articles on China and newspaper microfilm accounts of exactly what had happened in Tiananmen Square in June. Comparing them to Salisbury's book, I was at sea again.

I had a career-making assignment in my hands, yet I was choking. I wouldn't be able to call Mr. Anderson for advice until Monday, when it would be too late to make my deadline. Gerry, my fantasy writer father, was out of town and it was too late to call him at midnight, anyway. Instead I phoned my real dad, a night owl like me. I blurted out my problem, expecting him to say, "I told you so." But he was pleased that I was asking his opinion and agreed to help. I read him a few passages that confused me and asked, "What does this mean?"

"Arterior sclerotic dementia, I'd guess," he said.

"What?"

"How old is Salisbury?" he asked.

"About eighty," I said. "What are you talking about?"

"The onset of dementia. There's fifty different kinds. Could be Alzheimer's, strokes, alcohol. Does he drink? Don't all journalists drink?"

"Dad, don't diagnose him!" I screamed, sure that my father was making fun of me during my deadline crunch. "Please just tell me what that passage means."

"It doesn't mean anything," my father said. "It's a mishmash. He seems old, sleep deprived, out of it, and confused."

"Really? That's what I thought! But then I was afraid I was missing something." I lit a cigarette.

"Trust your own judgment," said my father, lighting his cigarette; I could hear him inhale long-distance.

"I can't write that it's a mishmash," I lamented. "I can't trash a famous eighty-year-old journalist's book in the newspaper that made him famous."

"Maybe that's why they gave the book to you," my father said. "They figured you'd be young, malleable, and afraid to kill it."

"Dad, stop insulting me."

"I'm not insulting you," he said.

"Look, it's the biggest assignment I've ever had, and it's from this new editor, so I can't screw up. It's not a horrible book. He's got the angle right politically — trashing China's corrupt, scared, and geriatric leadership. He's sympathetic to the students. He asked a Chinese supporter of democracy 'What's the news today?' The man replied, 'The news is that one point one billion hearts are dead.'"

"So use that quote and make your piece mostly about what happened in Tiananmen Square," my father threw out. "Like all those boring professors who use the *Book Review* as a platform for their own issues. At the end you can stick in that the author was in too much of a rush."

Well, when had Dr. Disease become such an expert at book reviewing?

"Thanks, Daddy," I said.

I spent the weekend piecing together what happened from the newspaper reports and weaving in Chinese history from Salisbury's other books. As my father suggested, I trusted my gut and threw in criticism toward the end, trying to be honest but kind: "Mr. Salisbury's firsthand account is written in a fast-paced, chaotic, and colloquial style, which often feels confused and hastily set down. Rushed into print, the book lacks coherence, an overarching synthesis, yet in the end the material is so fascinating and important, the rush seems justified." I ended by citing specifics that lent the volume flavor and authority and with the purple quote about hearts dying.

I faxed in my typed copy early Monday. Then I called to apologize to Mr. Anderson that it came to 1,500 words, longer than he wanted. He expounded on the importance of keeping one's work tight and succinct, quoting Samuel Johnson, who said, "I'm sorry I'm writing you a long letter, I didn't have time to write you a short one." I feared I'd screwed up, and assumed my piece would be cut to shreds. I waited for him to call me for three and a half weeks. But the call didn't come. He never said whether he liked the review. I expected the worst.

So I was astonished one warm Wednesday to get the mail and find an early copy of the September 10 *Book Review*, which included fifteen hundred of my words, with hardly any edits, under the headline "Present at the Suppression." One week later, I received a check for $350, the most I'd made from the *Times* thus far. I sent the clip to every editor I'd ever met and several who had previously turned me down — from *The Washington Post, Boston Globe, Village Voice,* and *US Weekly.* They soon all gave me assignments. I felt launched!

Unfortunately, as the professional rejections started to wane, personal rejections still had the power to floor me. I found out that George was having an affair with a wannabe actress and we broke up. I thought our different levels of ambition had doomed the relationship and debated whether I shouldn't have canceled that weekend in the Hamptons. But being honest with myself, I had to admit that I'd pick being in the *Book Review* over a boyfriend any day. (No wonder I wound up married to a writer who was a worse workaholic than I was. Interestingly, when I finally gave up book reviewing, Aaron started reviewing sports books and thrillers for the *Book Review*.)

After a few more assignments, I asked Mr. Anderson to lunch. He insisted that I call him Michael, and that he'd treat. We met at a diner near his office in Times Square. I'd envisioned a sixty-year-old, tweedy, rumpled, white, married dad from Connecticut, like my other newspaper editors. I was surprised to find a single, tall, thin, good-looking, bespectacled thirty-eight-year-old African American Manhattanite. He had a baby face, like a young Samuel Jackson, with a bit of his swagger. He wore a snazzy gray three-piece suit.

I felt too casual in my jeans, T-shirt, and cowboy boots, but then again, I'd become a freelancer so I wouldn't have to dress for an uptown office.

When I asked about his background, he gave me two- or three-word answers. It took several more conversations to get any juicy details out of him. Eventually I cobbled together his biography. He was the only child of a middle-class family from the south side of Chicago, in a neighborhood called West Chesterfield. His father worked for the post office. His mother worked for the State of Illinois Department of Labor. They divorced when he was an infant. Upon prodding, he said that his mother had remarried a man with three sons. He liked having brothers and a stepfather, but that marriage also ended in divorce and he didn't keep in touch with his stepfamily.

I invited him out to lunch again several times, but he declined. Whenever he'd call to give me assignments, I'd sneak in personal questions about his background, which authors he liked best, whether he was going home for Thanksgiving, if he had plans for Valentine's Day. Most of my colleagues were open and out there, like me. But Mr. Anderson ignored my intrusive inquiries, which drove me nuts. What was he hiding?

It wasn't until a few years later, when he allowed my journalism class to interview him for a profile, that he revealed more interesting personal tidbits: He'd learned to read at an early age, before he was three. He recalled his mother reading the *Chicago Tribune* and, later in life, the Sunday *New York Times*. Seeing *A Raisin in the Sun* on TV had profoundly moved him. He earned his BA from the Medill School of Journalism at Northwest University. Right out of college, he took a job as a cub reporter at the *Chicago Sun-Times*.

The most lit up I ever saw him was when he chronicled his first assignment: covering a mass murder. He froze at the scene, not knowing what to do. Luckily, the seasoned photographer assigned to the story saw his fear and took the rookie under his wing. He became an assistant professor of journalism at Northwestern when he was twenty-eight. His mother and grandmother passed away in the same two-year period. In 1984, he moved to California and worked for both the *Los Angeles Herald Examiner* and the *Los Angeles Times* before taking the offer from the *Book Review* on July 5, 1989, about a month before he'd first called me.

One day when I phoned to beg Michael for another assignment, he asked me about my writing workshop. Apparently Gerry, the *Book Review*'s longtime science fiction columnist, had told him all about our Tuesday night club. I invited Michael to come sit in. He didn't want to attend the whole session, but in the early 1990s, he started making cameo appearances at our Christmas potluck dinners and summer parties. A well-dressed, smart, single editor at the *Times* was popular with my freelance posse, and he ended up giving work to several members. Along with the workshop carpenter, mover, and accountant, it seemed apt to share a *Book Review* editor.

The females didn't pitch him article ideas; they often pitched themselves. At first, I had a bit of a crush on the mysterious, tall, and dashing Mr. Anderson, too. But I never told him or acted on it. I wanted to publish more in the *Times* and wasn't interested in "sleeping my way to the middle" (to steal an old line of Aaron's). I was having better luck with editors than suitors and didn't need to double the peril and risk my steady stream of bylines. Meanwhile, I'd been dating Hal, the charming playwright and poet from the group, and I was a serial monogamist. Plus, I didn't want to be one of those left-wing white woman who only dated men of different races to prove their liberal cred.

Michael was barely interested in me anyway, even as a bimonthly book critic. I envisioned him wanting a partner with the resume of Lanie Guinier who looked like Halle Berry. He wound up dating a woman from my writing group for six months, a skinny blond, the only female to wear miniskirts and high heels to the workshop. I wished I could say she was an idiot or groupie, but she was a globe-trotting archaeologist who published short stories in prestigious journals. Michael never once mentioned her to me, but a grapevine of disapproving workshop femmes fed me the gossip. Half were outraged at his taste (think: Arthur Miller and Marilyn), the other half worried she was too cold and didn't deserve him. We were all relieved it didn't last long.

I kept milking my *Book Review* clips, which continued to open doors. An editor at *People* assigned me *The New Emperors: China in the Era of Mao and Deng* by Harrison Salisbury. It was much more coherent than *Tiananmen Square*, perhaps because it rehashed the history he'd already written in his prize-winning earlier books. I called Michael to tell him about the assignment, adding that my first Salisbury review had probably made the editor think I was a China expert. He didn't sound so amused. I figured he wasn't impressed with my landing a clip in *People*, which he'd consider lowbrow.

An essay I published in *New Woman* magazine was optioned by a Hollywood producer for $2,000. The agent who handled the deal suggested I expand the story into a novel. I brought in chapter by chapter to the writing group, which gave me good feedback. Michael agreed to read the first draft. His criticism was negative and curt. He just said it didn't work. It needed reshaping, rethinking, and "a lot of cutting." I didn't believe him until a year later, when the agent faxed me rejection letters from all the major publishing houses. Even the editors who'd loved the story and humor ultimately said, "It just doesn't work." After several rewrites, the agent pretty much dumped me.

I lumped this latest disaster in with my disappointments from *Newsday*, *The New Yorker*, and my failed poetry book, feeling like a loser, "catastrophizing," as one self-help author called it. I embarked on a particularly depressing dry spell. Months went by when I couldn't get work. Then a friend offered me a $60,000-a-year job at his medical advertising firm. Although I wasn't sure which was a worse fit for me – copyediting or medicine – I mentioned it to Michael. He ordered me uptown to lunch that day. Crying, I poured out my whole saga about how I couldn't publish my novel. Agents and editors no longer returned my calls. I'd screwed up everything and felt like I should hang it up.

"Taking an advertising job you don't want would be idiotic. You're a writer," he said. "Nobody said this field was easy. But you have what it takes. There's no doubt that you'll make it."

"Really?" I sniffled.

"Yes, really," he handed me a Kleenex. "You're doing very well for your age. You've already been published in prestigious places, and your work is improving. It would be stupid to give up now. You have to be more patient."

He didn't say I was talented or special, or define what "make it" meant, but his conviction reenergized me. Like my father, Michael rarely offered compliments. I worried that being so raw, insecure, and pathetic around him would alienate him completely, but it had the opposite effect. He became more gentle, responding warmly to my vulnerability and making me feel soothed and safe.

He underscored his encouragement by handing me four books to review that day. Although he wanted only three hundred words on each book, I took it as a huge declaration: *The New York Times* loves you; it will protect you. He told me to use his name to try other editors at the newspaper but to show him my submissions first. I did, and he line edited, cutting extra words, cursing "the disease of American writing, verbosity." Soon my byline was appearing in other sections of the paper. I never considered advertising again, and I made a rule not to ever submit my work anywhere without having a tough editor go over every word first.

A few months later, I thanked Michael for helping me through such a rough time. He pretended he didn't recall my lunch full of weeping. Then he claimed he had done nothing remarkable. "It was obvious you weren't going to work in medical advertising," he said. "You kept saying that you could never understand the technical jargon, even though your father was a doctor. I don't think your conflict was about the job."

Wow – I hadn't been conscious of the connection to my father. How did Michael know that's what the conflict was really about? Maybe I feared the advertising job was the last chance I'd have to communicate with my dad, to share words or a field we could talk about. Having Michael, another father substitute, understand, speak my language, and "save me" was healing.

Coincidentally, Michael gave me another chance to share professional turf with my father. It was after a workshop buddy had recommended me for a job as the head researcher for Laurence Bergreen's 1994 biography *Capone: The Man and the Era*. The noted gangster had died of syphilis, one of my father's favorite subjects ever since he'd worked as a venereal disease control officer for the public health department in St. Louis in 1961. Dad used to joke that they'd stamped out an outbreak of syphilis in Louisiana by making a local bar offer a free beer with each penicillin shot. Instead of being conceived in romantic New York City, I had to make my debut in the state where my daddy was a VD official.

Larry Bergreen happened to be doing Capone research in Michigan that August, when I was visiting my family. So I invited him to come over for lunch. One mention that Capone had the "S-word," and Dad launched into a long, gross monologue on the affliction. "See, in the least harmful stage of syphilis, a boil or an open sore, teeming with spirochetes, a screwlike organism, appears on the genitalia," Dad shared gleefully, running to get a medical tome for visual aid, showing pictures of an open wound on a penis. "But the third stage becomes a form of dementia where the disease attacks the frontal lobes of the brain. . . . "

My father became the book's medical consultant. In his acknowledgments, Larry thanked me for being an "invaluable researcher." He also wrote, "Dr. Jack Shapiro contributed a great deal to my understanding of Capone's syphilis, as well as the social climate surrounding the disease. Capone's cocaine habit, an important aspect of his life in the 1920s, has been overlooked until Dr. Shapiro examined the medical records and brought it to my attention." My father got more lines of thanks than I did. At first I was thrilled. Then I was jealous. After the *Book Review* ran a long, positive piece on the bio by Robert Sabbag, my father called me, annoyed. "Larry got the reason for Capone's perforation of the nasal septum right. But the reviewer got it wrong," he said.

"Got what wrong?" I asked, trying to follow.

"Susie, look at the review!" he instructed. "The perforation of Capone's nasal septum was not due to syphilis, as Sabbag wrote. It was due to cocaine use, as I told Larry and he wrote in the book. See, perforation of the nasal septum is a common feature of late congenital syphilis but an uncommon feature of the late-acquired syphilis Capone had. Septal perforation due to cocaine results from topical, local vasoconstrictive action of cocaine, which shuts down the blood supply to areas of the nasal septum the drug touches. Since cartilage doesn't regenerate, the perforation doesn't heal."

"What?" He'd lost me after "perforation."

"The inflammatory response is ischemic necrosis! Give me your *Book Review* editor's name. I'm going to call him," my father yelled, as if he wanted to scold an intern who'd misdiagnosed one of his patients.

"Dad, you can't call him. If you write a letter to the editor, I'll get it to him."

At first it was cool to get my father involved in the making of a book, but I'd created a monster. When I transcribed my father's two-page handwritten scrawl, the medical jargon seemed incoherent. The last paragraph read, "The description of Capone's nasal septum by the examining physician, the normal sinus x-rays, plus the lack of clinical problems associated with the finding strongly suggests occasional cocaine use as the most logical etiology. Incidentally, I have also observed nasal septal perforation as a result of chronic snuff use (nicotine vasoconstriction), repeated trauma to the septum (nose picker's ulcer), chronic chrome fume inhalation, sarcodisis, and repeated tight anterior nasal packing (pressure necrosis)." He signed it "Jack Shapiro, MD, St. Louis City Health Department venereal disease control officer," still proud of this thirty-year-old label. Embarrassed that this medical mishmash was written by someone to whom I was genetically linked, I nonetheless did my daughterly duty and sent it to Michael.

"We love your dad's letter," he called to tell me.

"Really?" I asked. "Can you understand a word of it?"

"Of course we can. It's a great letter. We're running it next week."

Michael printed my father's response to the Capone piece in the same issue in which I had an "In Brief" review, so we were in the same magazine. It made me feel much closer to my father, as if our minds were touching.

After critiquing five Holocaust books in a row, I had Nazi nightmares and needed to lighten up. I begged Michael for poetry, to no avail. I'd been publishing comical first-person pieces, so I talked him into giving me humor collections. Initially he acted as if the genre were beneath the *Book Review,* but eventually he acquiesced and I got to do Al Franken, Dennis Miller, Cynthia Heimel, and the comedian Sandra Bernhard. I thought a review should reflect the author's voice, but Michael edited heavily. We had different senses of humor and he slashed all my cute jokes and wordplays. My piece on Steve Martin's book *Pure Drivel* originally ended: "Although it's doubtful this work would have been published with such fanfare had Martin not been a famous performer, one is also pleasantly surprised that a Hollywood star can write more than pure drivel." When the review ran, the last line was, "It's humor raised to the level of abstraction." I knew editors had the right to change my work. But since my name was on the page, I argued that Michael should show me changes before they ran. He eventually agreed.

After a few refreshing humorous reads, he started sneaking me Jews again. I objected and pleaded for poetry, but he said, "The most poetic and profound lines you ever write are about Judaism." In high school, Jack Zucker also used to say that my best poetry was about my kooky Hebrew relatives. When my students were confused about which of their work they should be revising, I told them, "Follow your poetry," meaning the best lines in a piece often indicated where the heart was and which direction to continue. But I later learned that most writers had no idea where their poetry was and often desperately needed guidance from editors, agents, mentors, and teachers.

Not that those relationships were easy. I was pleased to be assigned essays by Katha Pollitt, a provocative left-wing essayist and poet whose poetry class I'd once taken and enjoyed. You're not supposed to review the book of someone you know, and you never lie to your editor (which is worse than lying to your lover or shrink). So I disclosed that I was a Pollitt admirer who'd once been her student. Michael said it wasn't a problem, since most writers taught and it wasn't fair to punish them for it. I argued that her book deserved more space. He said the work had been previously published, so the higher-ups had decided on the three-hundred-word length.

Pollitt's entertaining, albeit biting, treatise trashed fellow feminists Camille Paglia, Carol Gilligan, Katie Roiphe, Sylvia Ann Hewlett, Deborah Fallows, Judith Wallerstein, Nancy Chodorow, Ann Crittenden, and Sara Ruddick for quoting inadequate studies or misinterpreting data. But Pollitt added such sweeping provocative statements as, "Wives describe themselves as less happy than do married men or single women . . . and they are much more likely than single women to be clinically depressed," and, "according to a *Woman's Day* survey, only 50 percent of wives say they would marry their husband again." I was dismayed to find no index or footnotes. So at the end of my otherwise stellar thirty-two lines, I added one nit. "Although she criticizes others for shoddy data, Ms. Pollitt's own statistics are not carefully annotated." I ended with, "Still, this is a small oversight in an otherwise cunning and complex collection."

The day after my Pollitt piece ran (cut to twenty-four lines, eight lines shorter than my original), a *New York Observer* reporter called me, quoting an angry letter Pollitt had written to the *Book Review*'s editor, Rebecca Sinkler, that the *Observer* had obtained. Pollitt trashed me as a ridiculous choice of reviewer and raged against my every word, though most of them were laudatory. "I did not expect that twenty years of reviewing for the *Times* would protect me from a bad review," she wrote. "But I guess I did think that you would not print vague, unsubstantiated, and reputation-damaging charges against someone who . . . you trusted enough to assign some fairly important books."

I was hurt that someone I admired hated my basically flattering, fair review. Yet I'd been a journalist long enough to know not to snivel or argue in print, especially to the scandal-hungry *Observer.* "My review was positive," I said simply, and then made sure to add, "I'm a huge fan of hers."

I called Michael, who conceded there'd been a stink about my review and asked me to document my points. I spent the day listing the numerous authors Pollitt had taken to task in her 186 pages. Then I listed all the sweeping generalities and surveys she cited without direct quotes, dates, magazine issues, page numbers, or any other facts that one could look up. I faxed it to him and then called him back, depressed that Pollitt had misinterpreted my review and ignored my praise. I'd inadvertently insulted an important *Times* writer and was nervous that the *Book Review* would hate my guts and never hire me again. I was paranoid I'd made Michael look bad to his bosses. But he said this kind of dumb argument happened there all the time.

"Don't worry about it. You handed in a good review. You're not even the one she's angry with," Michael consoled.

"I'm not?" I was confused. "Who is?"

"She's angry the editor didn't run a two-thousand-word rave by Gloria Steinem on the cover."

If it were up to me, I would have assigned Steinem a two-thousand-word cover piece on Pollitt's book. The *Book Review* did seem sexist, with mostly male authors and reviewers, despite its current female editor. "It was a good review," I repeated. "I called her funny and furious, said she has razor-sharp wit, was cunning and complex."

"Writers are never satisfied with their reviews, even the good ones," he explained. "Don't you know that by now?"

Again I found Michael's reassurance calming. I later wrote Pollitt a note, saying I was sorry to hear she'd misinterpreted my review and reiterating that I'd always been a fan of her work. To her credit, she wrote me back, admitting that she was upset that the *Times* didn't do her book justice. I felt further vindicated when someone anonymously sent me the *Publishers Weekly* review of her collection that said, "One wishes only that Pollitt had taken the occasion of book publication to supply the sources of her data or to direct the reader to the salient passages in the works she cites." Her paperback had part of my review on the back cover, alongside blurbs by Steinem and Susan Sontag. (Mine was the longest quote but had no name attached, just *"The New York Times Book Review."*)

My quotes landed on other book jackets, too. After I reviewed Al Franken's *Rush Limbaugh Is a Big Fat Idiot and Other Observations*, my "funny, angry, and intelligent" blurb wound up on the cover of his paperback. I felt like I was moving up in the world, but I was still not identified by name. Only the gorgeous photography book *Poyln: Jewish Life in the Old Country*, a National Jewish Book Award winner, quoted me on the cover *with* my moniker. It said: "Exquisitely detailed, haunting portraits of the lost world of Polish Jews." – Susan Shapiro, *The New York Times*." The Jews, whom I kept trying to avoid but whom Michael insisted I chronicled poetically, were the only ones to claim me.

I made the mistake of telling Michael I liked being quoted on paperbacks. "If you ever write something just to give a publicist a sound bite, you'll never work for me again," he threatened. He was always Mr. Moral and gave fascinating lectures to my NYU Journalism School classes on the ethics of the profession. He told them to steer clear of publicists and publicity, since being paid to write something positive, whether it was true or not, was the antithesis of what good journalists did. I was casual in class, wearing jeans, swearing, chewing gum. In contrast, Michael's suit, proud manner, and serious stance inspired one student to nickname him Abraham Lincoln.

He explained how more than a dozen *Book Review* editors chose twenty-five to thirty books a week from the almost two hundred thousand books published a year to be featured, and how pitching the *Book Review* was different from pitching other publications. It wielded so much power in the book world that you couldn't request a specific book, lest you loved, hated, shared an agent or editor with, or had slept with the author. So you had to pitch yourself and your expertise for titles they would choose. "Don't be afraid to send letters asking me for an assignment," he instructed my students. Several went for it, and he gave three of them book reviews that term. Word got around that he kept giving youngsters a shot. Having a whole bunch of pupils see print in the *Book Review* didn't hurt my reputation. My classes sometimes filled up months in advance. I was soon teaching two versions of the same feature writing class in a row, capping the number of students at twenty for each section and having waiting lists each term.

Though the $75 stipends I could pay my teachers were slowly raised to a whopping $100, Michael didn't care about the money and said he'd do it for free. I thanked him for his time, especially because he was now teaching his own Yale seminar on literary criticism. He said he wasn't doing it as a favor to me; he spoke at many NYU and Columbia classes, believing that part of working for such a significant institution involved encouraging educational study and meeting the public.

Carol, my redheaded friend from the soup kitchen, attended one of Michael's lectures and was awed. She sent him a candid letter about her past homelessness and poverty, with her clips from *The Forward*, *Cover* magazine, and *Wine Spectator*. He assigned her the memoir *Once a House of Fire*, a British women's story of violence, abuse, and poverty. Carol called it "mesmerizing, poetic, and filled with hope" in her review. I found Michael's perceptive assignment mesmerizing and poetic in itself.

Although he could come off as abrupt and harsh, Michael's sensitivity periodically peeked through. When I introduced him to Aaron, Michael deemed him "a good, sweet man" who "obviously adores you." Then, as if that were too emotional, Michael added, "And he's probably the only one who'll put up with you."

Aaron and Michael were the same age, and I was pleased when they bonded over their sports obsessions. I wasn't pleased when Michael sent Aaron a baseball book to review. Aaron was a notoriously slow writer who'd become a screenwriter because it was the only way he could earn a living. He spent four weeks on a three-hundred-word book review for $100, which I found a waste of his time. By now, spending twenty-four hours on a three-hundred-word review for $100 was a waste of *my* time. Aaron liked getting free books and getting paid to pontificate, but he promised he wouldn't make it a habit.

At my wedding, Michael hung out with Howard Fast, my mom,

and the *New York Times* Style reporter doing a "Vows" column on the event. When I later called him for work, he said, "Tell your husband to call me. I have another book for him." My spouse had enough work, I informed him. I was the book reviewer of the family! "Why? Don't you want your husband to support you?" Michael asked. It was so bizarrely chauvanistic, I was sure he was kidding. What better way to goad a proud feminist? He was kidding, wasn't he? I wasn't so sure.

His manner toward me appeared to change from supportive to sardonic. He once called me screaming that one of my idiotic students had sent him a pitch without her phone number or email address. He trashed me in front of my class, embarrassing me. I tried to make light of it. Most of my letters to him started with, "What an amusing parody of my phone message" and, "Thanks for telling me my lead sucks."

In early 2001, Michael sent me a posthumous Holocaust memoir by an Auschwitz survivor who'd blocked out the evil he'd witnessed in the camps. Fifty years later he dredged it up. After completing the book, the author had a heart attack and died. I was just turning forty, in the middle of a fierce midlife crisis that involved obsessively rehashing all of the decisions I'd made in my life. It seemed to me that the author's memory had killed him. I was enrapt, not with the atrocities of the Third Reich, but with the lines debating whether he should have relived all the pain he'd experienced. I took it as an omen: "Don't look back, the past can kill you." My review focused on the dilemma, the treacherous deep-sea dive of memory, the twisted search for vanished footsteps, the perils of digging too deep.

After I emailed it to Michael, his response was one word: "asinine." When I asked what was wrong with it, he explained that the book had been published in France three years before it came out in America. Well, how was I supposed to know that? It didn't say that on the galley. So memory hadn't killed him after all. It was an honest error, an interesting mistake, even. Had I wanted memory to kill him?

Surely I wasn't being asinine. Why did he keep suggesting I was incompetent, unintelligent, silly? I asked him where the hostility was coming from, but he pretended it was my imagination. His exaggerated insults appeared to indicate that he liked me better when I was weak, needy, and single. Did it bother Michael that I no longer needed him or treated him like a deity? Now that I was married, stronger, and more confident, he'd switched from good father to bad father. I'd introduced him to another (single and broke) female who idolized him, calling him "Mr. Anderson" and looking up to him as if he were God. He wasn't mean to her.

I used the "asinine" scene in my memoir *Five Men Who Broke My Heart*, when I was debating whether I should go back to meet the ex-lovers who'd hurt me most. Members of the workshop thought the editor character (whose name I changed) had come off as snidely amusing. When I sold the book, I offered to show him the lines about him in advance and alter anything he didn't like. He cryptically said he didn't care, that having a cameo in my book didn't affect him either way. I considered Michael an essential mentor, yet I didn't even know him well enough to determine if he was being honest or deceptive. I had no idea if he was angry or flattered that I'd written about him, or if something else was darkening his manner.

I told him all my secrets and problems; he never really confided in me. He'd mentioned that he moved from midtown to Washington Heights to a new apartment he described as "a hopeless mess" with "piles of material that seemed to sprout like fungus everywhere." Was it smaller than his other place? Did he dislike his new neighborhood? I learned from my colleague Barbara (another tall, skinny, white girl) that she'd dated Michael for a few months. Then it didn't work out. She volunteered that he'd been incredibly kind, but that she had two kids, was in the throes of a lousy divorce, and decided it was too soon to get serious with anybody. Had she broken his heart? Was being alone making him bitter? I'd found bliss with Aaron and wished Michael could find love, too. Being a sought-out bachelor at thirty-eight was different from spending your fifties alone. Did he resent that through the years my relationship status, career, and financial situation had changed while his didn't?

Sure, Michael's pithy "In Shorts" of baseball and basketball books ran in the *Book Review,* as did his long, impressive essays on James Baldwin and Richard Wright biographies, the latter on the cover. But otherwise his job had remained the same. Editor Becky

Sinkler left in 1995, replaced by Chip McGrath, who was followed by Sam Tanenhaus in 2004. New editors were hired above and below Michael, who hadn't been promoted. I guessed his irreverent attitude didn't make him team player of the year. After McGrath left the *Book Review*, I bumped into him at a party and asked what working with Michael day to day had been like.

"He was the most brilliant line editor there. His reviews were very impressive, too," McGrath offered.

"If he was so brilliant and impressive, why wasn't he chosen to take over when you left?" I asked bluntly. Since McGrath had switched from high-level *New Yorker* and *Book Review* editor to writer, I was no longer intimidated by him. In fact, he was doing articles while I had just published three books, so I wasn't an inadequate underling. The playing field seemed level.

"Michael was almost too critical," McGrath conceded. "Nothing could satisfy him or live up to his high standards."

"I've worked with him for years and love him. But I feel like I don't really know him. I've been trying to figure him out," I admitted. "He's told me a little about his past, so I assume that comes into play."

"Yes. Hard background. He was basically raised by his grandmother in Chicago," McGrath said.

Michael had never put it that way to me. I had the sense that he and his former boss were close in a reserved, overly cerebral, male kind of way.

"He's an enigma," I said.

"Yes." McGrath nodded. "Like Bartleby, the Scrivener."

"Who?"

"You haven't read *Bartleby?* By Melville?" McGrath appeared astonished by my ignorance. I'd read *Moby Dick* but not Melville's short fiction. I didn't point out that I had a degree in poetry, not fiction, but was glad he was no longer my boss or my boss's boss.

"So how do you like being a writer?" I switched the subject, wondering where the closest Barnes & Noble was.

"I wish I hadn't been an editor for so long. It's so much more fun to be a writer," McGrath told me.

"It's a harder life, though," I threw out.

"You think so?" He obviously didn't think so.

"Well, as a freelancer it takes a while to get steady work," I explained.

"My son started out as a staff writer," he said.

I realized that Chip had begun getting bylines as a contracted writer for the *Times*, while his son, Ben McGrath, began his career as a staff writer for *The New Yorker*. So much for level playing fields.

After McGrath walked away, I quickly befriended the brainy-looking guy in a bow tie standing next to the cheese tray, asking, "Who's Bartleby the Scrivener?"

"You haven't read *Bartleby?*" He looked as stunned as McGrath had.

"No. I haven't read *Bartleby,*" I confessed. "Does he have a difficult personality? Describe him."

"Meticulous. Hardworking. Amazingly stubborn. Impossible to manipulate," Mr. bow tie told me. "Whenever Bartleby's boss asks him to do something extra, he says, 'I would prefer not to.'"

I picked up a copy of Melville's short works at the Barnes & Noble on Fifth Avenue and 48th Street, signing seven copies of my book while I was there. (It was a new publicity trick I'd learned: When you signed copies of your books, some bookstores would put a SIGNED BY THE AUTHOR sticker on them and place them on a prominent table so they'd sell faster. Plus, signed books apparently were less likely to be returned to the warehouse.) At my apartment I read the story and called Michael at home, relaying that his old boss had described his editing as brilliant and his reviews as impressive. Now that I knew it wasn't a horrible insult, I threw in the whole Melville part.

"You've never read *Bartleby, the Scrivener?*" Michael was incredulous. "You told Chip McGrath that you had never read one of Melville's most famous stories?"

"I wasn't going to lie," I defended myself. "I finished *Moby Dick,* a miracle in itself. My master's degree is in poetry." *Not dead-white-male fiction,* I didn't say.

"I'm sure he thinks you're an idiot now," Michael added, less interested in McGrath's (I thought important) flattery than in making fun of the lapse in my literary knowledge. I sensed that Chip's approval both pleased and embarrassed him.

"Chip does not think I'm an idiot," I argued. "We had a good talk. He was very nice to me."

"Yeah. How long did he keep talking to you after you told him you were ignorant?" Michael kept ribbing me.

Not so long, I didn't admit. "He likes being a writer better than being an editor," I added.

"Who wouldn't?" Michael asked.

That was telling. Michael had started his career as a journalist. I bet that like McGrath, he was sick of constantly improving everyone else's work when he'd rather get the byline himself. My hunch was confirmed when Michael signed a big book deal with HarperCollins for the biography of Lorraine Hansberry, playwright of the award-winning 1959 play *A Raisin in the Sun*, the first drama by a black woman on Broadway.

Allowing himself to be interviewed for another author's profile in my journalism class, Michael was the most gregarious I'd ever seen him. He spoke passionately about the late Hansberry, admitting that something in the life of this "remarkably understudied writer" had "caught" him. She was also an African American writer born on the south side of Chicago. Like Michael, she'd lived in New York and Los Angeles and had been a newspaper reporter. He believed she was a "real daddy's girl," whose father's death when she was sixteen left an indelible imprint that permeated Hansberry's view of the world. Although she married Jewish literature student Robert Nemiroff, they divorced in 1964, and there was evidence that she was bisexual. She died of cancer in 1965, at thirty-four. Michael had found a journal Hansberry had kept of her last years, when she was confined to a wheelchair and wrote, "I am so young to be in such pain."

I bet he felt a connection to her writing ambition, class conflicts, choice of white partners, and tragic ending after so much early promise. I tried to solve the mystery of who Michael was by analyzing why he'd gravitated toward this particular subject. "She had a reserve," he said. "She was not a confessional person." Had he identified with her reserve?

I sensed he was struggling, but he never admitted it. He took a leave of absence from his day job to do research for six months, but he returned to work before he'd finished. I recalled the years when I couldn't publish my own book while helping students get agents and book deals. Was Michael locked in a similarly awful paradox? He had the power to make or break everybody's books in the most influential book rag there was, yet he was unable to complete his own. He insisted he had no emotional link to Hansberry, though, and that the only problem he had was finding enough hours to write while working full-time.

"You must be thrilled that P. Diddy, Phylicia Rashād, and Audra

McDonald are doing the new Broadway version of *Raisin*," I told him cheerfully before one of his lectures. "It's the hottest revival around."

"That's a ridiculous, stupid thing to say." He bit my head off. "Why the hell would I care about that?"

"Because a new generation will be introduced to your subject's most famous play?" I asked.

What I said wasn't ridiculous or stupid at all. No matter how much he disdained pop culture, his publishers would surely want to sell books. Had I hit a nerve because he hadn't completed his book in time to capitalize on the celeb-filled production? My colleague Barbara later said they'd seen the revival together and he'd hated it.

He showed up to the book party for *Five Men Who Broke My Heart* appearing happy, letting me know that another (female) *Book Review* editor had liked it and assigned a review. Indeed, February 29, 2004, was a historic day for me, because instead of penning the three-hundred-word review of somebody else's book, a three-hundred-word, fairly positive review of my book ran. (The reviewer called it "playful and entertaining.") It could have been more effusive, but it felt better to be the reviewed than the reviewer. Michael never brought it up again. I didn't either – until his next New School talk.

"Did you read *Five Men?*" I asked him.

"I tried to," he said, rolling his eyes. In front of fifty of my students. What a jerk.

"At least I finished my book and it made it into the bookstores," I wanted to retort.

I attributed his insult to my recounting his "asinine" quip in my memoir. He said he didn't care, but what went on behind the scenes at the *Times* was supposed to be sacred. Or he may have thought the story made him look bad. Still, it wasn't the last time I used Michael as a character.

After I gave up cigarettes, alcohol, and dope, my addiction specialist, Dr. Winters, advised me to also quit freelancing. "Why chase after bylines you already have for money you don't need?" he asked. "It's hurting you. It's too much stress." In *Lighting Up*, I included the scene where Michael called to give me a book review assignment and I said no to *The New York Times*. I'd cried not only because it was hard to turn him down after fifteen years, but because he was still asking me to do three hundred words for $100. In retrospect, giving up the instant gratification of fast clips to focus on longer work was the best career decision I ever made. Of course, I soon became addicted to doing book events and book deals. . . .

When I started researching my mentor project in the fall of 2005, I Googled the late Harrison E. Salisbury (who'd died in 1993, at age eighty-four). I immediately stumbled upon press for *Tiananmen Diary* — very negative press. *The New York Review of Books* called it "The Lost Weekend." The worst slam, in *The Nation*, was by the journalist Judith Shapiro. She said the book was a mess, riddled with mistakes. I looked up this other Shapiro. (Good last name for a writer – there were many of them, in all genres.) Wow, this Judith had authored *After the Nightmare*: *Inside China Today; Son of the Revolution; Mao's War Against Nature*: *Politics and the Environment in Revolutionary China*; and *Return to China*: *A Survivor of the Cultural Revolution Reports on China Today*. Man, she was the ultimate Asian expert – why hadn't the *Times* editors given Salisbury's book to her?

Aha! In a flash, I realized they'd meant to. I filled in the blanks of what had happened in 1989 with the very first review that Michael had assigned me. Brand new at the *Book Review*, he'd obviously mixed up the two female Shapiro critics. So when Michael had called me, he'd thought he was speaking to the Shapiro who was a China expert. It wasn't such a good way to meet a mentor after all.

I went to my clips files and read through carefully. Right after my fifteen-hundred-word Salisbury piece ran, Michael kept giving me assignments. But he went back to Jewish issues and the piddly three-hundred-word length. That was why I didn't get another one-thousand-word review for ten years – and that was from a different editor. That second long review was about a nonfiction book called *Even Cowards Get Cancer*, by the British journalist John Diamond, a chain-smoker who got lung cancer. My review, which ran December 1999, ended: "Diamond's memoir offers pain, joy, redemption – and a good reason to quit smoking this New Year's Eve." Coincidentally, that would be the subject I tackled in my next memoir.

Unfortunately, only my short reviews in the year 2000 were included in a thick *New York Times Book Review* anthology. But yet another editor there finally did assign me a short poetry book to review – a collection by Peter Balakian called *June-Tree*, which I called "intense, soulful, and moving." It felt appropriate that lovely poetry would be my last book review. It ran just before the *Book Review* got rid of the "In Brief" section in favor of longer roundup pieces, right before I gave up reviewing forever.

"When you gave me that first China book, did you confuse me with the China expert Judith Shapiro?" I asked Michael point-blank during a phone interview I'd requested about our relationship.

"Yes," he admitted. "It was a big mistake. There was a whole interrogation about it. Someone had confused the two of you and gave me the wrong name. Becky threw a shit fit."

I pondered whether that omission counted as the best lie he'd told me. Since I'd never asked him about it before, I supposed it wasn't an out-and-out prevarication. Still, that error had probably altered my reputation at the newspaper of record in ways I never knew.

"Were you mad at me?" I asked.

"No. I actually thought it was nice that the old guy got a good *Times* review for one of his last books," he said.

"So, are there other reasons why you've been so critical and sarcastic with me?" I asked him. "Why was your criticism always so harsh?"

"Injured pride will make you show the son of a bitch that you can do what needs to be done," he said. "You won't want it to happen again."

He made it sound calculated, as if an ornery old editor had done it to him and it worked. My father had a whole bunch of mean, older male mentors. I'd always thought he'd chosen them because his father, my Grandpa Harry, was angry and rarely said anything kind. It was all my dad knew, so he re-created their relationship by gravitating toward difficult, stiff teachers and advisers. When he buried his father, he found that two of his tough medical school professors were buried in the same cemetery. He told me, "All my fathers are dead now," a line I used for a poem. Michael had never spoken of his father, though I gathered his parents' divorce, when he was an infant, was difficult for him. How could it not have been? Had I chosen Michael because he could be as hard to please as my dad?

"You once told me you knew I would be a successful writer. How did you know?" I asked.

"You were very determined, eager, and reliable," he said matter-of-factly. "You always handed in work on time, with few mistakes."

"Did I stand out from other writers?" I couldn't help but ask.

"Your writing workshop stood out," he said. "I thought the literary landscape you created was remarkable, very important for a lot of people. It was an extraordinary accomplishment that you kept it going for eighteen years. You forget I've watched you grow up," he added.

Although we'd worked together for most of that time, he'd never once told me that he was impressed with my Tuesday night group before. I didn't want him to think I was special because I was a teacher or the workshop leader. Then again, he was a teacher and, in many ways, a leader, so it was a trait we had in common. Was that why he understood me? Why couldn't I understand him?

"After almost two decades of considering you a friend and mentor, you're still a total mystery to me," I admitted. "I have no idea what your motivations are, what makes you tick."

"So what do you need to know? Ask me now!" He sounded emphatic and more open than usual.

"Okay, I will."

If I were going to chronicle our connection with my usual psychoanalytic bent, I needed to fill in the blanks. We continued our conversation in the dispassionate roles of interviewer and subject. But I was emotionally curious to unlock the mystery man who had championed me, my work, and my students, only to reject me just as I was making it.

"Do you think you're a loner because you were an only child who grew up with divorced parents?" I jumped in.

"I have no idea," he said.

"Is your father still alive?" I asked.

"I don't know," he answered. I expected that he wasn't going to reveal anything more, but then he added, "I haven't spoken to him in twenty-one years."

"You don't know if your father is alive or dead? Oh my god. What a tragedy," I blurted out. That meant they'd last been in touch when Michael was about thirty.

"I never knew my father. I have no memories of my parents being married," he explained. "It's certainly disappointing, but it's not a tragedy."

"Have you ever been in therapy?" I asked, sure he hadn't.

"Yes, I have," he surprised me again. "But finding my father isn't an active issue for me. What would I say to him after decades – 'Why did you leave my mother?'"

"Was he at your mother's funeral?"

"No."

"Don't you want to know if he's alive?" I pressed him. "Won't you want him to see your book when it's published?"

"Maybe if I'm giving a reading in Chicago. . . . " He didn't finish.

I imagined Michael's fantasy was that his father would walk into the bookstore to find him standing at the podium, reading from his bestseller to a standing-room-only crowd. Or was I projecting the reason why I'd become a writer – to impress my hard-to-please father and finally win his love?

"My addiction specialist said addicts depend on substances but not people. You don't depend on people or substances, do you?" I asked. "I've never seen you smoke, drink, or take drugs."

"My grandmother smoked, which bothered me. My mother had an alcohol problem, so I'm intolerant of drunks and drug addicts," he said. "That's why I never drink or do drugs."

Was that why his grandmother had to raise him? Because his mother drank? "I never knew any of this. You don't ever talk about it," I said.

"I'm open with a small group of my closest friends," he argued. Somehow I didn't really believe he was.

"Do you feel a connection to Hansberry because she wasn't confessional or open at all?"

"No," he said. I wondered if his silence signaled the end of the conversation. But then he asked, "Why is your voice so full of anxiety today?"

I admitted that I was confused and hurt that *Lighting Up* wasn't doing well. I'd heard the *Book Review* was running a review in ten days, but I didn't know if it would be short or long, who'd critiqued it, or what was said.

"Now, that's stupid," he said. "How could it be a short review? When was the last time you saw an 'In Short' in the *Book Review?*"

Last Sunday, I thought. In each issue the paper now hired one person to write three-hundred-word reviews of five books under a heading different from "In Short." "It could be one of several books mentioned in one of those new nonfiction roundup pieces," I clarified.

"You shouldn't care what other people say about your work," he threw out.

"When your book comes out, aren't you going to care what important critics say about it?" I asked.

"No," he said. "With all the people you know in publishing, you can't get an early copy?"

"Nobody can get it until Monday," I lamented before hanging up the phone.

It was Friday, which meant I'd have to wait nervously the entire weekend. I ran out to an appointment. When I came home, I found an envelope Michael had sent by messenger that contained four copies of the March 13, 2005, *Book Review.* In a half-page critique, a female freelancer I'd never heard of called my book "frank and darkly funny." It wasn't an all-out rave, but I recalled Katha Pollitt's disdain for her good review and decided to feel gratitude for that pull quote, which I pictured on the cover of my paperback.

"Julie assigned the review. I had absolutely nothing to do with it," Michael insisted.

I appreciated his candor and thanked my lucky stars that Julie, my old and loyal *New Yorker* colleague, had been on my side. But I wanted to know why Michael – whom I thought was my ally – hadn't fought for either of my books to get space in the *Book Review*'s pages. Was he envious that I'd finished two books before his came out? Were my memoirs too confessional for his taste? Too girlie for him? Not worthy enough, in his estimation, for literary praise?

"Well, thanks for getting me early copies of the review. I'm so glad it's good," I told him, extremely relieved.

"Stop caring what other people think of your book!" he admonished.

Funny that this line was coming from my *Times Book Review* editor, who was the harshest critic I had ever met. Talk about asinine! "I'm human," I said. "It took me twenty-two years to get a hardcover. How could I not care about the critical response?"

"Look, you've come a long way and accomplished a great deal," he said. "You should be proud of that!"

Now that I was vulnerable, he transformed back into the gentle, understanding fatherly figure who made me feel safe again. He didn't have a father – I bet that was why he did it so well. He became what he'd needed himself.

"You hated that first novel I wrote that I made you read, remember?" I asked.

"It was dreadful," he admitted.

"What about *Five Men?*"

"It was less dreadful than your novel, but you needed more

distance. It was slow and you were too close to your subjects. *Lighting Up* is a much better, deeper book," he said. "The writing is slicker and doesn't have the taint of the first-time author."

You're dying for that taint, I wanted to say. "'Slicker' doesn't sound like a compliment," was what came out.

"It's more professionally written. It moves better. Your voice is more confident," he elucidated. "You've learned that the reader's interest has to be maintained, so there's more suspense and humor. It was consistent and entertaining."

I didn't tell him how much his review meant to me.

Months later, all the editors were asked to evaluate the much-praised and revised *Book Review* under the leadership of Sam Tanenhaus. Though I loved it and found it more engaging, I heard from several sources that Michael wrote a long, angry screed. He basically claimed that the publication had gone to hell because of the idiotic commercial direction its new editor had taken. Then he left. When I learned that his long tenure at the *Book Review* was coming to an end, all I could think of was one word: Bartleby.

Barbara, the woman who used to date Michael, said she saw a recent Internet posting mentioning that his Hansberry biography would be published in 2007. I left him a few phone messages, but he never returned my calls. All the emails I sent to his private address bounced back.

Not Related

HARVEY

SHAPIRO

In essence I met Harvey Shapiro the
day I moved to Manhattan on July 20, 1981, when I bought books for
my upcoming NYU classes. Sitting on a bench in Washington Square
Park, I examined the paperback *New York Poems*. The cover showed
a blue sky and a small crush of silver buildings underneath. I turned
to the table of contents and looked for my name. I wasn't in there,
of course. A twenty-year-old English major, I'd never published anything in a big-city anthology. But it was a habit I fell into after noting

that Shapiro's were popular in the poetry field. I'd discovered Karl Shapiro, David Shapiro, and Alan Shapiro. (I recently found Gregg, Myra, Marla, and Mordecai Shapiro poets on the web, too.) Sitting outside that summer day, I was struck by this additional member of the Shapiro poetry tribe. So who was the new guy?

His poem "Riding Westward" started: "It's holiday night / And crazy Jews are on the road, / Finished with fasting and high on prayer. / . . . I hope I can make it to Utopia Parkway / Where my father lies at the end of his road. . . . " He had an accessible and engaging voice, yet the double entendres made his words more complex than they first appeared. Were these East Coast Jews really crazy? Only high on prayer while driving? Was his father dead? Why was I sure their relationship wasn't utopian? It had a humorous tone, but wasn't Yom Kippur supposed to be the saddest day of the year?

Reading confessional poetry, I usually felt like half detective and half shrink, perhaps why a failed upper-middle-class Midwest princess had been so immediately taken by the dark genre. (Hadn't I flunked suburbia because I was too intense for small talk?) I envisioned Harvey as a sardonic New York Jew with father issues who was ambivalent about the pious people, probably some in his own family – just like mine.

His poem "National Cold Storage Company" detailed what was stored at this (literal, or was it mythical?) Brooklyn warehouse. "I myself have dropped into it seven years / Midnight tossings, plans for escape, the shakes. / Add this to the national total / Grant's Tomb, the Civil War, Arlington, / The young president dead. . . . " It seemed to address Kennedy's assassination, but the personal clues hooked me. Was the narrator an insomniac? What was he escaping? Were "the shakes" due to excessive alcohol? Or fear? His poem continued: "Above the warehouse and beneath the stars / The poets creep on the harp of the Bridge. / But see, / They fall into the National Cold Storage Company / One by one. . . . " Wait a second – were they committing suicide, as so many poets had done? Was he that sad, like me?

Friends my age followed rock stars, going to concerts, collecting T-shirts and autographs. I was a poetry groupie. Since Harvey lived nearby, I figured I'd run into him. Within months I'd met Joseph Brodsky, Galway Kinnell, Czeslaw Milosz, Sharon Olds, Yehuda Amichai, Grace Schulman, and Louise Glück. Many living poetry legends taught, lectured, or gave group readings – right in my neighborhood! I showed up, bought books, stood in line for hours to get a signature and a handshake. Several even stopped by to have a drink and eat my mother's food at poetry receptions I hosted at my place. But no sign of Harvey.

I was finishing my master's degree and dating Dan, the poetry professor, who was offered a Fulbright scholarship to study abroad for two years. When Dan asked me to go with him, I thought he was kidding. I was twenty-two and so enthralled with New York, where I'd just landed, I couldn't consider moving elsewhere. The relationship ended disastrously and Dan refused to speak to me – for decades. I was paranoid, selfishly fearing I'd be shunned by Dan's prestigious poet crowd.

"Don't worry. Everybody's too busy with their own fucked-up breakups to notice yours," confided Hugh, Dan's colleague. A good-looking, soft-spoken, award-winning, forty-two-year-old poet, Hugh assured me nobody hated me, that Dan would find another girlfriend in no time – which turned out to be true. When I showed Hugh some poems, I learned that he was as good a line editor as Dan (a hard commodity to find), so I glommed onto him as a new comrade-in-arms. I was delighted to discover that he knew my high school English teacher Jack Zucker – *and* he was close to the mythical Harvey Shapiro! Indeed, Harvey had been his mentor and father figure since Hugh had taken Harvey's poetry workshop at Columbia University in 1966.

"Was Harvey a good teacher? Did he like your work? Were you his favorite student? How many people were in the class? How old were you?" I asked.

"I was twenty-six and Harvey was forty-two then," Hugh answered slowly. (We lived at different speeds. I'd cram in a hundred words for every one of Hugh's.) "There were twelve students in Harvey's class. He felt connected to me when he learned that I'd studied with his friend Louis Zukofsky as an undergrad. Harvey and I would go for drinks after class." Hugh showed me a few slender poetry books by Harvey, who'd given up teaching to work at *Commentary*, *The New Yorker*, and *The New York Times Book Review*, where he was now top editor, assigning Hugh poetry books to critique.

Scanning autobiographical traces in Harvey's poems, articles about him, and *Who's Who in America* furthered my imaginary ties to him. His parents were from a village near Kiev, like my grandparents. He was born in 1924 in Chicago, where my father had gone to medical school, and spoke Yiddish before English, as my mother had. His clan had moved to New York in the 1920s, around the time my Grandpa Harry had landed in Ellis Island. Harry hated running Shapiro's Window Shades and seemed eternally bitter and in a bad mood. Maybe I wanted this Shapiro I'd never met – with a name just a few letters different from Harry's – to be my successful poet grandfather. Harvey's father, Jacob Shapiro, came off as emotionally difficult, too, like my father, Jack Shapiro. Even *their* names were similar.

I was fascinated by all the potential bonds and begged Hugh to let me know the next time Harvey was doing a reading, so I could meet him. But Hugh was the most shy and reserved writer I knew. (He once attributed his slow, quiet pace to his mother's depression when he was born.) Alas, initiating social or career introductions wasn't Hugh's forte, and my two years at NYU and almost four years at *The New Yorker* passed sans even one sighting of Harvey.

I had a little luck publishing poetry in small journals, but the most I was paid for a poem was $100 from *Cosmopolitan*, so I needed a real job. (All poets did. Galway Kinnell said he had to teach because he couldn't support a family on his book advances – and this was after he'd won a $300,000 MacArthur Foundation grant.) In 1987, I took a position promoting programs at Jewish social welfare agencies funded by UJA-Federation. I visited the Educational Alliance on the Lower East Side, where my parents had met as teenagers.

My stories were picked up on radio and TV and by the Jewish Telegraphic Agency. But a piece I'd done on a kosher battered women's shelter caused controversy. (Jewish men weren't supposed to beat their wives. Apparently it was bad juju to let the world know some did.) But I refused to rescind my story. The next morning a note was on my desk. Instead of the expected "You're fired," it said, "Great work, keep it up." It was signed by Jeanette, the head of my department, my boss's boss. She was a pretty, slim, classy executive in her fifties, my mother's age.

I thanked Jeanette, befriended her, and soon asked for a favor: a month long leave of absence so I could go to Israel. She okayed the trip, and since the organization funded programs there, she assigned me enough work to pay for my stay. When I returned, I told Jeanette about my visit, where I'd interviewed the majestic poet Yehuda Amichai at his Yemen Moshe home for a magazine article. (My connection to Amichai, in his sixties and happily married, was platonic and professional, though I admit to a crush.) I'd also caught up with my Tel Aviv cousins. Being with my extended family made me feel lonely in New York, where I was a workaholic who lived alone. Jeanette was divorced; her daughter was studying abroad. It was the first time she'd lived by herself. She was lonely too. We had something else in common – we'd both recently slept with new guys who had potential.

When she summoned me to her office the next week, it sounded urgent. Had I forgotten to double-check statistics for my AIDS story? "Can I call him, or do I have to wait for him to call me?" Jeanette asked. I'd been wondering the same thing about my own Romeo. By the end of the day, they'd both called. By the end of the month, Jeanette and I were gossiping like teenagers about our new boyfriends.

"I'm so into him I'm flipping out," I told her.

"I'm deeply involved too," she said.

We were a weird duo. I was living in a tiny studio, wearing all black and chain-smoking cigarettes and dope at parties filled with radical artists and activists. Jeanette, who'd been a New Jersey homemaker, lived in a spacious three-bedroom, three-bath on the Upper West Side. She wore pastel designer suits and had perfectly coifed short light-brown hair. Unfortunately, both of the guys we'd been so excited about turned out to be creeps who cheated on us.

Since I mentioned that I'd fixed up several marriages, she asked me to play matchmaker for her, too. Screw the cads we'd just split from! We planned a singles party in September 1988. When she asked, I didn't even know whether I had an electric or gas stove. Luckily, she was a food maven who knew how to make many Jewish recipes, so she suggested we host a break the fast, the meal after Yom Kippur, at her huge Riverside Drive place. She'd cook and pay for everything; my sole duty was to provide the guys. Only one problem: Where would I find nice Jewish bachelors thirty years older than I was who were successful enough for Jeanette? I called my old poet pal Hugh, who was still unmarried. In a stroke of genius (or was it selfishness?), I asked him to bring his friend Harvey, who I'd heard was separated from his wife. I don't know if it was the promise of single women or free food at fancy uptown digs, but this time Hugh came through.

I'd wanted to meet Harvey for seven years. By inviting him now, was I trying to be the matchmaker who found him a wife? Or was I really fixing him up with myself? Since I had such high expectations, meeting him in the flesh was bound to be disappointing. Yet what could be a truer link than loving someone's poetry? I practiced telling him how, since we had the same name, I'd looked him up in that first anthology and discovered "Driving Westward." Then it hit me that tonight, this very night, when I was finally going to hang out with Harvey for the first time, was Yom Kippur, and he was driving in from Brooklyn. How unbelievably perfect! It was fate! As Hugh introduced Harvey and we shook hands, I blurted out, "It's holiday night / And crazy Jews are on the road / Finished with fasting and high on prayer!"

Luckily he didn't think I was a stalker. He seemed charmed. It turned out he was more attracted to me than to Jeanette, who wasn't quite his type. (He liked artsy intellectuals.) Jeanette said he wasn't quite her type, either. (She didn't like artsy intellectuals.) So after our dual break the fast fete, I claimed Harvey as my new best friend. (Later that year, I did introduce Jeanette to the guy she married.)

Over the next few months, Harvey invited me to readings at PEN American Center and the 92nd Street Y, literary awards ceremonies, and tony book parties – you name the place, Harvey got invited. He'd switched from the *Times Book Review*, where I'd already broken in, to the Sunday *New York Times Magazine*, where I hoped he'd help me break in. He introduced me to many of his fellow editors. When I contacted them, they'd jump to attention. Harvey and I had the same last name, and I was almost four decades younger than he was, so everyone assumed we were related. I didn't tell them otherwise.

"This is my daughter, Susan Shapiro," he told a guy at the Brooklyn diner. "Have you ever met my cousin, Sue?" he asked another patron. I penned a poem to him called "Not Related": " . . . Not sure what to call this visiting girl / he told his friends who stopped by our booth / 'This is my niece from the Village,' or / 'Have you met my daughter?' Last time / he called me his second cousin. . . . / In his living room I took his torn / blue paperback collection from the shelf / called *Battle Reports*. He signed it, / kissed me on the lips at the door, / said 'Published before you were born.'"

He did kiss me on the lips – twice. The first quick pucker was a goodbye gesture at his place, as I was on my way out. The second kiss, at my apartment, after we got stoned on high-class Hawaiian weed, came with a gentle proposition, something like "You're so beautiful, we should be together." He wasn't much taller than my five feet and seven inches; he had gray hair and a weird little Santa Claus mustache and beard. Yet I'd really sparked to him. He was sexy, brilliant, alive. Hanging out together, we'd catch an early theater or performance piece, stop by a reading or book party, grab a bite, catch a late movie, and then dissect the work we'd witnessed — all on the same night! I'd pay for one, he'd pay for another, or we'd get on guest lists for free tickets — he more than I, of course. He had more energy and creative appetite than any guy my age. Yet the math stopped me.

I was twenty-seven, so he was thirty-seven years older than me and really could have been my grandfather. I did prefer older men (father issues redux, I'm sure). But I told Harvey the truth — that the three-and-a-half-decade gap was too much to conquer. He took it in stride, except for a few snide comments reminding me of his ornery side. Once, when I said I had no plans for the summer, he said, "You really should find someone to travel with already." A different time, at his place, when I'd been careless with my cigarette ashes, he said, "We're not dating. You don't have the right to destroy my table" (another line that wound up in a poem).

I told my shrink that a randy sixty-four-year-old was interested in me. She asked if he was available. When I nodded, she said, "Well then, good for him." But I needed a mentor more than I needed a boyfriend. My track record in love wasn't so hot. My relationships with my gurus were more enduring. Plus it was the longest I'd ever pursued a mentor before and I didn't want to screw it up. Harvey was dating lots of women anyway. He morphed into a mix of trusted adviser, protector, and close confidant, proving he was well worth the wait.

I was soon invited into his inner circle, where I learned more about him. He'd married his wife, Edna, in 1953, and they'd lived in the Village at Patchin Place, across the courtyard from e. e. cummings and just above Djuna Barnes. His first book, *The Eye*, came out in 1953. Harvey had two sons close to my age, Saul and Dan. He'd split from Edna a long time before, but they weren't yet officially divorced. After the separation, he'd apparently had a lot of intense love affairs. His friends joked about his legendary exploits, but that was clear from his risqué poems.

"Adaptation of a First Grade Composition" began: "I suppose I used you / The way an Indian used his buffalo. / I have come in your queenly cunt, / Your tight asshole of an Indian princess." The complete text of another poem read: "Cynthia got herself off in the stacks / at UCSD. This thought warms me / as I sit by myself in the library at Duke, / remembering her voice and her careful diction / describe how the desire to manipulate / her clit came from the heavy breathing of lit." At one point, Virginia Hamilton Adair, a poet near his age, wrote of his work: "Shapiro's women seem to be equal parts goddess and whore. . . . This vision is too limited, but it is at least frank — not hostile, just frank." The sexual words he used seemed to me tinged with anger: "cunt," "tight asshole," "got herself off," "clit," "muff." Or was I just from another generation?

Speaking to my journalism classes, he blew my students away with his piercing candor. He admitted he liked to drink and feared he wouldn't be able to craft poems without booze, and that he could never pay his rent with his writing. Students in the continuing education classes especially related to his double career and how he'd kept a day job while typing poems late at night.

"All the editing helped my poetry," he insisted. "When you learn to edit others, you learn to edit yourself. I had two kids to support. I wasn't a suffering artist. I always led a bourgeois life. By choice, not by chance."

His day gig made cameos in his verse. "Working Days" was set at a three-martini lunch at Schrafft's, in mid-Manhattan, with editors Charlie Palmer, Barney Lefferts, and Sherwin Smith. "I was a guest in their Wasp heaven. / They might have chosen a better Jew to chronicle them. / But they had their own phrases. / I admired them because / Their hatred of what they did for a living was pure. / Newspaper men working for an editor so dense, he would / Remark of any sentence that contained a subordinate / Clause: 'This is something for *The Partisan Review.*'"

Like begging a rock star to play his greatest hits, I made him repeat stories of the literary lions he'd known. He was the poetry editor and ad salesman at the inception of *The Village Voice* in the 1950s, where he told his colleague, fellow *Voice* founder Norman Mailer, that publishing a page of bad reviews of Mailer's 1955 novel *Deer Park* in the *Voice* was a silly gimmick that wouldn't work. "I was totally wrong," Harvey said. "It made him famous." In 1960, after James Dickey trashed Allen Ginsberg's poem "Kaddish" in *The New York Times Book Review*, Harvey defended its importance in *Midstream* magazine. When Martin Luther King Jr. was jailed, Harvey called the Southern Christian Leadership Conference to ask King to write a jailhouse letter for the *Times Magazine*. "Another editor rejected it, out of blind stupidity," he said. *The New Leader* took "Letter from Birmingham Jail," and it was an instant sensation. In the 1970s, Harvey went to the Oval Office to interview Jimmy Carter, who recited Dylan Thomas. "When the peanut business was slow, he'd sit on bales of peanuts and memorize Thomas's poetry," Harvey said with a smile.

He told my students never to be intimidated by *Times* editors, mostly middle-aged married guys from the suburbs who desperately wanted to run pieces about what was happening with hip young people. In fact, he'd commissioned the eighteen-year-old Yale college student Joyce Maynard to write about her life in a cover essay. Her pixielike picture wound up attracting the attention of J. D. Salinger, with whom she had an affair she later chronicled in a memoir that mentioned Harvey.

After he spoke to my class, I took him to dinner to get precious time alone to pick his brain. He'd made Joyce Maynard famous; I wanted him to discover me. I nervously brought up the possibility of my writing for the *Times Magazine*.

"It'll never happen," he said.

"Why won't it happen?" I asked, hurt by his terse rejection. I pulled from my briefcase a stack of pieces I'd sold to his newspaper's op-ed, book review, and "City" sections, along with other top publications.

He was unimpressed. "You in the *Magazine* will never happen. No shot in hell," he repeated, in his typically blunt, no-bullshit fashion. "I'm not going to lie to you."

While he took a cab back to Brooklyn, I walked home crying, wishing he'd lied. He'd just told my green, clipless students they had a shot to break into his magazine but told me — a well-published journalist by now — that I had "no chance in hell." His curt, hurtful tone echoed that of my grandfather and father. With the help of therapy, I'd quit dating jerks — only to gravitate toward the same kind of macho gruffness in gurus. Was I forever trying to win over my father by proving I was as tough as my brothers? I still needed to show that I was thick skinned, that mean words wouldn't scare me off, that I could play with the big boys.

Fortunately, I'd already learned that sycophants were useless, and most of the advice that had improved my life had been harsh and downright painful to hear. I had sweet friends and fawning students who told me how great I was. But surrounding yourself with ass-kissers could turn you into Michael Jackson. I depended on my mentors to tell me the ugly, unadulterated truth so I could appropriately and sanely navigate this competitive city's cutthroat business scene. It kept me real and humble, with low expectations, so I was no longer too surprised, shocked, or disappointed by rejection.

At the same time, by this phase in my freelance career, I was sure that no never really meant no. It meant ask again later, in a different way, offering a new pitch, spin, updated lead, or revised piece so timely, hot, or exclusive it couldn't be refused. Writing could always get better, especially if a smart critic told you how to refocus or recast your idea in a fresh way. Aside from asking for criticism from my workshop and my husband, I'd paid professional ghost editors to fix my work line by line. If that didn't do it, there was also the inane power of using celebrity endorsements or better connections. Harvey's pronouncement did indeed turn out to be a lie, though he ended up getting me in the *Times Magazine* almost by accident.

I'd been doing book reviews and author profiles for Peter, a wonderful *Penthouse* editor, who assigned me a piece on Judith Regan. She was a gorgeous, provocative Simon & Schuster "editrix" (a "Page Six" colloquialism she inspired), who was as potty-mouthed as Howard Stern, one of her authors. Publishing Stern's book, along with bestsellers by Rush Limbaugh and Beavis and Butt-head, caused Regan to be labeled "culture vulture," "guerrilla publisher," " tabloid-trained carpetbagger," and "the demise of Western civilization."

During our first conversation in the winter of 1994, Judith told me Howard was "a tongue-down-your-throat kind of guy," while Rush was "more sensual and romantic," and revealed that she hadn't had sex in a year, since her divorce from her abusive husband. Using the word "motherfucker" constantly, she claimed she worked so hard so she could earn "fuck-you money" to quit any job she pleased. When I asked how she could predict if a manuscript was going to be a best-seller, she said that upon first reading, it had to "make my nipples hard." What a dream interview!

Thanks to my outspoken subject, the thirty-five-hundred-word piece I handed in was the bounciest prose I'd ever crafted. I received a check for $5,000, a ton of money for me at the time. Yet month by month I was disappointed that my perky profile was not printed. I asked Peter when Judith Regan would run already.

"It's not going to run," he said. "I just don't have room for it. I'm sorry."

"You've officially killed it?" I was stunned. I could see slashing something boring or badly written. But this piece was ready for prime time! Harvey had taught me the term "killed," which meant that editors decided an article would never run, and the rights reverted to the author. I wanted it confirmed before I sent it out again.

"Yes, it's killed. Why?" Peter asked. " Do you think you can sell it elsewhere?"

"Yeah, I do." Semi-heartbroken, I was determined to find my hot profile a new home, pronto.

"You have my blessing to shop it elsewhere," he said. " Good luck."

I was grateful to be paid so much money I didn't have to return. Yet I was eager to see my long prose in print, especially when I heard that media mogul Rupert Murdoch was stealing Regan away from her high-profile Simon & Schuster job. He did this by offering Regan a five-year, multimillion-dollar deal, her own imprint, ReganBooks, at his publishing house HarperCollins, a TV talk show, and promises of "media synergy," meaning she'd be able to buy TV and film rights to books she'd commissioned. As Regan got hotter, my orphaned interview got hotter too, and I didn't want to sit on an explosive story. Harvey knew every editor in the city, so I asked his advice about where to resubmit my article. Should I try *People* magazine? *The Village Voice? The New York Observer?*

He suggested Wayne Lawson, literary editor of *Vanity Fair.* But before we got off the phone, he said, "Let me take a quick look at the piece and I'll tell you for sure." I faxed it to him. (He'd become proficient on computers several years before I'd mastered cyberspace.) He called me back an hour later.

"So what do you think of my article?" I asked.

He said it made his nipples hard, and if I could confirm the Murdoch deal and update it right away, he'd pay me $3,500 and run it quickly. He, as in *The New York Times Magazine!* "But," he added, "take out the motherfuckers."

I toned it down for the newspaper of record, but I left in a few wild and crazy lines so as not to forfeit the raunchy flavor, reflecting Regan's spiky persona if not her real personality. I figured they'd cut out the raciest parts. My rewrite was accepted, and a $4,000 check came one week later. I thought the $500 increase was an accounting error and called Harvey to report it. He said it wasn't a mistake. I'd never been paid so promptly or earned higher than the contract stipulated. I got $1,000 more for syndication, which meant I'd now made $10,000 from one piece. The apex of my thirteen-year New York journalism career was happening because of my fellow Shapiro poet. The world was fair after all!

I wasn't sure if Harvey's "It'll never happen" had fueled my desire to prove him wrong. People always underestimated me, especially my father. During a recent argument, my dad told me, "Shut up, you're stupid, you don't know what you're talking about." I thought, *That's why I'll be a successful writer: to show my father I do know what I'm talking about, that my words aren't stupid.* If they were printed in the smartest publication in the world, they couldn't be stupid, right?

My profile of Judith Regan was illustrated with a picture of her in a regal white gown, looking like Joan of Arc, standing next to a real lion. A second photo showed her staring adoringly at Murdoch, her boss and obvious replacement daddy. I was pleased that one R-rated anecdote survived. Regan had told a story about being arrested and strip-searched in Utah in the late '70s, allegedly for making an illegal left turn. Represented by the American Civil Liberties Union, she sued, won, and said proudly, "You can no longer get fingered for minor traffic infractions in Utah, thank you, Judith Regan." I pointed it out to Harvey, who had thought "fingered" meant "nabbed" and had left it in. When I told him her original phrase had been "finger fucked," he laughed heartily but told me to keep that little factoid to myself.

Although I tried to use my cynical reporter's eye to not make it a puff piece, I was happy to learn that Regan requested rights to use my article in her press kit. I knew I wasn't supposed to care what my subjects thought, but I did. (And I was flattered to be interviewed by Regan on her Sirius radio show thirteen years later, just weeks after she was fired over the O. J. Simpson *If I Did It* book fiasco. It didn't surprise me that Murdoch betrayed her, or that a powerful businesswoman wasn't allowed to have as big a mouth or ambitions as the men she worked with, and thus took the fall.)

After my Regan piece debuted in July 1994, I'd taken Harvey's advice to find a guy to travel with and was staying in L.A. with Aaron, who was working on *Seinfeld*. I'd felt intimidated dating a guy on the staff of the number one comedy in the country. Breaking into such a prestigious magazine gave me confidence that my career was happening, too. To congratulate me, Aaron bought me a watch I still wear and said he was proud of me. (The trick to landing love seemed to be picking a man like my mother, not my father.)

Back in New York, Aaron and I dined with Harvey at Knickerbocker, but they could barely hear each other over the loud jazz piano. Because Aaron's field was TV comedy, Harvey assumed he would be goofy or nonliterary. Surprised by Aaron's knowledge of John O'Hara, obsession with World War II, and love of poetry, Harvey gave Aaron the thumbs-up. Aaron read his poems and was equally impressed. Since Aaron was an antisocial misanthrope who hated crowds, he was grateful he didn't have to attend the countless fetes and literary events I dragged Harvey to as my date.

Harvey invited me to the *Times* magazine's fun holiday parties at Sardi's Restaurant and helped me sell them five more pieces. After the "Endpaper" editor turned down my humor essay about trying to quit smoking, Harvey informed me that person was switching departments and I should rush my piece back to the replacement editor, Penelope, who was "young and kooky like you." Plus, he informed me, she'd recently quit smoking herself. Bingo! She bought it, and that piece led to my quit-smoking memoir. But Harvey also let me know that other editors there didn't necessarily love my work.

Both Aquarians, Harvey's birthday and mine were a few days

apart in January, and we sometimes celebrated together. In 1996, turning thirty-five, I was in the mood for a blowout. But, newly engaged, Aaron and I were saving up for the down payment on an apartment. Harvey was turning seventy-two, still unmarried, and feeling financially flush. We made a pact echoing the party plan with Jeanette, where Harvey and I had first met. This time Harvey paid for most of it and I planned it. I found a huge loft on Greene Street in SoHo to rent from 8:00 PM to 3:00 AM. My artist friend Rina made a cool invite that looked like a newspaper listing. Under "Entertainment Events," it said, "Susan Shapiro & Harvey Shapiro's 107th birthday party." It was freezing and snowing that night, and I was disappointed that fewer than the two hundred people we'd invited came. But my (mostly young, female) friends were impressed with the acclaimed older poets and journalists. Harvey's (mostly older, male) friends dug getting high, drunk, and loose on the dance floor with so many hot, pierced, mini-skirted babes.

At my July wedding, Harvey was one of the elder statesmen. Since he was a World War II vet with a surprisingly conservative political streak, I worried when I saw him having what looked like a serious tête-à-tête with my cousin Howard, the infamous communist who was still left of left. Yet soon they were nodding and laughing, as if their relief that I wouldn't be an old maid had transcended their old party lines. In one of my favorite wedding pictures, my two important father figures stood next to Aaron's and my real fathers.

That was the same season a small press finally published my poetry manuscript *Internal Medicine*, the revised version of my NYU master's thesis, a mere fifteen years late. Harvey's blurb on my back cover read: "Susan Shapiro's family is full of good stories, and she tells them honestly and well, as if life in America was as interesting as life in the shtetl. In troubled and moving lines, she gives you the color and passion of her own Greenwich Village days." When his new book came out, we did readings together. After one at Posman Books, I asked what he'd thought of my selection. "Well, you just don't have enough music," he said. I was hurt again by his bluntness. But he was right. He had more ardor for poetry than journalism, while I'd turned out to be a more passionate prose writer than poet.

As Harvey retired from *The New York Times* and I got a bit more juice in the biz, I tried to hook him up. My Barnes & Noble community relations manager pal set up Village readings for him and made sure the store carried his books. I published laudatory articles about him, as did some of my students. I recommended him to my NYU boss, convinced he'd make a good professor. But the head of hiring didn't make a fuss over him, and Harvey wasn't willing to fill out forms and jump through hoops for a position he didn't need. He obviously had other priorities.

In 1998, Harvey sounded excited for me to meet Galen Williams – the only woman he'd ever formally introduced me to as his girl-friend. She was a pretty, vivacious, divorced landscape architect with two grown sons. Harvey boasted that she'd single-handedly founded the nonprofit organization Poets & Writers, where they'd originally met. In her early sixties, she was age appropriate, though she looked much younger. After our first double date, I whispered to Harvey, "Man, Galen has great energy!" He said, "Funny, she just said the exact same words about you."

Officially retiring from *The New York Times* in 2003, Harvey became immersed in editing *The Poets of World War II*. In interviews he told of enlisting after his first year at Yale. At nineteen he'd become a radio gunner with the Air Force, flying thirty-five missions in a B-17 and winning a Distinguished Flying Cross. Harvey's green hardcover proudly displayed the work of many of his fellow veterans, including Karl Shapiro and George Oppen, who'd served in the antitank company of the 103rd Infantry division in Germany until 1945, when he was seriously wounded by shell fire. A communist who moved to Mexico to avoid an FBI investigation, Oppen won a Pulitzer Prize in 1968 for his poetry. Oppen gave Harvey a nice (albeit understated) book-jacket blurb for his latest book, like the endorsement Harvey had given me. Harvey later told me that he'd taken Oppen's lines from an introduction he'd given for a reading at the Guggenheim.

It turned out that Oppen had been an important mentor and father figure to Harvey. Did anybody ever get the real father they wanted? We'd both picked paternal poetry figures to nurture us. Yet having a real poet as a dad wouldn't solve the problem, either.

I flashed to the haunting poem "Flight" that Franz Wright had written to his father, James Wright: "Since you left me at eight I have / always been lonely / star-far from the person right next / to me, but closer to me than my bones you / you are there."

My favorite stanza in Harvey's war poem "Battle Report" read: "In the absence of pain he continued, / The oxygen misting his veins like summer. / The bomber's long sleep and the cry of the gunner, / Who knows that the unseen mime in his blood / Will startle to terror, / Years later, when love matters."

As he aged, love did seem to matter more. Aaron and I were in Florida at the same time as Harvey and Galen; one night we all took a midnight stroll on the beach. Harvey held Galen's hand. I held Aaron's. In fifteen years of friendship, it was the first time we'd both been content in lasting relationships. After so many hits and misses for both of us, it seemed like a miracle.

When they weren't traveling to Florida, California, or Paris, he and Galen split their time between her East Hampton house and his floor-through in Park Slope. I was an ardent Greenwich Villager who turned down his invitations to Long Island, but Harvey was the only one I'd trek to Brooklyn for. At his latest cocktail party, I felt lucky to get to mingle with the writers Hilma Wolitzer, Maggie Paley, Phillip Lopate, and James Atlas, as well as *New York Times* editor Jack Rosenthal. Harvey's events were always filled with literary stars. Yet working at *The New Yorker* had taught me the downside of being surrounded by people of letters: It was hard to compete. Did Harvey wish he'd won wider acclaim? He wrote: "Oh, to be a Nobel Laureate looking back. / How serene I would be, and with what / clarity I would view all around me, / illusion and non-illusion. / And with what / justice I would pronounce judgment on my life."

I was worried about being judged by Harvey. In 2003, after selling my sex memoir about remeeting my exes, I was sure that Harvey and his crews — the serious-older-poet brigade and the elitist *New York Times* guys — would look down on my genre, style, and subject matter. Embarrassed, I didn't bring up my news to anybody at a reception for his World War II anthology. But his friends already knew, kissing, hugging, and high-fiving me, shouting, "Mazel tov!" and patting me on the back. "Harvey told us you got a $50,000 advance! Wowie, you're rich, girl! I'll be happy to get $1,000 for my new book," one said. *Yeah, but your new book will be poetry,* I thought. When I compared it to the six-figure advances of some of my colleagues and students, I'd actually felt a tad disappointed with mine. But it amused me that Harvey, usually discreet about business matters, had spilled in public the price my hardcover had garnered. It was worth it for the implication that I'd done well in his eyes.

He cheered me on at subsequent readings and book bashes. Though not an avid TV watcher, he also managed to tape, catch, and praise Aaron's TV shows, and he was especially jazzed by Aaron's grisly *Law & Order* episode about psychotic serial killers who murdered a slew of prostitutes. A seventy-nine-year-old serious poet who could get psyched about TV murder and mayhem? Harvey never ceased to surprise me.

His divorced was eventually finalized, and Edna passed away in 2005. When I questioned why he didn't marry Galen, he told me to mind my own business. I analyzed whether his mother issues were still getting in his way. After all, in one of my favorite poems of his, about how his baby sister had died, he wrote: " . . . My mother / when she saw me said, Why did God / take away my beautiful child and give me / this ugly baby instead? And she turned away, / not to touch me / for the first few months of my life. / This is family history." As my father used to say, "If you don't have your mother's love, you have nothing."

Then I recalled the rift over the division of Howard Fast's estate when he'd left his second wife of seven years his house and assets. It had hurt his kids, who thought that a child's eternal adoration should be rewarded more than the last years with a younger lover. So I kept my mouth shut, wondering if — unlike Howard — Harvey was being responsible, putting his lifelong obligation to his children and grand-children first.

Harvey certainly celebrated Galen in his new poems. "Part of an Infinite Series" began: "She raises her nightgown / over her head / like the beginning of a Greek trilogy. / She raises her night-gown / over her head / like the Opening of the West. / She raises her

nightgown / over her head / like a shout in the East Village. . . . "
I smiled reading fourteen stanzas that started this way. In "For Galen
& After O'Hara," he admitted: "I did not take my walk today. / . . . But
I did spend most of the morning / in bed with you making love / while
the bright March sun . . . / blazed . . . I luxuriated in that sun, / seated
by the dunes, aware of the halcyon sea, / idly turning the idea-less
pages / of the Ideas Section of the Saturday *Times* / almost unaware
of my luck and you." There was a new wistful, romantic quality to his
work. Though perhaps it was too much sweetness to bear unless he
could take a swipe at his old employer in the same line.

A special reading at St. Mark's church on January 28, 2004,
was held for Harvey's eightieth birthday. I was hurt that I wasn't
asked to be one of twelve readers. Now that I was a memoirist, did
they forget I'd also written poetry? And that I'd already penned the
poem "Not Related" for him? Okay, so the other readers were his
former students, old colleagues, or big-shot literati. But I noticed a
female Asian poet I didn't recognize. Was the fact that she was a
woman what bothered me, or that she was young and good looking,
with multicultural cachet?

I could handle being less important than Harvey's partner, his
sons, his daughters-in-law, and his grandchildren (which mirrored
how edged out I'd felt by my father's obsession with his grandkids).
But who was this young, dark-haired poet on Harvey's roster, whom
I'd never seen at any of his readings? Some Knopf chick who'd won

highbrow prizes when I wasn't looking? At home, like a jealous lover, I Googled the interloper. She was indeed the author of big books, the winner of prizes and grants. Harvey's latest collection had a blurb from her. Talk about not being able to compete.

When Harvey and Hugh gave an intimate, candle-lit reading at the Cornelia Street Café in the fall of 2005, Harvey looked pale and said he hadn't been feeling well. A week later, Galen called to say Harvey needed serious surgery at an uptown hospital. Hugh and I ran up to see him with flowers and books. Luckily he recovered quickly. But months later, he landed in the hospital once more, this time in Westchester. Hugh arranged a ride for us to visit. But a message from Galen said it wasn't "a good day for friends to come, only family." This pattern was repeated several times, until I gave up attempting to visit.

Again I noted who counted as family: his sons, their wives and kids, plus Galen, her sons, their mates and kids, and Hugh. Not me. When Harvey was released from the hospital, he and Galen went to Florida for three months. He didn't return my emails or messages. Along with worrying about him, I felt rejected. He'd been there for me for two decades, but this wasn't his gig anymore. He'd helped me all he could. Now I had a husband, agent, book editor, and shrink who took good care of me, and students it was my job to assist. I didn't really need Harvey anymore. That was the problem with mentors – unlike real mothers and fathers, they had every right to walk away and not look back when their work was done.

Harvey and my other advisers had filled in what I couldn't get from my own relatives. So it was dumb and self-defeating to re-create the domestic rivalries I'd escaped in my original family, but I couldn't help feeling left out. In Theodore Roethke's poem "Elegy for Jane (My Student, Thrown by a Horse)," the teacher is self-conscious about the depth of his mourning, lamenting, "I, with no rights in this matter, / Neither father nor lover." I wasn't mourning, because Harvey was alive and completely healed. I had christened him my poet father, editor, mentor, fun date, journalism guru, and special friend, but it was sinking in: We really were not related.

Hugh wasn't really related by blood or live-in relationship, either, but he'd been at all hospital visiting hours and bedside vigils. He'd already won the adopted-child spot. Hugh was male, the fantasy son, more important than the daughter. It seemed as if I was forever the loser in some ancient sibling hierarchy. In Transactional Analysis, it was called a "life script." Colloquially it was the story of my life. Indeed, I'd begun my poetry collection with "Father's Skeleton," about the night my brother Brian was accepted to medical school and my father brought home his old study skeleton for him. "Remember the tibia, femur, and fibula / like a nursery rhyme I missed / while you danced father's skeleton / to your room and locked the door / that night father gave you his bones." So in my jealous-sister eyes, Hugh was getting what was left of Harvey.

Condemning myself for relieving such petty competitions,

I reread Harvey's bold and affecting words about his older sister who'd died before he was born: "I was conceived on the night / of my sister's funeral. / As a replacement, I suspect. / But she was very beautiful / my mother said, and when I was born / I was quite ugly . . . / . . . My mother, / when she saw me said, Why did God take away my beautiful child and give me / this ugly baby instead. And she turned away, / not to touch me . . . " Neither of us had been our parents' favorite child, and it consoled me to think that Harvey, more than anyone, would understand how it felt to be passed over, seen as less important, discarded, or ignored. This poem alone, which I adored and reread often, taught me a writer's divine reparation: You turn your worst pain into your best art.

Anyway, Hugh had discovered Harvey twenty years earlier than I had, when he'd been his star student, and he'd been loyal to Harvey far longer than I had. Clearly he deserved this place of honor. Since Hugh's real father was deceased and I still had a good (albeit distant) living one, Hugh needed Harvey more than I did. While checking facts for this chapter, I once again took to picking Hugh's brain about Harvey. So I'd been relegated to the place where I'd started, just a member of Harvey's fan club and audience, a groupie. Yet ultimately, the adult part of me realized how lucky I was that Hugh had shared Harvey with me at all.

During a phone conversation, when I admitted how left out I'd felt, Harvey said, "Look, Sue, I was flat on my back with tubes in me. You're too high energy and draining. I wasn't rejecting you, I just wasn't up for it." Okay, I understood his point. Compared to the unobtrusive Hugh, the quietest person I knew, I could see where my talkative, emotional personality might be viewed as too intense or extreme. Not that Harvey had a modest, retiring presence himself. He was actually quite a gigantic, passionate, quirky, memorable character, as were most of my role models. Whose goal was it to be subdued, pale, normal, and blend in with the crowd? Not mine!

At the same time I thought it was important to hear – and really listen to – critiques from people you admired and then to acknowledge your flaws and limitations. At least that way you wouldn't be shocked by strangers' reactions to you and could seem in the joke. I'd even included a scene in *Lighting Up* where I asked my shrink why he'd called me one of his most taxing patients. He'd answered, "You have a chronic anxiety level connected to a hyperactive mind that's plugged into a very analytic level of consciousness. There's no rest or rhythm. It's all high pitch. There's a continual idiosyncratic intensity that's exhausting."

In March 2006, Harvey's new handsome hardcover, *The Sights Along the Harbor,* came out just as he returned to New York. Now that he was better, he courted my overly energetic aura and called, emailed, and sent me invitations to multiple events as if nothing had happened, as if his surgeries, death scares, and difficult out-of-town recovery had just been a little vacation. Although he was walking more slowly now, with a cane, the attention and press for his book sprung him back to life. He was buoyant at his crowded readings and book parties. When toasting his publisher, Wesleyan University Press, he thanked them for putting out nine volumes of his through the years, but he added that along the way it had rejected nine of his other manuscripts.

This struck me as very significant. Not everything you write will be brilliant, acclaimed, and get the reception you desire, but that's okay. Keep working and going down the list, taking acceptances where they come. Every page you craft doesn't have to wind up bound in big hardcovers. Some of Harvey's poems ended up in paperbacks by Sun Publications and Hanging Loose Press, two small Brooklyn publishers. Some poems from those paperbacks made it into his hardcover *Selected Poems* anyway.

The *Times Book Review*, his old alma mater, finally gave him a rave, his best review ever at age eighty-two. Under the title "City Boy," the critic wrote: "Gnomic and beatific, salty and bawdy, puckish and waggish, kvetching and kibitzing . . . Shapiro is a veritable dynamo and a venerable American original whose small poems at their tonic best are as large as life." The editors ran a cute picture of him at nineteen, when he was in the army.

I passed out the review to my New School class the week Harvey was coming to speak to them again. One of my undergraduate students didn't understand that it was a picture from the 1940s and told him she was stunned to see a much older man walk into my classroom. "Don't I look like that guy anymore?" Harvey asked her, pointing to his young photograph, roaring with laughter.

Then he regaled everyone with his war stories, poetry wisdom, advice, and gossip from fifty years in the newspaper trenches. The only thing that marred my night was when someone asked him if he was working on new poems for his next collection. "No, I think this will be my last book," he said.

How to Have a Protégé

Feeling exhausted and drained from editing one hundred new students' essays in the fall of 1996, I was muttering to myself that I'd never offer to aid another aspiring writer – no matter what – when my phone rang. The lilting voice on the line introduced herself as Isabel Steinberg, assistant to Ruth Gruber, who'd given her my number. She said she was an eighteen-year-old college freshman from Illinois, studying poetry at Columbia, who wanted to ask me a big favor. Damn, I could never ignore a protégé of Ruth when I myself was a protégé of Ruth who'd used Ruth's name countless times. Alas, I was karmically bound to assist her.

So what was it this uptown wannabe poet wanted from me? Another part-time job to pay for her poetry habit? My editors names? Attention and approval? Between trying to encourage members of my Tuesday night workshop and keeping up with my NYU and New School classes, I was already overloaded. In my put-upon mood, I prayed she wasn't going to ask me to read and edit her experimental poetry opus, eight-hundred-page great American autobiographical novel, or memoir about her fucked-up family. Aside from teaching to pay my bills and reciprocating the generosity of my workshop colleagues, I had no interest in getting into the mentoring business.

I wasn't a best-selling author with any clout. Nor was I an agent, editor, or producer who could officially buy or sell anyone's magnum opus – not even my own. Yet after I'd had a bunch of pieces in the *New York Times Magazine*, requests from strangers had been coming daily, as if a professional writer were obligated to evaluate every striver's early pages for free. (As a special favor, Aaron had once critiqued his brother-in-law's dentist's screenplay. The dentist wound up sniffing that a former third-string critic for a Connecticut newspaper had been much more encouraging – and then questioned Aaron's thirty years of TV/film credentials.)

After fifteen years in the big city, I felt stuck in an aggravating career phase. I had tons of work and clips. But toiling seventy hours a week was earning me less than $30,000 a year. Thus, at age thirty-five, I wasn't even grossing my age. Not even with extensive publications, teaching awards, and stellar evaluations from students in four classes I taught three terms a year as an adjunct instructor. I'd had no luck landing an assistant professorship (with an annual $75,000–$100,000 salary for one-third my course load) or a hardcover deal with a New York publisher, though I'd helped many colleagues sell their books. I had recently line edited manuscripts for three Tuesday night workshoppers, recommended ghost editors and agents, gotten them press, held their hands through the whole publishing process, and then thrown them book parties. Like the wedding planner dying to be the bride, I was living a frustrating paradox. I assumed my hard work and helpfulness would come full circle, but so far they hadn't. In ways overanalyzed in multiple therapy sessions, this inability to get what I needed translated into feeling unwanted and underappreciated by the world.

"Ruth gave me *Internal Medicine*, which I really love," Isabel said. "My favorite part is the argument with your mother, when you cut your faces out of all the old photographs in your family albums. That line really blows me away."

Okay, she had my attention. Good ploy, quoting my poem to hook me. Upon first meeting Harvey, hadn't I captivated him by reciting his crazy Jewish poem back to him? I even liked her use of present tense, especially potent because my slim paperback, recently put out by a tiny Maine press, seemed to have arrived stillborn. Indeed, Ruth was one of the few who'd reviewed it, and only for *Hadassah* magazine. My book editor had sent the reviewers' copies out late. Even my former pupil working at *Publishers Weekly* (whom I had first helped see print) claimed it had shown up past deadline and thus was completely ignored.

"I also love Grandmother Sophie, when your mother warns you, 'The Goodman women are witches,'" Isabel continued. "And what a perfect metaphor when you and your mom stay up all night playing Scrabble, your 'words and emotions twisted like challah bread you break and break between you.'"

Had she memorized the entire collection? My poems were so confessional, her comments carried an unexpected intimacy, as if she'd just met my mother, my late grandmother, and the rest of my blood relations. The praise was a bit much, but I wasn't used to people I'd never met calling to rave about my poems, and her voice sounded so chipper and earnest. Who didn't want adulation? I flashed to the theory of my *New Yorker* boss, Helen, who thought we became writers because of some pathological hole in the heart that craved the undying adoration we'd missed as kids.

What was this girl's name again? Isabel Steinberg. I wrote it down on a Post-it near the phone. Lovely first name, and she was obviously a fellow Yid. She'd managed to flee the Midwest for Manhattan, poetry capital of the planet, which felt kind of fearless, if I recalled my own footsteps. She was accepted at Columbia, already knew Ruth, did her homework before initiating contact, and was ambitious too. I used to tell Romeos who tried to pick me up with good lines, "Flattery will get you everywhere." Okay, I could read a few of her poems, if I had time.

"Listen, Ms. Shapiro . . . "

"You can call me Sue."

"So, Sue, about the favor I mentioned . . . "

I braced myself for whatever imposition she was about to propose. At least she had the courtesy to kowtow a bit first before basically asking, "Can I have your job, your connections, and your life?" (I'd done this enough times myself to know that when you called someone older in your profession to promote you, that was, on some level, what you were really requesting.) It was amusing, since I'd been feeling like such a failure. I wanted to say, "Sure, I'll help you be just like me − a has-been who never quite was."

"We're doing a reading at Columbia next week, where each student picks a poet they admire and reads four or five poems from their book. I wondered if you'd give me permission to read from your collection," Isabel asked.

That was all she wanted? Really?

"You only need my permission?" I was skeptical that I could worm my way out of this unwritten helping-another-protégé-of-my-mentor contract so quickly.

"Yes, I just wanted to make sure it would be okay with you," she said.

That sounded too easy. Where was the rub? Then I realized Columbia was a hundred blocks away and she'd expect me to go to this thing. After attending thousands of literary events, I'd grown tired of long group readings by well-known poets. Lately I'd been so busy with work, I preferred to stay downtown. Don't tell me I'd have to schlep way the hell to West 110th Street for an amateur – and probably endless – reading by students, and not even my own students.

"I'd have to come to the reading?" I asked. "All the way uptown?"

"No, no. You don't have to come uptown. Ruth said you turn into a pumpkin above 14th Street," she quipped. "All I need from you is your permission."

An hour later Isabel was sitting across from me on the leather couch in my living room. She was a pretty, short-haired brunettete with no makeup, wearing blue jeans and a casual flowery top. She was thinner than I was, and taller, maybe five foot nine. There was something graceful and willowy about her; she could have been a model. I offered her a soda and popcorn left over from the writing group the night before. "So you're right off the boat from Illinois," I said.

"Well, before I came here, I spent a semester studying in Europe. Then I was at Tel Aviv University over the summer," she said. "I'm fluent in French and Hebrew."

Before I could say that I too had studied abroad and knew French and Hebrew, she added, "You mention Tel Aviv and Paris in your poems. Did you like Tel Aviv better than Jerusalem? What's your favorite place in the world? Don't you love Baudelaire's *Les Fleurs du Mal?* Who's your favorite poet?"

She asked as many questions and spoke as quickly as I did, which I found endearing. "Lately, Yehuda Amichai," I answered.

"Oh my god, he's a genius! I'm a huge fan of his work too!" She lit up, as if it were an astounding coincidence that two Jewish poets liked the best poet in Israel.

"Love is finished again, like a profitable citrus season," I recited one my favorite of Amichai's.

" . . . or like an archaeological dig that turned up / from deep inside the earth / turbulent things that wanted to be forgotten," she jumped in.

It was a nice reprieve from my boring day-to-day chores, and I was easily distracted by Isabel's youthful energy and adoration. She made me feel important, as if I were sort of famous. I remembered how hitting it off with a mentor used to feel like falling in love. Every dumb thing you had in common loomed gigantic. "Don't tell me you like chocolate, too? So do I! What a wild concurrence! It must be fate!" It was fun being on the other side, able to make her day by just being friendly.

She was obviously on her best behavior and wanted me

to like her. Nobody used connections and flattery to seek out someone more experienced in her field for just a brief chat. I wondered if, from her angle, this was an audition, interview, or crucial exam — like the bond an infant at a third-world orphanage felt toward the parent who could potentially adopt them. I'd read that the smartest, most intuitive babies learned to seduce with their smiles and charm, which could literally save their lives. *I'm special*, their body language would shout with every turn and wink. *Pick me! Pick me!*

Isabel had been struck by the poems on my mother. About twice as old as she was, I could have been her mom. If I wanted to, it would be easy to nurture, support, and hook her up. Yet aside from getting a kick out of her over-the-top compliments on a bad day, I debated what good taking on a pseudo-teenage daughter would do me. I'd felt so liberated as a working woman with no children I was responsible for. Aside from encouraging my favorite undergraduates in my courses, I'd never really had a protégé before. Was I courting a potential headache? Did I owe it to all the gracious gurus who'd taken me on and guided me?

She recited Amichai's first stanza in Hebrew with an accent that was flawless, like a native's. What stood out most was how quickly she spoke — in Hebrew and English — even faster than my rapid-fire pace. I recalled how, as a little girl, I'd memorize and recite long poems to get my parents' applause. It was the only time they'd put down the newspaper, shut off the TV, and turn their attention away from my younger brothers. I'd long ago connected my fast-paced speech to growing up with too many siblings too close in age. Thus I was still performing, rushing to get my words in edgewise. I guessed Isabel had also been usurped or interrupted.

"My favorite place is right here, Greenwich Village," I answered her earlier question. "What about you?"

"I don't know yet. I want to keep traveling, writing, and translating poetry. I'm hoping to go to Asia next year. Then Africa. Maybe I'll study Italian or Spanish next. Or Arabic. What do you think?"

"I think hyperactivity can be a way of hiding," I threw out.

"As if achievement were redemption?" she quoted from another of my poems.

Yes! Exactly! I'd graduated college at twenty, finished my master's degree, and taken the *New Yorker* job at twenty-two, using external achievement to compensate for what was missing, as she did.

Like a psychoanalyst doing an intake session with a new patient, I inquired about her background. She'd grown up feeling lost in a crazy dysfunctional family, with a bunch of siblings still in the Midwest who didn't really "get" her. After her parents' difficult divorce, her father remarried someone Isabel wasn't close to. Her dad was smart but emotionally distant. (Was there anyone I'd ever been drawn to who described their early years as joyous and functional? I kidded my students that having a horrible childhood was a prerequisite for our profession, and that if they grew up happy, they'd have to work harder to overcompensate.)

It was easy to understand why Isabel had been gallivanting around the world. A beautiful teenager could always find a bed, a meal, and an adventure. I'd globe-trotted too and then moved seven hundred miles east when I was her age. But despite her engaging warmth and easygoing banter, I sensed the baggage she carried was heavier than mine, filled with more sorrow. Whatever had silenced or squelched her had been so extreme, she needed to be heard in multiple tongues, in many countries.

"So, I actually have one more favor to ask you," she said.

I knew it. What had I unwittingly gotten myself into? Here was where I'd have to spend hours editing for free, I was sure.

"Can I write an article about you?" she wanted to know. "I just did a piece about Ruth for this glossy national Jewish magazine." She pulled a clip from her backpack. She kept copies of her work near her, like I did, as if she might be asked for proof of her achievements at any minute, as if a published piece were your ID. "The editor said I should query her with some more timely ideas. You have the great new collection out, so what do you think? Can I pitch you?"

"Sure, you can pitch me." I was pleased to be in the same category as Ruth, and that the favor Isabel asked for was easy and would benefit both of us. She'd get a check and a new clip, and I'd get some much-needed press for my poems.

A week later, after the editor said yes, Isabel came back downtown to interview me. She fired away questions for hours, furiously scrawling notes, asking perceptive follow-ups, hanging on to my replies. It was the most details anybody had ever asked about my work, and my answers appeared to fascinate her. Not that it was really about me. She was searching for a role model to provide direction. She reminded me of myself fifteen years earlier, so I found her hunger endearing.

As promised, she dropped off a copy of the magazine when the piece came out. Her long, chatty, quote-filled profile started: "Susan Shapiro's Greenwich Village apartment is guarded by a fortress of books." Underneath my name was the hyperbolic headline "The Truthsayer." I didn't know whether that was Isabel's title, or if the editor had taken it from the paragraph that read: "Shapiro explains the mind-set of conservative Jewish suburbia as a state of constant fear that the Cossacks are on their way. 'But I didn't want to pretend,' Shapiro says. 'I wanted to write the truth.'"

She wrote that I'd escaped my childhood home early but couldn't flee my upbringing, which followed me, haunting all of my work. She made a crack about how fast I spoke: "When Shapiro talks about her poetry, she decreases the speed of her speech from twenty miles per hour to a more reasonable fifteen." Funny, because her piece was a bit jumbled and read as if it were on speed. Still, it came off as exuberant and very complimentary, used a sexy author's photo of me, and mentioned my collection several times. Thanking Isabel, I related how much I enjoyed her profile. She sounded so happy that it pleased me. I was touched. It wound up creating a bond between us – as if an artist had painted a flattering portrait that I liked and exhibited openly. If our meeting had been a test, Isabel had excelled. Boy, was I easy. She was in the door, every door.

When she asked about my journalism classes, I let her attend whichever editors' lectures she wanted for free. When she inquired about the Tuesday workshop, I invited her to join and she became part of my workshop family. Although my cousin Molly had joined at fourteen, she hadn't been around lately. Thus Isabel was the new baby, a fresh-faced, idealistic eighteen-year-old in a sea of cynical, rumpled middle-agers and senior citizens coming to my apartment every Tuesday night. In my midthirties, I'd never seen myself as middle-aged before. I flashed wistfully to my student days at NYU, where I was the youngest person attending the book events of my literary idols. Had the student become the Svengali?

Isabel came every week and clicked with Gerry, who, like me, was taken by her poems. They were rough, yet deep and sophisticated – filled with foreign words and phrases, political outrage, allusions to literal and emotional devastation. She was a bit too gung ho – wanting to read many poems and stories every single Tuesday. Sometimes she'd show up with thirteen or fifteen pages that were only one-and-a-half spaced – too much for a newcomer, way over the ten-double-spaced-pages limit we'd set. But I liked that she'd rewrite each draft a hundred times, like I did. Without giving up space to get my work critiqued, I tried to squeeze in as much of her poetry and prose as we could. If we didn't have time, I'd go over her pages and mark notes for her on my own.

Asking more personal questions and piecing together hints between the lines, I learned that her mother wasn't just colloquially "crazy," but mentally ill. In her poetry she nailed the sad slippery drama of her mother's delusions and fantasies, eviction notices, troubles staying sane. She mentioned that she and her siblings had never eaten in her mother's kitchen at the same time. Nobody prepared meals. They'd sneak in to grab food for themselves, eating it quickly while standing at the fridge. No wonder she'd been so taken with images of my mother feeding me, how we'd eat and argue late at night in a warm suburban kitchen I would leave but kept returning to.

Within a few years, poems that Isabel brought into the workshop were accepted by out-of-town journals and won small literary prizes. I wasn't sure if I was jealous because her poetry had more innate music than mine did, or because Daddy Gerry had taken to her the way he'd once taken to me. I was also bizarrely envious of her family's troubles. Compared to divorce, remarriage, madness, and mayhem, my background seemed too pedestrian to wring much dark beauty from.

I wasn't conscious of being more attached to her than to anybody else in the group. But I missed Isabel, and felt a little deserted, when she went on a trip abroad in the fall of 2000. She came back all aflutter about a lanky Israeli filmmaker named Elan Rem, three years her senior. I figured he'd be one of many lovers, but she wasn't into playing around like I had. Instead, at twenty-two she got engaged, inviting me to their small wedding in his Israeli hometown. (Had she planned it on foreign soil so it would be impossible for her mother to attend?)

In debt from our apartment's down payment and in major workaholic mode, I barely considered the invitation. Gerry and his wife attended; Isabel had adopted them, and vice versa. Her deepening links to the workshop tribe made me wonder about the nature of all the interconnections. If Ruth were her grandmother, Gerry and Barbara had become her fantasy parents. So who was I to her? A teacher whose classes she'd never officially enrolled in? Her cool aunt in the Village? She had real siblings, but they were in noncreative professions in different states. I guessed that I'd become like a surrogate writer sister in the big city. Not that I was so supportive when she asked my advice on work or love.

Of course, my own choices colored my opinions. I'd married at thirty-five, a good age for creative souls to wed, according to Rainer Maria Rilke's *Letters to a Young Poet*. I'd kept my name and was taken aback when she changed her byline to Isabel Rem. She probably adopted her husband's moniker because it was shorter and more eloquent than Steinberg. But I wasn't an advocate of serious career women giving up their names or autonomy to marry early. I warned my female students of the Sylvia Plath syndrome – beware trying to juggle an ambitious husband, multiple books, and babies, all before you turn thirty. On the other hand, Isabel and my cousin Molly had both come from broken families. Thus, the illusion of a happy intact clan loomed larger for them than someone like me, who'd felt claustrophobic amid too much domestic interdependency.

I kept trying, unsuccessfully, to slow Isabel down. But she kept rushing, letting me know she'd crafted the whole fifteen-page story she brought into the workshop that afternoon, writing and talking way too fast. Clearly, I recognized bad habits in Isabel that I didn't admire in myself. Take more time, chill out, wait till next week. The group isn't going anywhere, I told her. A mentor was someone whose hindsight became your foresight, right? Her poetry impressed me, but I didn't really get her fiction. She liked my first-person essays but never really got my fiction either, so we were even.

One Tuesday night, Gerry called her third-person narrator "forced" and "unnatural." The next Tuesday, Isabel's story was in the first person, and the Tuesday after that, second person. A week later she used the voice of the male character, then the maid, then the child. I didn't like any of the versions and got annoyed, suggesting that if she could change the voice that quickly so many times, it wasn't ready to show. If she didn't know whose story it was, then why bother telling it at all? I had the opposite problem – I was reluctant to alter narration in my longer work and usually settled on the original draft's first person, refusing to try anything else. I should be more open, Isabel argued, probably correctly.

Yet I was selling several pieces a week to *The New York Times* and other top publications, and I wanted the group to be professional. I wasn't running an experimental, free-form creative salon. With my impatient personality and lack of tolerance for ineptitude, it was good that I didn't have children. Gerry, a very involved father of four, was more patient and open to artistic experimentation. But just because Isabel was talented and in her twenties didn't mean I wouldn't hold her to the group's high standards or would lie to her about her work. It wasn't healthy for a mentor to be a cheerleader who fed your ego; it was just the opposite. Hadn't she called me the truthsayer?

Over lunches at my local diner and during long walks through the Village, I let Isabel pick my brain and gave her my honest assessment of her career prospects. The poetry she wrote and translated was excellent, and we celebrated when her latest book of translation found a home at a small university press. But I reminded her that poetry rarely paid the bills. Despite her finishing a rough draft of one adult and two teen novels, and finding an agent through the workshop, I wasn't convinced her fiction would ever support her. (Was I projecting, since I'd never had luck with novels either?)

I encouraged her to try journalism, editing a first-person piece she sold to *The Forward,* where I'd often been published. Someone who crafted good poetry could usually ace prose. Yet personal essays had to be personal, and she was limited by her reluctance to reveal anything dark about her family or her husband in print. She was more comfortable spilling secrets in her poetry, in which everything was cryptic and shrouded in mystery. This was where we diverged, since "Lead the least secretive life you can" was the mantra I maintained.

In summer 2003, while quitting all my long-term compulsions, I also gave up the writing workshop. The *New York Times* article about the demise of the eighteen-year group cited Isabel, now a Columbia graduate student and teaching assistant. She pondered how she was going to adjust without getting her Tuesday night fix. The last line was her quote: "I'm going to need therapy."

Aha! I bet that was my role – amateur therapist! After the group ceased, she still called me with her problems, the way I'd have tune-ups with my old shrink. When Isabel was upset that a bunch of her husband's relatives came to stay at their too-small apartment for two weeks, I suggested he put them up in a hotel or cheap sublet. "But he moved to this country for me and he misses them," she argued. I insisted that a husband had to put his wife's feelings first and make sure she was comfortable in her own home. When she complained that she was broke, I took her out to eat and gave her books and names of editors to try, reminding her that journalism paid more than poetry. She said she always felt inspired and challenged after she left me. I liked playing provocateur, and I was tickled when a new student emailed that after my first class, she felt as if I'd put her fingers in a light socket and all the strands of her hair were standing on end. Isabel and I no longer hung out weekly, but I hoped to stay a strong, illuminating force.

In his great book *The Writer's Journey*, Christopher Vogler points out that Glinda the Good Witch appears only three times in *The Wizard of Oz*. First she gives Dorothy the red shoes and yellow brick road to follow, acquainting her with the unfamiliar rules of the weird new land. Then Glinda blankets the sleep-inducing poppies with white snow, protecting the young heroine from harm. Finally she helps Dorothy return home to Kansas with the help of the magic red shoes. With my acolytes, I liked to see myself as Glinda. My idiosyncratic, three-tiered advice to Isabel (and any young scribe who asked) was something like:

1. Avoid negative relatives as much as possible.
2. Hang out with writers in the magical land of Manhattan at all costs.
3. When you're stuck, seek out several older, encouraging witches and warlocks. That way, when one gets sick of you, you can rotate.

Several former workshoppers disappeared postgroup, but Isabel remained omnipresent and supportive, emailing to salute my good reviews, showing up to my readings and book events, pitching a piece on *Lighting Up* to *The Jerusalem Post*. It was sweet that she wanted to recast me almost a decade after her first profile. I said fantastic, asking just to fact-check her article before she handed it in. She said sure, and we made a plan to meet.

At the interview she shared exciting news. A well-known female poet had picked her for an award through a prestigious literary organization. The eighteen poems Isabel had submitted would be published in a "chapbook," a pocket-size paperback booklet with an introduction by this Famous Poetess. Isabel hoped she'd be able to use this important name's endorsement as a blurb for full collection she'd publish in the future. There was to be a reading and ceremony in December for her and five other winners at the New School, where I taught, six blocks away. My New School bosses were involved with this annual program. I hugged and congratulated her.

I had mixed feelings but wasn't sure why. Because a national figure had chosen Isabel's poems, whereas my poems had never won any major sanctions? Or because I felt replaced in Isabel's heart? Gerry was her most important guide, but he'd been everyone's pretend papa, including mine. I worried that Isabel would no longer need me at all, now that a more acclaimed older female writer was her champion. If Gerry and the Famous Poetess were her poetry parents, I'd be relegated to serve merely as Isabel's mentor on the side for first-person prose.

Pondering my ambivalent reaction, I realized that the New School cosponsored this contest for students like Isabel, who didn't even go to the New School. But they'd barely noticed my books, though I'd been teaching two popular classes a term there for twelve years, since 1993. They had offered me a visiting professorship to teach seminars in its MFA creative nonfiction program, which I loved. But that hadn't led to an invitation to join the faculty, and the only reading they'd asked me to do was in their cafeteria, not in the main auditorium, where Isabel's event would be held. Did that hurt my ego?

Luckily, these were just fleeting pangs in the otherwise miraculous summer of 2005. With three books out in a row and a new one in the works, I couldn't contain my joy. Aaron landed the best TV staff-writer job of his career and, to top it off, we bought the apartment next door at an insider's price. He was moving his office home, so we were combining both apartments. Despite warnings that contractors took twice as long and charged twice the amount of their original bids, our two-month construction went beautifully. (Turned out renovation was quite the satisfying activity for an impatient addict: "Take that wall down." *Bang. Bang.* All gone.) We soon had a three-bedroom, three-bath, twenty-three-hundred-square-foot loftlike space, lined with built-in six-foot wooden shelves. After a combined fifty-five years in Manhattan, Aaron and I finally had enough room for all of our books!

After our lunch interview, I invited Isabel to be the first to see my freshly expanded, remodeled, repainted place. We were thrilled for each other. I said I'd be at her December reading and marked down the date, though it was two seasons away. Marveling that my enlarged space would be ideal for literary soirees, I heard myself say, "Maybe I could throw you a little reception here after your reading. We could invite everyone from the old workshop."

I had no idea what my schedule would be in six months, and it was too early to plan for the next winter — I didn't know which nights I'd be reading or teaching yet. Plus, Aaron hated social events, barely knew Isabel, was psyched to be rid of my workshop, and wouldn't sanction a reunion. Still, in my expansive mood, I felt proud of Isabel and grateful that she'd pitched another article on me. It wasn't easy to get ink on a book that had been out six months and wasn't a best-seller. I hoped foreign press would add to my internet sales. As she left we kissed goodbye, promising each other everything. I'd send her a copy of the new project I was working on. We'd talk more about her potential party. She'd get me an advance draft of her chapbook, along with a copy of her profile of me before it was submitted.

Hanging out with someone in her twenties made me feel younger, as if I were reliving my early days in Manhattan. Yet in my forties I'd acquired experience, books with my byline, money, a strong marriage, and now a magnificent work and living space. I was elated, feeling as if all the good karma I'd ever built up had come through. When I shared my excitement with Dr. Winters, he warned me to avoid any grandiosity or exaggeration and make room for disappointment and chaos, or else I'd wind up getting slammed. I had no idea what he meant.

Two days later, scanning the first draft of Isabel's profile, I was flattered that she called my work "funny, witty, and lightning fast." But as I read on, I was dismayed to find several mistakes and lines that seemed off. She talked about how I'd used addictions to "alleviate a desire to pursue other goals," which wasn't right. I'd explained how cigarettes had alleviated anxiety, how in the past I'd had a fear of certain kinds of success, and that quitting my addictions had been like clearing away a smoke screen. She'd combined sentences that didn't gel. Instead of focusing on how I'd managed to quit unhealthy habits (the whole point of an addiction memoir), she'd overemphasized the parts about "my crazy Jewish clan." Was she stuck on my old poems and that preconception of me or projecting her own story onto mine? She'd crafted it too quickly, her habit.

She also didn't mention that since I'd stopped using toxic substances, wonderful things had taken their place — such as book and movie deals and a better marriage. Instead of touting my triumphs, she'd made five references to my mother's overfeeding me and ended with a discussion of my "weight issues," as if I were struggling with obesity. At five foot seven and 130 pounds, I didn't think I had any serious "weight issues." I feared she'd taken casual comments I'd made at lunch totally out of context. Her piece was obviously well intended and I really wanted to like it, but I just didn't — which put me in a quandary.

The mentor-protégé relationship sometimes takes a tragic turn, according to *The Writer's Journey*. "Hercules had an alarming tendency to do harm to his mentors," Vogler warned. "In addition to painfully wounding Chiron, Hercules got so frustrated at music lessons that he bashed in the head of his music teacher Lycus with the first lyre ever made." Though I figured it was just a messy rough version she'd rushed, deep down I wondered if Isabel's piece were subconsciously hostile.

Some workshop members had resented my transformation to a smoke-free, sober, hardcover author with expanded bank accounts and square footage. Striking out on my own meant that on some level, I'd left them. When I picked up on hidden subtexts, Dr. Winters said, "It's never your imagination, but then you always overreact." I didn't want to overreact. Isabel and I had been close for ten years. But my role was that of workshop leader, journalism teacher, and mentor — I critiqued her work. Yet it felt ungracious to trash a piece that promoted my book. She had called it "funny, witty, and lightning fast" after all, giving me a good pull quote. She correctly disclosed that she'd attended my writing group and classes, in keeping with my long-standing philosophy that you should never to lie to your editor or your shrink. But what about lying to your protégé? If I told her it was fine and didn't correct the mistakes, personal facts about me and incorrect-recovery gibberish would run in an important newspaper.

This is why it's difficult to write about someone you know, and why many editors insist that journalists have no connection whatsoever to their subjects, even when you disclose your bias. In 1981, the novelist E. L. Doctorow, an NYU professor, allowed me to interview him for a school journal, but only if he could have the final edit. I agreed. When I'd asked him about successful schools of authors in this country, he said there were two: "one who summers in Martha's Vineyard, the other who summers in the Hamptons." When I showed him my final piece, he edited out that line, my favorite.

"Why would you cut that out?" I asked him. "It's funny."

"It's too sarcastic and elitist," he said, explaining he didn't want to come off as flippant or obnoxious.

The copy that ran was boring, earnest, and politically correct. I later learned it was bad practice to show your piece to your subject before it saw print. Under duress, you could let someone check his or her quotes, but the narrative wasn't up for discussion with the subject (just your editor.) Now on the other side, I wanted to protect myself. When somebody without much experience, like

Isabel, asked to profile me, I agreed only on the condition I could check facts before it ran.

Hurrying on deadline, everyone made mistakes. I flashed to a newspaper story I'd once penned about the thirtieth-anniversary reissue of *Up the Down Staircase*. The author, Bel Kaufman, was a Jew who championed the causes of our people, but I'd erroneously implied that the teacher character in her book was Jewish, too. Kaufman, a schoolmate of Ruth's, saw me at one of her book parties. "The teacher wasn't Jewish!" she yelled. "I made sure that I didn't make her Jewish!"

I apologized profusely. Initially I thought she was making too much of a fuss out of a tiny error nobody would notice. Wasn't she pleased that I was raving about a new paperback edition three decades after her book's original publication? Then again, for writers, words counted. I sent Kaufman a note of apology, reminding her how much I admired her and her book. The next time I saw her, she was charming and friendly, as if nothing had happened. Was I being the exact same kind of fussbudget to Isabel? Had I turned into an ungrateful, anal, nit-picking control freak insistent that my exact words, intention, and image be captured the way I wanted them to be? Perhaps no writers ever liked anything written about them and always thought they could craft it better themselves.

I decided to tell Isabel the truth, so she could make changes before handing it in. I calmly asked her to not send in her interview yet. I thanked her for the positive, great tone but pointed out the mistakes and misleading lines that could be improved. She sent me back a curt email saying that her piece was fine and she didn't have time to revise it. In her next note she dismissed the new project I'd given her to read, saying she thought it didn't work at all. It was juvenile to say that she didn't like my book because I didn't like her article. The problem with hanging out with younger people was that they sometimes seemed so young.

In teaching me not to be too impulsive, Dr. Winters had come up with a technique for my cyber correspondence. If I received an email that upset me at 9:00 AM, I practiced answering on a blank letter, without the address. I wasn't allowed to send my response until 5:00 PM. The later drafts were much shorter and nicer. Isabel needed someone like Dr. Winters to chill out her abrupt emotional overreactions. But *I* was *her* Dr. Winters. Wasn't I?

As far as I knew, she'd published only five or six articles, most of which I'd edited line by line. Why would someone with little experience assume she could nail a twelve-hundred-word profile in a first draft in a few days? I'd sold hundreds of profiles in two decades, and I usually couldn't do it that fast. That was why I'd started the workshop to begin with, to get feedback from sharp critics who'd help me improve. Why didn't she show it to Gerry or other colleagues for their comments? I emailed Isabel again twice, but she didn't answer and never showed me her rewrite.

Confused by this uncomfortable twist, I mentioned it to Haylie, a seasoned journalist from the Tuesday workshop. "Isabel's always been too thin-skinned about criticism," Haylie said. "Once, after the group, when she didn't like my comments on one of her poems, she told me, 'You don't understand what poetry is.' She struck me as very naive and emotionally unformed."

Not long later, my Tel Aviv soulmate Joanie sent me a copy of Isabel's published profile, which was a little better than the first version. Yet I was dismayed that some errors I'd pointed out went uncorrected. She'd kept in the misuse of the word "alleviated," along with the other lines she'd smashed together into one nonsensical statement. She still ended with my mother's overfeeding. Her mistakes were more troubling this time because I'd already fixed them. Why didn't she listen? Stubbornness? Did she think she knew my life better than I did?

I reminded myself that nothing was worse than having your book overlooked, and this was a nice full-page piece with a pretty picture and a copy of my book jacket. If you didn't read it carefully, it came off as lovely and positive. An acquaintance who saw it congratulated me "on the rave." Most of the people I'd assisted hadn't given me any press (such as the ingrate at *Publishers Weekly* who'd totally snubbed my poetry collection). Isabel had managed to publish two pieces implying I was a serious author, attempting to pay homage. I stopped arguing semantics, especially since nothing could be changed after an article ran, anyway. I assumed she'd eventually come around and apologize for disregarding my notes, or explain she was on too tight a deadline, or admit that she'd found my critique of her piece upsetting.

During the fall, I included her in group email invitations to my readings and book events, which she ignored. I found it ridiculous that her way of dealing with our spat was to avoid all contact, and I had an impulse to call her and say, "What the heck is your problem? Why are you avoiding me?" Yet it took two not to tango. Before I contacted her again, I pondered my own actions and emotions in the conflict.

Mentors were not always mature, sane, and fair, according to Vogler. They could be human and disappointing, as in *Mr. Smith Goes to Washington,* when Jimmy Stewart's hero learned that his senator role model was actually crooked and cowardly. Rumpelstiltskin helped the heroine spin straw into gold but then demanded too high a price for his favor. The musician character Svengali in George du Maurier's novel *Trilby* became so obsessed with his student he doomed them both. Were my expectations for Isabel and her profile of me too high?

Sometimes, like parents, mentors had a hard time letting go. If Isabel needed to rebel, run away, or demonize me for reasons I didn't understand, I should give up on my desire for a direct confrontation and let her go. With so many kind colleagues and appreciative students clamoring for my attention, I decided to disconnect emotionally and forget about it.

In November I helped Danny, a fellow journalist, plan a Barnes & Noble reading in the Village for a biography he'd spent six years on. Since Aaron was a fan of Danny and his book, he didn't mind when I invited everyone over after the reading for what would be the first party in our newly renovated place. That same week, my agent sold my new project, a (hopefully) humorous look at love and marriage, which chronicled how I'd been fixed up with my husband and had set up twelve marriages — including my editor Dina, who'd recently married one of my husband's former comedy-writing acolytes.

Okay, so out of all my ideas, I worried that fix-ups was the lightest. If I died tomorrow, did I want to leave the world the equivalent of a *Cosmo* article? It wasn't that I couldn't sell a serious novel or nonfiction tome; it just couldn't be next. My agent said, "Get a bestseller first. Then you can do anything you want."

That week my L.A. pal Gary called with the news that #1 *Single*, the TV dating show he was producing, starring the singer Lisa Loeb, had been green-lighted. Loeb was a Jewish, brainy, suburban-bred doctor's daughter with three siblings, and she loved my books, he said. Thirty-seven and single, she wanted to meet a nice guy and settle down. Since I was the self-proclaimed "fix-up fanatic," did I want to be on her show and introduce her to some great available men? Five minutes on *The Today Show* had shot my first memoir to number seventy in reader ratings on Amazon.com (which lasted two whole hours, I knew from webstalking myself). And that show was at 6:00 AM, agonizingly early for a late nighter. I'd never been offered any evening airtime that could be filmed at my place. Jazzed that someone well known whom I admired was a fan of my work, I agreed to play matchmaker on national TV.

The December date that Lisa's producers chose was the same date I'd committed to Danny's reading. Since Danny and his crowd were mostly single and Jewish, I triple booked. At 6:00 PM was Danny's Barnes & Noble reading, at 8:00 PM I'd throw him the reception, and at 10:00 PM Lisa, her posse, more solo guys, and the camera crew would show up. My editor and her new husband were coming by for the spectacle.

While I was on deadline for my new book, finishing my winter term, planning this event, and too busy to see straight, Isabel resurfaced. A few days before Thanksgiving she emailed, apologizing for being out of touch. She'd been away because of a family illness, she said. She reminded me that her award ceremony was a week away. When I looked at my calendar I saw that it was the night of the reading/reception/reality TV extravaganza I'd just planned. I recalled that I'd kind of offered to throw a little soiree in her honor. Since I hadn't heard back from her in months, I no longer had the time or desire.

But it went deeper than that. I'd intentionally relegated the whole poetry world, as well as the Tuesday workshop, to my past. I preferred to be with my husband, my book editor, current colleagues — who made me feel cherished and admired. I wasn't interested in going to the New School on a night I didn't have to teach to hang out with former friends I was no longer that close to. I didn't have to see a one-time protégé who'd blown me off read poetry with her new God on a stage that was never offered to me.

I didn't begrudge Isabel the spotlight. She was a talented, hard-working, up-and coming twenty-eight-year-old poet who deserved to be picked by the Famous Poetess. I wished her success, but from a distance.

I returned Isabel's note, claiming I'd forgotten about her reading. That was a lie. I'd made a conscious decision to move on without her. Like an ex-lover who'd already gotten closure, I had no intention of backtracking. She pretended she'd forgotten my offer, too. She said she was planning to have dinner at a nice restaurant with the poetry bigwigs afterward. Good, so she didn't need me there anyway. I was relieved.

Then she extended another invitation. It seemed her family was coming to town, so she was throwing a Saturday evening fete at her place that she wanted Aaron and me to attend. Gerry and other Tuesday-nighters would be there, as well as her classmates. The last thing I was in the mood to do on Saturday — our one date night — was to rush one hundred blocks uptown to mingle with a group of poor but noble poets half my age. I made an excuse to get out of it. Isabel emailed back, saying how much it would mean to her if we could at least stop by. Damn it. Priding myself on being a dependable and loyal person, I felt guilty and acquiesced.

I showed up armed with two bottles of wine and a book by Elizabeth Bishop as a congratulatory present/peace offering, though neither of us acknowledged that anything negative had transpired. I'd never visited Isabel's small uptown apartment before; I'd always made her trek down to see me. It was also the first time I met her relatives and fellow Columbia classmates. She introduced me to everyone there as if I were a VIP. They all knew about me and the Tuesday workshop. It occurred to me that she'd grown tired of attending my downtown events. She'd wanted me to reciprocate. Fair enough. I bought her chapbook and made a big fuss, asking her to sign it for me.

As she pulled out a blue Flair pen and began an inscription, she recounted meeting my New School bosses at her poetry dinner, relaying how highly they thought of me. Then she asked if I'd recommend her for a teaching job there. She'd acted bizarre toward me for six months, and now she wanted another favor? When she handed her book back to me, I read what she'd written: "Dear Sue, to one of the most enduring admirers of my work and one of the best role models of a passionate writer. I admire you very much. Love, Isabel." Interesting that she began by calling me her admirer, switching our roles, rewriting history. Yet she also wanted me to use my connections to get her a job at the school where I taught at the same time.

The gathering had seemed nice and bearable — until I looked over at her shelves and couldn't find any of my books there. Had she hidden the hardcovers I'd signed to her? I turned to the acknowledgment page of her chapbook and saw that Isabel had thanked Gerry, his wife, and the Famous Poetess, along with several Columbia teachers and chums. But my name or a mention of the workshop wasn't there. What was that about? I'd been thanked in numerous books by workshop authors – including Ruth and Gerry. I'd thanked the workshop in my books. I'd never listed Isabel specifically, but one was supposed to offer gratitude to one's mentors, not one's protégés. I'd been a good disciple myself, always showing appreciation for the elders who helped me. I could teach a class on how to be a classy protégé that Isabel should take. Was she telling me she was no longer under my wing in any way?

Fine. I no longer wanted her to be. But then why had she made such an issue of my coming up here? Was my attendance, with my husband, a feather in her cap? Or was this some kind of subconscious payback? I wasn't the least bit hungry, but I began eating too much cheese, salami, and pickles, as if her article had willed me a binge-eating disorder. I couldn't wait to get back to my own neighborhood, feeling as if I were stuck in a bad remake of *Up the Down Staircase*. Or was it *All About Eve*?

Then again, hadn't I been a promiscuous protégé myself? I'd cast a wide net, juggling many editors, older colleagues, and superiors simultaneously, deserting a few gurus gone wrong, always searching for more gurus gone right. I couldn't expect her to be a serial monogamist when it came to mentors when I wasn't. These kinds of adviser-advisee relationships weren't like marriages, with the external steps of courtship, engagement, vows, separation, divorce, and alimony. They were more like free love from the 1960s, or polygamy, or the vague perimeters of friendship. Sometimes old friends took a back seat to brand-new ones, right?

At home, I read Isabel's poems carefully. I recognized some from early drafts she'd brought into the workshop. She'd taken our advice and they were now tighter, shorter, more melodious. Her pages were beautiful, graceful, worthy of the awards and praise. I slipped her tiny chapbook into my poetry shelf, filing it alphabetically, where it belonged.

On Monday I wondered whether to recommend Isabel for the teaching position. It would be easy for me to focus on our miscommunications, continue feeling slighted, and simply blow off her request. But wasn't a mentor — of any duration — supposed to be a source of wisdom and transcendence? I tried to come out of myself, dig deeper, find a more analytic perspective. I'd had a nurturing link with Isabel for a decade, when she'd been the kid sister of my workshop family. She'd published two basically laudatory profiles of me, using what little power she had to promote my work. Yes, I wished she'd been able to face disagreements head-on, not flee whenever an interaction became uncomfortable. Yet I'd had twice her years to figure out coping mechanisms, not to mention good therapy. Despite some superficial family feuds, I was lucky I'd had a warm, wonderful mother who'd adored me. Isabel's original maternal bonds had been damaged. Maybe that made it harder for her to maintain intimate ties with a strong, intense female figure like me.

I considered ways I might have hurt her without meaning to. She may have felt abandoned when I'd terminated the Tuesday group, not blessed her by name in my books, criticized her fiction and her profile of me, and started making real money from my nonfiction. Although I still read and wrote poems, I didn't regret forsaking the poetry scene and all the suffering and snobbery that went with it. My preference for having my prose packaged in splashy hardcovers could have come across as arrogant. Had I embraced my recent financial upswing a little too gleefully? She may have thought I'd sold out. (I joked that I'd been trying to sell out for years, but nobody was buying.)

I didn't know if Isabel and I would wind up dear lifelong colleagues, or if we'd never be close again. Either way, I summoned all the sage, judicious lessons from my own magnificent role models, who tended to err on the side of generosity. I decided to be as kind and selfless as they had been to me. I emailed my New School bosses, telling them how brilliant, talented, and special I'd found Ms. Isabel Rem.

Dr. Winters once mentioned taking his young daughter along on a four-day jaunt to California. "But of course, now the trip has to be all about her," he'd added, sounding resentful. I didn't have the responsibility of children to take care of. So who needed the burdens and dramas of fake offspring? Sitting down at my computer, I erased the whole Isabel saga from my mind, swearing off this entire mentorship stuff. I promised myself that I'd steer clear of all needy younger artistic souls from now on. They were too hungry, screwed up, and draining. I had my own hungers to satisfy. It was so much sweeter and easier being a protégé.

When the telephone rang, it was Johanna, an adorable, bright young student, the star of my current class. What was so important that she couldn't email but had to call me at home early Monday morning? It seemed that a magazine editor she'd just met had told her to pitch some author profiles for an upcoming issue, and Johanna had the brilliant idea that she could do a piece about me. She was right around the corner, calling from her cell phone to see if she could stop by for just a second. . . .

How to Get Great Gurus of Your Own

Right after *Five Men Who Broke My Heart* came out, my editor forwarded me a five-hundred-page manuscript from a young guy from Texas I'd never met. His cover letter, addressed to me, bragged that he'd enclosed his true-life story about the five women who'd broken his heart — the male version of my memoir — which he forgot to mention he had bought, skimmed through, or even liked. He was sure I'd want to read his project cloning mine and help get it published. I was semi-amazed he thought I'd find this strategy endearing when I was more apt to call my lawyer than my agent.

Having a mentor seems such a brilliant idea that many people, like Mr. Texas, fall under the illusion that it's an easy process, and assume everyone will jump at the chance to offer career connections and advice for free. Yet it's actually harder to land a good mentor than a good marriage partner. Luckily, having multiple mentors works better than having multiple marriages, and you can approach, court, and juggle several guides simultaneously.

But before you ask anyone for assistance, beware. Feeble attempts to network, charm, and cajole luminaries often lead to humiliating blunders. One young journalism school graduate recently posted a Craigslist ad titled "Seeking Mentor" that read: "I want to meet someone who is a published author because i know that in order to be successful you have to find out what successful do and take action." (Suggested action: Take a proofreading class.) My buddy Rich Prior, a producer at Sirius Radio, recalled the time he was speaking to a campus group and a senior came up to him and said, "Unlike all the others in the audience who left, I stayed for your *whole* talk." The kid seemed to want a medal for his endurance, along with a job, and didn't even realize he'd already turned off Prior completely.

So instead of estranging the superiors you mean to impress, you need to get a clue. Here are some careful, canny, and classy ways to coerce someone older or wiser into promoting you professionally, along with surefire methods to immediately alienate all VIPs in your path.

1. ACT ENTITLED, GET DELETED: Despite your certainty that you're a genius worthy of immediate attention, successful people are very busy doing their own work. That's how they became successful. So make sure you're not coming across as arrogant, presumptuous, impatient, self-involved, flippant, insulting, demanding, or delusional. Don't assume anybody will assist you out of benevolence or awe, or because you're so incredibly cool and special. Thousands of recent graduates are begging anybody with a job, company, or name in any field for the same favors. Just because you choose someone doesn't mean they'll choose you. Unless you're approaching your Uncle Dave or your mom's old college roommate, assume you'll have to earn the ear or energy of higher-ups.

I'm not an agent or an editor who can buy or sell books, yet I get a ridiculous amount of requests to read unsolicited manuscripts and proposals. Recent emails began: "I've just completed one hundred thousand words of my debut novel, which I'm sure you'll find talented and worthy of your expertise. . . . " and "Though I've never read any of your work . . . ," which both fell under the heading "Letters We Never Finished Reading . . . "

2. REAL LIFE IS NOT A REALITY SHOW: Donald Trump will

probably not invest in your real estate scheme. The chances of Oprah's inviting you on her show to push your product are slim. And I'm betting Salman Rushdie won't read your unpublished one-thousand-page opus in twenty-four hours and call his publisher with a fawning blurb. Yes, once in a while, pursuing a long shot will pay off. But it's easier and faster to first focus on admirable individuals already in your world – a kind boss, coworker, successful older relative, neighbor, doctor, or teacher you admire.

I met most of my mentors at school and work, the best places to mine for powerful allies. The only gurus I didn't meet that way were Howard Fast, who was my cousin, and Harvey Shapiro, who was the former professor of a good friend, so I had a personal introduction. Even so, it took me seven years to finagle our first face-to-face meeting.

3. BE UNPREPARED AT YOUR OWN PERIL: In one of my NYU journalism classes, all the young women expressed interest in internships, jobs, or clips from the ultrahip *Jane* magazine. Yet nobody was having luck with the busy editor, Esther Haynes. Before approaching Haynes, my student Pamela first did a little research and found a funny *New York* magazine feature article Haynes had penned about a jailhouse love triangle involving the club-kid-turned-murderer Michael Alig. By coincidence, Pamela had once had an odd conversation with Alig at a Chelsea bar and was thus able to start her missive to Haynes: "I loved your piece on Michael Alig – who I've actually

met. Boy, is that guy obsessed with urine!" Pamela was in Haynes's office the next day and wound up selling her an essay for $1,000. Yes, Pamela was lucky, but she wouldn't have uncovered the perfect factoid to share had she not taken ten minutes to do her homework.

Check libraries, bookstores, websites, and Google to learn more about the person you want to hire or inspire you. If he's a professor at your university, look up a description of his classes and try to sit in on a lecture. If she's a published author, read her books and bio, and attend a reading. Most editors also write. So pitching someone without familiarizing yourself with their publication – and their bylines – is just plain lazy.

Contributing to someone's pet charity could also make you memorable. Neelou, a student last term, came to a soup kitchen reading I hosted at Holy Apostles and bought a copy of Food for the Soul. She emailed me to say how much she enjoyed my anthology and then asked for my advice. I wound up editing a rewrite of her essay and giving her the name of an editor to contact, whom she sold it to. I didn't help her only because she'd come to an event important to me. But by attending, she sure stood out from my eighty other students and earned my interest and gratitude.

4. DON'T DEMAND TOO MUCH TOO SOON: Proposing a weekly column to an editor you've never met is like asking a cute stranger, "Will you go out with me every Saturday night for the next three years?" That kind of overkill, which makes you look too needy and

insecure, will make someone run the other way. Instead, for your ini-tial attempt, pitch one short piece, and if it goes well (like a good date), you'll surely get another chance. Similarly, inquiring whether a CEO you don't know will schedule a private meeting with you could be conceived as intrusive or inane. However, attending a public speech he's giving and shaking his hand later might elicit a generous instinct. Keep initial requests small and nonthreatening. Wanting a known novelist to edit your manuscript-in-progress and recommend her agent is unrealistic. But buying her book and asking for her sig-nature could be endearing. Once you've made a good impression, ask the person about his or her next event, or if she or he has a card, blog, or website, which may offer channels for keeping in touch. Build up to asking for bigger favors.

5. DON'T BE A STALKER: Sending a fan letter or email is a much better strategy than showing up at someone's home or office without an appointment. Don't phone anyone you don't know directly unless you have a very close contact (as Isabel had when she called me). Instead compose a short, sincere note you can send to his or her office, agent, manager, or network. Briefly express honest appreciation, mak-ing sure you spell the person's name, company, or book title right. Like many authors, I put an email address on my website. Though I'd usu-ally ignore a total stranger's request for my editor or agent's name, I answer nice fan letters from anybody who appears sane.

Someone who came to one of my seminars and wanted more

advice afterward feared that flattering me would make her seem like an ass-kisser. I told her, "Better to be a kisser upper than a self-involved egotist."

6. CONNECTIONS CONNECT YOU: Don't mention the person who sent you on line sixty-seven of your letter – since most readers won't get that far. The first sentence out of my protégé Isabel's mouth was, "Ruth Gruber gave me your name," which instantly made me think, *Darn, I have to help this person.* Why? Because Ruth helped me. When I contacted my cousin Howard Fast, my initial salutation was "My mother is Mickey Shapiro." I knew Howard thought my mother was saucy, so that pretty much nailed me a first meeting. Lavishly praising the person you know in common is common sense. Saying anything that can be construed as remotely insulting about the name you just dropped is, to quote one of my mentors, asinine.

If you don't have a direct in, try an indirect one. My students start letters to editors who've been guest speakers, "Thanks so much for taking the time to speak to our class. You were inspiring." Or, after checking with me, they write: "My professor Susan Shapiro gave me your name." (And not: "My professor Susan Shapiro suggested I send you my work so you can publish it, give me lots of money, and make me famous.") If you have no literal link but the person is from your hometown or you both graduated from the same school, mention that. Or begin with facts and flattery. "As someone who loved your recent L.A. lecture . . . " isn't bad. It could win you a smile, a handshake, words of encouragement, a business card, or a flyer to the next event. There is only one faster way to endear a writer to you than starting with, "As someone who bought your book and loved it. . . . " That is: "As someone who bought five copies of your book for my friends. . . . "

7. ENOUGH ABOUT YOU: Don't ever begin with how great you are. Saying, "As a recent honors graduate of Columbia University, who double-majored in English and philosophy," and then going on to list all of your impressive accomplishments, will not impress anyone. If the potential helpmate you're approaching doesn't know you, they don't yet care about your grades or resume. On some level you're pretty much implying, "I want your job. I want your salary. I want to be the next you." Are you contacting someone running a charity mentorship program or round-the-clock free career service? No? Then have the brains to praise your target's accomplishments *before* launching into how important you are or will be.

This continues to be true during the course of your relationship. My former student Jody recently sent me a long email chronicling every freelance gig she'd had and lost in the seven years since she'd taken my class. At the end she asked to meet so I could help with her next move. I wished her well but said I was too busy with work deadlines and my current classes. It was true. But had she Googled me first, she would have found I'd sold five books since she'd last seen me. Starting her correspondence with "Mazel tov!" may have gotten her further than "Help me, hear me, feed me."

Naked ambition is ugly; myopia and self-involvement will get you nowhere fast. According to the Robert Greene bestseller *The 48 Laws of Power,* the individual you hope will be your boss, big sister, or pipeline to prosperity is the master you must bow to. One executive I know says if the first lines of the cover letter contain three "I's" in a row, the answer is already no.

8. DON'T TRASH YOURSELF: It stuns me how many aspiring writers unconsciously shoot themselves in the foot by beginning a letter to an editor, "Though I've been rejected every time I've sent out my work . . . " or, "Though I'm sure you're not looking for a new freelancer without any experience. . . . " Self-deprecating humor can be engaging when it comes from Chris Rock or Ellen DeGeneres, but don't try it with someone you don't know. The loser, slacker, nebbish, neurotic role that works in Woody Allen movies, Philip Roth novels, and David Sedaris essays is rarely endearing in person. Admitting you've been a goof-off, lazy, depressed, heartbroken, fired from previous jobs, an alcoholic, or a drug abuser isn't so compelling, either. Be conscious of your fears and your tendency to reveal way too much, or tell off-color jokes, and other methods of self-sabotage.

9. TRY HUMILITY: If you desperately feel the need to share tales of yourself and your many achievements, don't show off or exaggerate. "I just finished my third experimental science fiction novel, written in German and Spanish, which my professor E. L. Doctorow thought was brilliant" means little if these tomes remain

unpublished. Unless you're applying to graduate school, "I was Phi Beta Kappa" makes you sound like a young, competitive blowhard. Remember, you're not greeting your father or your Aunt Carla, who already care. You're approaching someone you admire and whom you'll never get to know if you don't rein in your self-regard. Understatement is preferable, along with making your motives clear. "As an aspiring editor who just finished NYU journalism school, I would be honored to meet you if you ever have five minutes" isn't a terrible way to *conclude* a call, email, or letter. Writing "As a business major who followed your brilliant recent leveraged buyout in the papers, I wondered if you ever needed an intern or unpaid assistant" might lead to a response, an interview, or an internship.

10. NO CONTACT SANS CONTACT INFO: If you want a response to your letter, why are you leaving off your phone number and address? Why not attach a self-addressed stamped envelope? Don't include an email you don't check often or write down an office number if you can't take calls during the day or check messages only on weekends. I know someone who sent out a stack of resumes, then left the country with no laptop or plans to check voice mail or messages for fourteen days. How self-defeating was that? If you want a reaction, make sure you can be reached easily. Put your first and last names, address, phone numbers, email address, and fax number on any letter, card, or cybernote. Be careful about sharing links to risqué websites, MySpace pages, or embarrassing videos of overly pro-

vocative photos of yourself. Don't assume everyone communicates the same way and loves email, instant messaging, or faxing and has a cell phone or BlackBerry. Some Luddites my age still prefer regular mail. At the end of my classes, I send back the last assignments to all of my students who put addresses on their papers. The rest are lost, tossed, or deleted.

In *About Writing*, the prolific author Samuel R. Delany says: "It's not my job to copy names and return addresses from envelopes onto manuscripts when the writer was too lazy or too thoughtless to do so. . . . When I receive an envelope in the mail, . . . open it, and remove a manuscript with no name on it, I throw it away immediately. . . . Don't let a copy, hard or electronic, get six inches away from your keyboard without containing your name and address, snail mail and email. Make this a habit." Make this mandatory!

11. YOUR MENTOR ISN'T YOUR HOMIE: Would you tell your co-op board or college admissions committee you had an abortion? Or once tried Ecstasy, bulimia, or cutting yourself? No? Then use discretion with your mentor, too. Even after you meet, click, get aid or a job from your guru, don't spill your guts. You may eventually be asked about your personal life. Please remember that you're not talking to a blood relation, who will think you're adorable no matter what, or your therapist, who is paid to hear all of your problems. A busy professional could run the other way if you seem too needy, neurotic, or pathetic. If you're trying to publish your memoir about the roots

of your needy, neurotic, pathetic personality, that's even more reason to keep the craziness on the page. While acting out may get you a referral for a good counselor or psychopharmacologist, nobody wants to go to bat for an emotional basket case.

12. ISSUE PROPER INVITATIONS: Once you've established contact with a human you hold in high esteem, by all means extend offers that pay the person homage. Especially if real payment is involved, too. Most of the editors and agents I've asked to speak to my classes and seminars said yes. To coerce them, I've used connections and flattery and phrased my questions specifically, as in, "It would be an honor if you'd consider speaking to my journalism class on Monday, May 9, from 7:00 to 8:00 PM, and I can offer a one-hundred-dollar stipend." After the lecture, I ask if I can treat the speaker to drinks or dinner, and I send a thank-you note. Asking Ian Frazier to speak to my class led to his inviting me to coteach his class, which led to the miraculous book we did together.

13. SHOW UP, SHUT UP, ANTE UP: Paul, a former protégé, called to say he was sorry he missed my recent readings, panels, and book party. Then he asked for my *New York Times* editor's name and my take on how to break into the newspaper of record. I said, "Sorry, I'm on deadline" (a writer's best alibi). I was miffed that he couldn't make it to my six local book events, but – a week later – thought I'd come through for him with another big favor. He might have saved the day by simply saying, "I just ordered your book from Amazon.com. Can't wait to read it."

You have to remember that the person who has the least power in any relationship has to compromise and come out of himself the most. So if you're on the side seeking advice, sympathy, connections, or praise, know that your esteemed guide always has the upper hand. You should expect to attend your mentor's events (preferably with a group of your friends!), travel to his or her turf, walk in bearing presents (even if it's just a congratulations card and Korean deli flowers), offer to treat, supply transportation, and give more than you get. Most important, ask questions and listen more than you talk. If Paul ever asks me why I no longer make time for him, I'll spell it out.

14. RETURN THE FAVOR: Older, powerful people need young blood for fans, assistance and to keep current. I was happy to publicize the projects of my mentors. Now many students I helped get internships a decade ago have risen to the ranks of senior editors, and every former pupil I've asked to speak to my class has come back. My one-time student David Goodwillie invited me to his book party, gave me a signed copy of his memoir, *Seemed Like a Good Idea at the Time*, and thanked me in the acknowledgments even though he'd taken my course six years before. Moved by his gratitude, I invited him to participate in a reading I was doing with my mentor Harvey Shapiro, whom David had met through our class and admired. The whole evening was a lovefest. Mentors, like elephants, have endless memories, and there's no time limit to generosity.

Reaching out to those who went out of their way for you — even decades later — could lead to important lifelong links.

15. BE THE MENTOR YOU WANT: No matter what your age or background, consider teaching, tutoring, volunteering to aid those in need, or becoming a big brother or sister to kids lacking a strong role model. Don't forget that the cosmic principle of karma involves circular deeds that create your destiny. So whatever you put out there eventually comes back to you. Being a giving, selfless person who does kind deeds for those less fortunate could be exactly what will make the perfect guru turn around and take you on.

Acknowledgments

I would like to express my deepest gratitude to:

MY DREAM TEAM: my perceptive agent Elizabeth Kaplan, visionary editors Jill Rothenberg and Laura Mazer, brilliant webmaster Eric Shapiro, hardworking foreign-rights guru Diana Finch, and fabulous photographers Danny Brownstein and Mike DeBruyn.

MY "CORE PILLARS" WHO BELIEVED IN THIS BOOK FROM THE START: CR and Fred Woolverton.

MY BOOK-EVENT ANGELS: Lisa Applebaum, Donna Rauch, Amy Stanton, Keith Hewitt, Daryl Mattson, Meesha Dibner, Lita Weissman, Chris Johnson, Keith Chandler, Laurie Smith, Max Roberts, Jeffrey Penque, Sarah Jackson, David Greenstein, Rachel Dorman, Susan Corcoran, Linda Friedman, Sharon Preiss, Steven Greene, Dite Van Clief, Elliot Rabin, Rachel Kramer Bussel, and Mediabistro's miraculous Laurel Touby, Carmen Scheidel, Taffy Akner, Jessica Eule, and Mara Piazza.

MY BEST CRITICS: Alice Feiring, Rich Prior, Kate Walter, Tony Powell, Liza Monroy, Kristen Kemp, Harold James, Stan Mieses, Jill Hamburg-Coplan, Nicole Bokat, Devan Sipher, and Gerry Jonas.

MY TEACHING COLLEAGUES: Jackson Taylor, Laura Cronk, Robert Polito, Deborah Landau, Luis Jarmillo, Mary Quigley, Elizabeth Maxwell, Bob Blaisdell, Sara Goff and Alice Phillips.

MY FAVORITE EDITORS: Julie Just, Claire Lambe, Christopher Moore, Margo Hammond, Frank Flaherty, Mackenzie Dawson, Jerry Portwood, Nicole Davis, Esther Haynes, Bruce Tracy, Sarah Kricheff, Chrissy Persico, Faye Penn, Joanna Douglas, Elizabeth Shaw, and Danielle Perez.

MY WEST COAST FAMILY: Jane Wald, Kathryn Glasgow, Gary Rubin, Gary Kordan, Jody Podolsky, Alison Powell, Caren Emmer, Timmy, Lori Monheim, Leah Solo, Amy Alkon, Anita Rosenberg, Lynn Isenberg, Julie and Scott Greenwald, Sally Helfer, Andrea Wachner, Cliff Schoenberg, Ruth Andrew Ellenson, Amy Klein, and Rachel Sarah.

MY LONG-SUFFERING NEW YORK CONFIDANTS: Ivy Landsman, Dagmar Schwartz, Mike and Amy Schwartz, Gabi Rem, Stacey Greenwald, Stacey Kramer, Ryan Harbage, Serena Richards, Wendy Shanker, Rob Bates, Diana Schwable, Rasha Rafaie, Seth Kugel, Roberta Bernstein, Sherry Amatenstein, Emma Segal, Karen Salmansohn, Lisa Rosenthal, Larry Bergreen, Tory Connolly Walker, and Molly.

MY EAST COAST FAMILY: LuLu Rubin, the Kahns, the Brownsteins, the Zippers, and the Goodmans.

MY NEW EAST COAST SUPPORT SYSTEM: Charlotte Abbott, Kimberly Auerbach, Hilary Davidson, Megan Gillin-Schwartz, Jane Warshaw, Pamela Ryckman, Felicity Loughrey, Sarah Norris, Karen Neary, Tiffany Dubin, Marci Alboher, and Mark Hollander.

MY BELOVED ETERNAL MIDWEST SUPPORT SYSTEM: magic hair stylist Robert Stephanian, Karen Buscemi, Krysten Weller, Judy and Jim Burdick, LuLu Rubens, Suzanne Altman, Andrea Miller, Nancy Newman, E. J. Levy, Cindy Frenkel, Jill Margolick, Helen Zucker, Karen Sosnick, Howard Lutz, Scott Grant, Robin Singer, Dave and Judy Roberts, Arlene Cohen, Teri Morof, Lynne Scheiber, Ronit Pinto, Laura and Lina Berman, and all the Shapiros, especially The Fab Five: Andrea, Sammy, Dara, Benny, and Abe.

About the Author

© DAN BROWNSTEIN

Susan Shapiro has written for *The New York Times, The Washington Post*, the *Los Angeles Times, The Boston Globe, Newsday, The Nation, The Observer, The Village Voice*, Salon.com, *The Forward, Glamour*, and *Jane* magazine. She is coeditor of *Food for the Soul* and author of *Lighting Up, Secrets of a Fix-Up Fanatic*, and *Five Men Who Broke My Heart*, which was optioned by Paramount Pictures. She lives with her husband, a TV writer/producer, in Manhattan, where she has taught at NYU's Journalism School, the New School's MFA program, Holy Apostles, and Mediabistro. You can visit her website at www.susanshapiro.net.

Selected Titles from Seal Press

FOR MORE THAN THIRTY YEARS, SEAL PRESS HAS PUBLISHED
GROUNDBREAKING BOOKS. BY WOMEN. FOR WOMEN.
VISIT OUR WEBSITE AT WWW.SEALPRESS.COM.

Single Mom Seeking by Rachel Sarah. $14.95, 1-58005-166-9. A single mom who knows the difference between "going to bed" and "putting to bed" shares her heartfelt and hilarious take on the challenges of balancing motherhood with dating.

Getting Unstuck Without Coming Unglued: A Woman's Guide to Unblocking Creativity by Susan O'Doherty, Ph.D. $14.95, 1-58005-206-1. This encouraging and practical book is about understanding blocks in the creative process and getting to the bottom of what causes them.

Incognito Street: How Travel Made Me a Writer by Barbara Sjoholm. $15.95, 1-58005-172-3. From the founder of Seal Press comes this eloquent coming-of-age travel narrative about her beginnings as a writer.

The Anti 9-to-5 Guide: Practical Career Advice for Women Who Think Outside the Cube by Michelle Goodman. $14.95, 1-58005-186-3. Escape the wage-slave trap of your cubicle with Goodman's hip career advice on creating your dream job and navigating the work world without compromising your aspirations.

Single State of the Union: Single Women Speak Out on Life, Love, and the Pursuit of Happiness edited by Diane Mapes. $14.95, 1-58005-202-9. Written by an impressive roster of single (and some formerly single) women, this collection portrays single women as individuals whose lives extend well beyond Match.com and Manolo Blahniks.